Singapore FOR Kids

Illustrations by TRIGG

© Third edition 2000 by Nicola Supka

Published by Times Books International
an imprint of Times Media Private Limited
Times Centre, 1 New Industrial Road
Singapore 536196
Tel: (65) 2848844 Fax: (65) 2854871
e-mail: te@corp.tpl.com.sg
Online bookstore:
http://www.timesone.com.sg/te

Times Subang
Lot 46, Subang Hi-Tech Industrial Park
Batu Tiga, 40000 Shah Alam
Selangor Darul Ehsan, Malaysia
Tel & Fax: (603) 7363517
e-mail: cchong@tpg.com.my

Printed in Malaysia

ISBN 981 232 127 6

Singapore FOR kids

A Parent's Guide

Nicola Supka

TIMES BOOKS INTERNATIONAL
Singapore • Kuala Lumpur

CONTENTS

Acknowledgements

I would like to acknowledge the many and varied contributions made by the following people:

My husband, Godfrey, for his faith in me and unfailing support (also for being my technical and marketing advisor);

For suggestions and materials: Meg Green, Clara Pong, Tan Poay Lim, Rosalyn Tay, Jenny Hulton-Smith, Lesley Burnett, Louise Dubec, Sally Lavin, Susan Fitzpatrick, Ilsa Sharp, Karen Johnson and Linda Crawford;

All the organisations (over 800 of them) that supplied information for inclusion in the book;

Everyone who contributed an anecdote on parenthood: Patricia Koh, William Xavier, Jenny Hulton-Smith, Rosalyn Tay, Bernard Harrison, Lai Ah Eng, Claire Chiang, Diana Ee-Tan, Ruby Lim-Yang, Sandra Chua, Caroline Wong, Jean Marshall;

All my friends, in Singapore and elsewhere, for the words of encouragement;

The staff and volunteers of Landmark Education, for their wonderful programmes that gave me the confidence to make it happen;

Rory—it would never have happened without you—and Jinkee, for looking after Rory every morning for months, and so making it all possible;

My publishers, for having the courage to commit to publishing this book on the basis of a synopsis from a first-timer;

My editor, Sunandini Arora Lal, for her helpful comments on the manuscript.

Medical advisor:

Dr. Paul Zakowich, a board-certified specialist in Internal Medicine, practising at the Mount Elizabeth Medical Centre

Other advisors:

On child care provision: Ministry of Community Development, Child Care Services Branch

On library facilities: The National Library Board

On Singapore events and festivals: Singapore Tourist Promotion Board

On employing a maid: The Expat Maid Agency

Government sources used:

I would like to thank the relevant ministries for permission to use information from the following:

Ministry of Education pamphlet: "Schooling in Singapore: Primary Education—An Information Guide for Parents"

Singapore Civil Defence Force leaflet: "Everytime we attend to a non-emergency call, we take longer to get to you"

ABOUT THIS BOOK

IS THIS BOOK FOR ME?

If you're a parent of children under 12, or planning to have a family soon, YES! *Singapore for Kids* is a "pick and mix" of information that offers something for everyone.

One of the challenges of producing *Singapore for Kids* was writing for both local and foreign parents. Some of the information in the book, such as places to visit and the shopping guide, may not be new to local readers. However, the book also contains previously unpublished information, such as the survey of preschools and the list of support services for families, which is useful to everyone.

Most local parents have the benefit of an extended family living in Singapore—grandparents, aunts, uncles, sisters and brothers. This is an important support structure, although no doubt the source of stresses and strains as well! On the other hand, most foreign parents have no relatives living here, and fathers often spend a considerable

amount of time away on business, leaving the mother to look after the family alone. It is perhaps for this reason that I looked to include information such as "access with strollers" and "(baby changing) facilities". Many of the organisations I contacted did not provide any such facilities and did not consider them important.

As there are a growing number of nuclear families in Singapore, local parents increasingly need these facilities too. I hope that this book, by publicising those organisations that provide suitable facilities for young families, will encourage more places to be family-friendly.

SOME PRACTICAL DETAILS

Finding the places

To assist you in finding the places mentioned in the book, each entry includes the sector code. This is the first two digits of the postal code and replaces the old system of "district codes". A map showing the sector code boundaries can be found at the back of the book. Full addresses and telephone numbers for all the organisations featured in the book are to be found in the List of Addresses at the back of the book.

Costs quoted in the book
The fees quoted in this book, whether for preschool care, birthday parties or swimming pool entrance, are given only as a guide and are subject to change.

"See also"
Some organisations provide a range of services relevant to families, such as a play centre, party organisation and parenting workshops. To help you find all the details, many entries in chapter 1 have a "See also" section, which refers to other relevant entries in the book. To find individual pages, refer to the index at the back of the book.

ABOUT THE THIRD EDITION
This latest edition incorporated new and revised information. As always, my publishers and I are keen to receive your feedback.

CHAPTER ONE

EDUCATING YOUR CHILD

This chapter is a guide to educational and play activities for newborns to 12-year-olds. It is structured as follows:

Preschools
A guide to preschool options with descriptions of the activities and facilities offered by over 400 preschools

The Primary School System
An introduction to the primary school system and the process of getting your child into the school of your choice

International Schools
A summary of educational provision for expatriate children

Play Centres
A guide to centres with activity sessions and/or indoor play facilities

Creative Classes
A listing of centres that offer classes in art, dance, drama and music

Enrichment Classes
A guide to classes that reinforce what the child is learning in school or preschool

Sports Activities and Facilities
Suggestions on where you can go for sports ranging from beach volleyball to ice-skating

Libraries
A look at the facilities and activities provided by community libraries

PRESCHOOLS

Suddenly your little baby is all grown up and ready for preschool. You have so much to think about: Which educational approach is the best? Will he be happy there? Is it close enough to home or work? Will he make friends easily? Will he like the food? This guide to preschools will help you make the right choice for you and your child.

Singapore has some of the best preschool facilities in the world. It's also extremely well regulated, ensuring that child care facilities are clean, provide suitable equipment and have sufficient and suitably trained staff. Child care is also affordable, although high-cost luxury preschools exist too.

WHAT ARE YOUR PARENTING BELIEFS?

Some parents believe that young children learn best through play, and therefore that the curriculum should be full of water play, sand play, Art and Craft, Music and Movement. For these parents, a garden for the children to play in may be an essential, and access to computers is probably an irrelevance. Others want a more structured setup so they can see clearly what their child will achieve in terms of language, maths and so on. These parents may want their children to have tests at kindergarten level and may be interested in enrichment activities, such as science and drama.

Most of us want a bit of both, believing that a balance of structured activities and play is important to our child's development, but the exact mix each of us is looking for may be quite different. That's where this guide can help. You can see at a glance which preschools in your area offer the right mix of activities and facilities.

Please note that the information provided here is intended only as a guide and cannot be guaranteed. It is based on questionnaire responses received from preschool centres and not on personal visits. Always confirm the details with the individual preschool concerned, as many things, particularly costs, change frequently.

WHAT IS A PRESCHOOL?

This book's definition of a preschool includes all kinds of child care facilities for children from 18 months to six years, from one-hour to full-day sessions, costing anything from $30 to over $1000 a month. So hopefully there is something for everyone.

Following are some general definitions.

11

CHILD CARE CENTRES

The majority of preschool child care is provided by child care centres. They are regulated by the Ministry of Community Development and provide full-day (and in some cases half-day) care for children from 18 months or two years up to primary school age.

KINDERGARTENS

Kindergartens generally accept children from three to six years old (although age limits vary) and provide part-day (three to four hours) or occasionally half-day care. Confusingly, the word "kindergarten" is also used to describe an age group. Kindergarten 1 (K1) refers to children aged four to five years, and Kindergarten 2 (K2) refers to children aged five to six years.

PLAY GROUPS

Preschool centres that provide part-day care, or offer play facilities for young children attending with their parent or carer, may be called "play groups". Again, this term is also used to describe an age group. Play group (PG) refers to children less than three years old (i.e., under Nursery age).

MUM WATCH OUT FOR MONSTERS

TR194

Since these definitions can be rather confusing, the preschool centres have been grouped according to the number of hours for which they provide care. The categories are as follows:

Full day: up to 12 hours a day
Half day: five to six hours a day
Part day: up to four hours a day

PRESCHOOL OPTIONS

FULL DAY

Full-day preschool is the most popular option for mothers who return to full-time work and therefore need full-day care for their children throughout the preschool years. Hundreds of child care centres ap-

---

What Does it Mean to Be a Dad?

The day Darryl arrived, they were conducting a ground breaking for a new wing at the hospital. I thought it was rather symbolic. There we were, moving from couple to family: it seemed like a pretty earth-shattering transition to me! In the event, there was no rush of emotion, no overwhelming sense of new responsibility, no immediate change. Heck, was I being cheated of my "moment" or wasn't I tuned in enough? What I found myself tuning in to, instead, was the closing ceremony of the Seoul Olympics on TV. . . .

When my own son was born, I would have liked to have told my dad what it was like being his son, but sadly he died six weeks too soon. My family came from Goa, India, and travelled all over the world. I grew up in Singapore, considered not Goan but "Other Race", a classification that doesn't give even a hint of my rich and complex family history. How am I to pass this proud heritage on to my boy who is racially half Chinese but who culturally seems to be dominated by his Chinese side?

– William Xavier

William Xavier is a TV presenter and businessman. He has one son, Darryl, eleven years old.

proved and regulated by the Ministry of Community Development provide this level of care.

HALF DAY

Half-day care is a less expensive option and one that is favoured by working parents who have relatives or a maid to assist with child care, and who feel that their child will benefit from spending more time in the home environment. A number of child care centres offer this half-day option.

PART DAY

The part-day option is favoured mainly by non-working mothers who want their children to have some preschool education but who have chosen to care for their preschool children at home for the majority of the time. Centres offering part-day care are not regulated by the Ministry of Community Development. Kindergartens are regulated by the Ministry of Education and generally provide care four hours a day for children three years and over. Younger children are catered for by a smaller but growing number of play groups, some of which are run by expatriate women from their homes and others that are conveniently located in shopping centres. In addition, the PAP Community Foundation (PCF) runs over 300 education centres offering two- or four-hour child care programmes.

MAJOR PRESCHOOL PROVIDERS

There are several large preschool organisations in Singapore. They include the following:

- People's Association
- PAP Community Foundation (PCF): 310 education centres
- Presbyterian Welfare Services (PWS)
- NTUC Childcare Co-operative: 25 child care centres, including three workplace centres
- YMCA
- YWCA

The NTUC and the PCF are included in this survey.

SURVEY OF SINGAPORE'S PRESCHOOLS: KEY TO THE TABLE

Questionnaires were sent to hundreds of preschool organisations. The responses have been compiled in the form of a table, which you will find at the back of the book. The information was compiled in 1997 and fully updated in 1999. Preschools are listed in sector code order, to help you find those nearest to your home or workplace. The first two digits of the six-digit postal code form the sector code. For instance, the address of Brookvale Creche is 111 Faber Drive, Singapore 129423; its sector code is 12. The map following the table shows the sector codes of Singapore.

This is not a complete guide. However, the survey table gives a representative picture of child care provision and some ideas about what to expect and look for when selecting a preschool for your child.

1. HOURS OF OPERATION

The table specifies whether the preschool offers "full", "half" or "part" day care. See "What Is a Preschool?" for definitions of these terms.

2. AGE

The age range for each preschool has been summarised using the following codes:

Age range	Level	Code
18 mths.-3 yrs.	Play group	PG
3-4 yrs.	Nursery	N
4-5 yrs.	Kindergarten 1	K1
5-6 yrs.	Kindergarten 2	K2
6-7 yrs.	Primary 1	P1

You will need to check with individual preschools regarding their cutoff dates for each year's or term's intake.

3. COST

Fees quoted are generally monthly or termly and do not take account of government subsidies payable to working mothers and single working parents (where the child and at least one parent are Singapore citizens or Permanent Residents). These subsidies are currently $150 per month for full-day care and $75 per month for half-day care.

Abbreviations used:

pa: per annum
p6m: per six months
pt: per term (10 weeks unless otherwise stated)
p8s: per eight sessions
p20s: per 20 sessions
pm: per month
pd: per day
ps: per session

A non-refundable registration fee is generally payable. It may not be listed in the table. Call the individual preschool for details.

Additional charges that may be payable and, in most cases, are not listed here include library deposit and charges for uniform, stationery, other materials and insurance.

4. RATIO

Teacher-to-child ratios indicate the usual number of children being cared for by the teacher(s). For example, if a class has 16 children, 1 teacher and 1 teacher's assistant, that is a ratio of 1:8. Some preschools have the same ratio for all age groups, some have indicated the average ratio across all classes, others have indicated the ratio for each age group (i.e., for Play group "PG", Nursery "N" and so on). These ratios vary slightly from day to day. The figures given here are intended only as a guide and are not guaranteed.

Ministry of Community Development (MCD) regulations require that child care centres maintain the following teacher-to-child ratios:

Age group	Ratio
18 mths.-2$\frac{1}{2}$ yrs.	1:8
2$\frac{1}{2}$-3 yrs.	1:12
3-4 yrs.	1:15
4-7 yrs.	1:25

Child care centres that maintain these ratios are indicated in the table as "MCD". Many child care centres offer better teacher-to-child ratios than the MCD minimum, and their ratios are indicated in the table (see "Top teacher-to-child ratios").

Preschools that are not child care centres are not required to maintain these ratios. However, most of them have ratios that are better than the regulations require anyway.

5. ACTIVITIES

Language teaching

Most preschools teach children to speak, read and write English and Mandarin. However, some preschools offer other languages. These are indicated in the table using the following abbreviations:

A: Arabic
H: Hindi
J: Japanese
Mly: Malay
T: Tamil

See "Choosing the Right Preschool" for details of preschools that offer languages other than English and Mandarin.

Optional extras

Many preschools offer a range of additional activities, sometimes known as enrichment activities. Some of these, such as Cooking and Science, are part of the curriculum. Others, such as Speech and Drama, are generally optional and involve an extra charge. Drama may be in English (E) or Mandarin (M). Any additional charges for these activities are indicated. Trips to places of interest, undertaken by many centres, also involve an extra charge. These costs clearly vary and are not included in the table.

Tests

Those preschools that include tests as part of the curriculum are indicated in the table. Generally these are undertaken once or twice a year and only at the K1 and K2 levels. Other preschools have alternative ways of assessing children's progress.

6. MAIN LANGUAGE

The main language of communication used by teachers is underlined, for example:

English is main language

If the preschool offers a bilingual programme, the two languages used are underlined, for example:

Bilingual English/Mandarin programme

or

Bilingual English/Japanese programme

✔ J

If parents can choose the main language of communication, no language is underlined, for example:

English or Mandarin programme

✔ ✔

The Family Place offers alternative language programmes, it has two entries, one for each programme.

In some cases, the percentage split between English and Mandarin is indicated in the "Notes" column.

7. FACILITIES

Food and drink

A tick in the "Food & Drink" column indicates that some food and/or drinks are provided. Always check with the centre to find out what exactly this includes. All child care centres provide three full meals a day and have to meet both nutritional and cultural requirements, but other preschools may provide only snacks, especially if the child is there for three hours or less.

Transport

A tick in the "Transport" column indicates that a bus service is provided. This always involves an extra charge. Call the individual centre for details of its transport arrangements.

Garden or outdoor play area

A tick in the "Garden/Outdoor Play Area" column indicates that the preschool provides safe, accessible outdoor play space. Centres without their own outdoor play areas may take children on trips to a local public park.

17

Sharing the Load

I took my daughter out of full-time child care when her baby brother was born. She now attends a kindergarten every morning and gets to see Lai Hsin in the afternoons. Lai Lin was never very happy in day care. She would often say the day was too long (it was from 10 to 5) and she wanted to come home. She's now much happier, and the children already play together remarkably well. As parents we all worry about sibling rivalry, but I'm convinced that by spending more time together my kids will become the best of friends!

With the growing number of nuclear families in Singapore, I believe it's important to form bonds with other families in the neighbourhood. We all have a tendency to stay within the family unit and be fearful of "intruding" on our neighbours. Bringing up children can be hard work, but when you combine forces with your neighbours, as we have, and share the load (such as dropping and fetching the children to and from their various classes, and having them play together) life becomes much easier for parents and richer for the children.

– Lai Ah Eng

Lai Ah Eng has a Ph.D. and is a founder member of AWARE, amongst her many community commitments. She has two children—Lai Lin, 7, and Lai Hsin, 4.

Gym equipment

A tick in the "Gym Equipment" column indicates that the preschool provides some indoor or outdoor play equipment, which may include items such as a slide, swings, ride-on toys or a climbing frame. Preschools run by play centres usually have access to a play maze.

Library

A tick in the "Library" column indicates that library facilities are provided for the children. This may consist of library shelves in individual classrooms rather than a separate room.

CHOOSING THE RIGHT PRESCHOOL

TOP-VALUE PRESCHOOLS

There are some wonderful preschools in Singapore offering immaculate facilities, oodles of enrichment activities and many highly educated teachers. The only problem is that some of them cost over $1000 a month, way beyond what most parents can afford. Luckily, there are also plenty of good-quality preschools offering good value for money.

Top-value preschools are defined as those offering:
- full-day care at $400 or less a month,
- half-day care at under $300 a month,
- part-day care at under $350 a term for every-day care (or pro rata for less than five sessions a week).

Their fees are marked in bold in the table, for example:

Full: $400 pm
Half: $270 pm

Please note that in many cases these preschools' costs have been subsidised to provide affordable places for children of needy families. Also, that fees may vary depending on age and other factors.

TOP TEACHER-TO-CHILD RATIOS

Many of the preschools with the best teacher-to-child ratios are also the most expensive. That's not surprising, as clearly more staff are needed to maintain a good teacher-to-child ratio. What is more interesting is that some preschools have managed to maintain good teacher-to-child ratios while keeping costs relatively low. The teacher-to-child ratios in the table are intended only as a guide. Don't expect them to be adhered to exactly, as class numbers vary from day to day.

The teacher-to-child ratio was included in the survey because it is a useful objective measure of a preschool's quality of care. However, it is certainly not the only one and should not be considered in isolation. Other factors include the size of the group or class, the quality of activities and facilities provided and, perhaps most important, the professionalism and enthusiasm of the teachers.

Those preschools with overall teacher-to-child ratios of 1:10 or better have their ratio(s) marked in bold. If they have top ratios for only certain age groups, only those ratios are in bold. For example:

PG   **1:4**
N   **1:5**
K1   1:15

Preschools that have ratios between 1:8 and 1:12 for under three-year-olds only are not considered as having "top" ratios, as this is the MCD required ratio for child care centres.

PRESCHOOLS WITH ENRICHMENT ACTIVITIES

Nearly all preschools in Singapore offer a balanced and wide-ranging curriculum that includes Music and Movement, and art and craft activities. Many also offer Science, Cooking and Computer classes. See the table for details. Listed below are centres offering additional enrichment activities.

An asterisk in the following list indicates that an additional charge is payable. See the survey table for details. Otherwise, the activity is offered free of charge as part of the curriculum.

Speech and Drama in English (E)

1-2-3 Kids Childcare & Development
Adventist Child Development Centre
Cambridge Child Development
Care Corner Child Development*
Good Shepherd Childcare*
Honeykids Child Care & Development
Intellect Child Care & Development
Junior Playworld Child Care & Development*
Kinderjoy Educare*
Kinderland Child Care*
Little Fairyland Child Care & Development
Mothergoose Child Development
NTUC Childcare Co-operative Childcare Centres
Pat's Schoolhouse (all branches)
Praises Child Development Centre*
Playhouse Child Development
Sasco Child Care*
Tenderluv Daycare Child Development Centre*
The Children's Place
The Little Skool-House By-the-River
The Moral Child Care Centre*
Wonder Kids Child Care & Development*
Young Talents Child Care & Development*

Speech and Drama in Mandarin (M)

1-2-3 Kids Childcare & Development
Cambridge Child Development
Eternal Life Assembly Child Care*
Mothergoose Child Development
Pat's Schoolhouse (all branches)
The Children's Place

The Little Skool-House By-the-River
Young Talents Child Care & Development

Exercise Programme (Gymnastics/P.E.)
Children's Cottage
Eastmen Child Care & Development
Julia Gabriel Communications
Kinderland Child Care
Pat's Schoolhouse (all branches)
St. Clare Kindergarten

Children's Music Course
Kinderland Child Care*

Swimming
1-2-3 Kids Childcare & Development
Kinder Corner 1
Playhouse Child Development
The Little Skool-House On-the-Green

PRESCHOOLS OFFERING MINORITY LANGUAGES

Malay
Joytech Child Development Centre
Jude Child Care & Child Development, Pasir Ris (upon request)
Taman Bacaan Child Care & Development (bilingual English/Malay programme)
Taman Bacan Sang Nila Utama Child Care (bilingual English/Malay programme)
The Children's Learning Centre
Wonder Kids Child Care & Development
Some PCF Education Centres

Tamil
New Life Kindergarten
Some PCF Education Centres

Arabic
Jude Child Care and Child Development (Pasir Ris)
Wonder Kids Child Care & Development

Japanese
Eton House Pre-school (Newton)
Pat's SchoolHouse, Halifax Road
The Family Place
The Little Skool-House By-the-River

French, German, Dutch
Kindergartens of the French, German and Swiss, and Dutch schools respectively (see "International Schools")

MONTESSORI PRESCHOOLS
One advantage of Montessori preschools is that, because of their emphasis on children working at their own pace, they generally have excellent teacher-to-child ratios. The following preschools are included in the survey. Contact any of them for

more information about the Montessori approach to preschool education.

Full Montessori preschool offering full- and half-day care

Ichiban Montessori Child Care Centre

Full Montessori preschools offering part-day care

Bridges Montessori
Greentree Montessori Kindergarten
Montessori Creative World (two branches)
Sunshine Montessori House
The Montessori Workgroup

Child care centres offering some Montessori activities as part of their curriculum

1-2-3 Kids Childcare & Development
Pitter Patter Child Care & Development
Playhouse Child Development

EXPATRIATE-RUN PRESCHOOLS

There are several private, expatriate-run preschools, which generally offer part-day care for small groups of children in the organiser's home. Very few of them are included in the survey, but you can get lists from parent volunteers via the various national associations (see chapter 5).

Most of the international schools offer preschool education for children from the age of three or four years. See "International Schools" for details.

SOURCES OF FURTHER INFORMATION

The Ministry of Community Development's Child Care Services Branch provides information on all child care centres registered with it (of which there are several hundred). Its database is updated every month. Call the Child Care Information Service ☎1800 258 5812.

The *Directory of Schools and Educational Institutions,* produced annually by the Ministry of Education, has a list of over 80 privately run kindergartens; it is available to members of the public for $2 from Reception at the Ministry of Education headquarters in Kay Siang Road. Call the ministry's free hot line ☎1800 473 6420.

New preschool centres are opening all the time. There are several parenting magazines published in Singapore that include occasional articles on preschool provision and often refer to new centres. These magazines are: *Motherhood, Young Parents* and *Today's Parents.* They are available from most bookstores and kiosks.

THE PRIMARY SCHOOL SYSTEM

AN OVERVIEW

All children here receive at least 10 years of general education, of which six are in primary school and four in secondary school. The main aim of primary education is to give children a good grasp of English, their mother tongue and Mathematics.

Primary education is divided into a **foundation stage,** from P1 to P4, and a two-year **orientation stage,** from P5 to P6:

Stage	School year	Age of child
Foundation	P1	6 yrs.+
Foundation	P2	7 yrs. +
Foundation	P3	8 yrs. +
Foundation	P4	9 yrs. +
Orientation	P5	10 yrs.+
Orientation	P6	11 yrs. +

PRIMARY SCHOOL SUBJECTS

As well as ensuring children gain a firm foundation in English, their mother tongue (Mandarin, Malay or Tamil) and Mathematics, schools provide classes in Civics and Moral Education, Science (from P3), Social Studies (from P4), Art and Craft, Music, Health Education and Physical Education. These continue up to P6. Children whose mother tongue is English may choose the second language (from Mandarin, Malay or Tamil) they wish to study.

THE ORIENTATION STAGE

At the end of P4, each child is assessed on his or her performance in English, the mother tongue and Mathematics. Based on this assessment, the school recommends to parents the stream that their child should attend in P5.

THE FOUR LANGUAGE STREAMS

EM1

Children who do very well in English, their mother tongue and Mathematics are recommended for the EM1 stream, in which both languages are studied at the Higher level.

EM2

The majority of pupils are recommended for the EM2 stream, where the school decides whether they need additional lessons either in English or in their mother tongue.

EM3

Those children who are less able to cope with languages and Mathematics are recommended for the EM3 stream, which offers Foundation English and the mother tongue at

Examination (PSLE) at the end of P6. Its purpose is to assess each child's suitability for secondary school and place him or her in the right secondary school course for his or her learning pace, ability and inclinations.

There are three types of secondary school course: Special, Express and Normal. The Special and Express courses lead to the GCE 'O' level examination in four years, whereas the Normal course leads to the GCE 'N' level in four years with a fifth year leading to the GCE 'O' level examination. Within the Normal course, there are Academic and Technical options.

Basic Proficiency level. The teaching of the mother tongue emphasises oral and aural skills, reading and listening comprehension, and conversation.

ME3

Schools also provide ME3 classes, providing there is sufficient demand. In the ME3 stream, pupils study their mother tongue at the Higher level and Basic English. The teaching of English in this stream is the same as that of the mother tongue in the EM3 stream.

THE PSLE

All primary school pupils sit the national Primary School Leaving

PRIMARY SCHOOL REGISTRATION

THE OFFICIAL REGISTRATION CRITERIA

Parents can register their children for the primary school of their choice according to the following registration phases (registration is held on consecutive dates in the order of the list below):

Phase 1

For a child who has a sibling studying in the school of choice

Phase 2A
For a child with a parent or sibling who has studied in the school of choice, or with a parent who is a member of the School Advisory/ Management Committee or staff of that school

Phase 2B
For a child with a parent who is directly connected with the school

It's OK, Teacher

Sarah had just started school, and her teacher was always angry. Angry about poor handwriting, angry when the children brought the wrong books to school, and angry when they did not follow her instructions.

That morning, the teacher was angry with Sarah because she had not done her corrections as instructed. The teacher yelled and screamed. "Come here, Sarah! Don't ever come to school without doing your corrections! Put out your hands. This will teach you a lesson." The teacher smacked Sarah's tiny hands with a wooden ruler—1. . . 2 . . . 3 . . . 4 . . . 5.

Satisfied, the teacher flung Sarah's book across the room. Holding back her tears, Sarah walked to the back of the classroom to pick up her book. She looked at the book and saw it was not hers. She told the teacher that she had made a mistake and it was not her book. The angry teacher was not at all sorry. Instead, she bellowed: "Whose book is it?"

"It's Susan's book," whispered Sarah.

"Susan! Come here!" shouted the teacher. She gave Sarah the wooden ruler and said, "Take it and beat her five times."

Sarah turned away and whispered, "No, it's OK, teacher."

– Patricia Koh

Patricia Koh is principal of Pat's SchoolHouse and has three daughters aged 23, 22 and 9 years. She has been working in the preschool education field for over 25 years. The above events took place in the Singapore primary school that Patricia's niece attended.

Phase 2C

For a child who is ineligible for or unsuccessful in earlier phases

Phase 2C Supplementary

For a child who is unsuccessful in gaining a place in the school of choice in Phase 2C

Phase 3

For a child who is neither a Singapore citizen nor a Permanent Resident

If the number of applications exceeds the number of vacancies in any phase, priority is given to children living close to the school of choice.

WHAT PARENTS CAN DO

There is likely to be a great deal of competition for places at the school you would prefer your child to attend. If this is the case, and you do not have the advantage of being in Phase 1 or 2A of registration, here are some suggestions:

1. **Start early.** Call all the schools in your neighbourhood at least two years before your child is due to start primary school, and decide which of the schools you prefer.

2. **Assess your chances of success,** based on the school's performance and popularity, and the number of available P1 places. Call the Ministry of Education for up-to-date information, on its free hot line ☎ 1800 473 6420.

3. Find ways to **develop connections** with the school of your choice. You may already have some connections with the school and simply need to build on them.

4. If "connection building" isn't your style, **volunteer your services** for anything from tutoring to fund raising. Don't be a shrinking violet—make sure that people notice what you are doing, in order to have a better chance of getting your child into phase 2B.

5. Last but not least, if you don't live close to your school of choice, consider moving there. **Proximity to the school** could make the difference between your child getting a place and losing it.

When your children reach secondary school age, you will go through another school selection process. This task will be made easier, however, by reading the *Straits Times'* annual guide to secondary schools. Published during August as a supplement to the main paper, the guide includes information on the strengths of each school and rankings for Special, Express and Normal schools based on various criteria.

FOR FURTHER INFORMATION

The majority of the information in this section is reproduced from "Schooling in Singapore: Primary Education—An Information Guide for Parents" produced by the Ministry of Education, Public Affairs Division. This pamphlet is available free of charge.

The *Directory of Schools and Educational Institutions*, as mentioned earlier, is produced annually by the Ministry of Education and is available from the ministry's headquarters in Kay Siang Road. The directory lists a range of educational institutions, including private kindergartens, all primary and secondary schools, foreign-system schools, special education schools, fine arts schools and language schools. The principal's and vice-principal's or supervisor's name, and the school's name, address and telephone and fax numbers are given next to each entry.

INTERNATIONAL SCHOOLS

Expatriates who intend to stay in Singapore for only a few years usually prefer their children to attend an international school rather than become integrated into the local system; this makes it easier for them to reintegrate into the school system of their home country or into international school in the country of the family's next posting.

Most of the international schools provide preschool care from the age of three or four. However, until the age of seven, children may attend a local preschool instead. There are plenty of preschools (either local or expat-run) that cater to the needs of expatriate families (for example, that do not focus on the study of Mandarin). See "Preschools" for further details.

For expatriates making Singapore their permanent home, or those who expect to be here for the majority of their children's school years, the choice is a different one. If the school fees are to be paid by the employer, international school may still be an option. Otherwise, parents would usually be best advised to get their children Permanent Resident status and integrate them as soon as possible into the local system, preferably from Nursery age (three years), since the teaching of Mathematics and language skills, including Mandarin, starts then and success in these subjects is key to success in the PSLE (see "The Primary School System").

AN OVERVIEW

There is an excellent range and quality of expatriate schooling available in Singapore. However, places are often limited, so it is important to plan ahead where possible. Contact the schools you think sound suitable, arrange to visit them, and then put your child's name on the waiting list of one or more schools of your choice.

Schools providing instruction in English follow either the US, Canadian, Australian or British system of education. Some schools, such as the Overseas Family School and Chatsworth International School, cater to children from all English-speaking countries by providing a mixed curriculum. Most schools have ESL (English as a Second Language) tuition to assist children with language difficulties. There are also schools providing instruction in other languages: French, German, Dutch and Japanese.

Where school fees are given they are intended only as a guide. You should always contact the school directly for confirmation. School fees vary widely, so depending on whether your company pays all or part of them, it may pay to do some research.

All foreign nationals attending school in Singapore must hold a Student Pass. The school admissions office should hold the necessary application forms.

SCHOOLS OFFERING TUITION IN ENGLISH

AUSTRALIAN INTERNATIONAL SCHOOL
✉ Sector 22

Language of instruction
English

Curriculum
New South Wales

Subjects
Maths
English language
Other languages: Mandarin
                 Japanese
                 French
                 Indonesian
Art
Music
Computer classes
Tests twice a year
Camps and overseas trips

Age
3 to 19 years

Cost
Kindergarten (3 to 5 years): $2780 per term
Thereafter: average $3500 per term
There are four terms per year.

Teacher-to-child ratio
1:25

Notes
1000 pupils
Mostly Australian teaching staff
Has own music centre, gym, pool and fields
Three trained ESL teachers and intensive language centre

CANADIAN INTERNATIONAL SCHOOL
✉ Sector 59

Language of instruction
English

Curriculum
Canadian

Subjects
Maths
English language
Other languages: Mandarin
                 French
Art
Music
Computer classes
Tests from 11 years
Field trips

Age
3 to 18 years

Cost
Call Admissions ☎467 1732 for details.

Teacher-to-child ratio
1:10 to 22

Notes
700 pupils
Over 80% Canadian trained teaching staff
Internet access from classrooms
Students from over 40 nationalities
Mother and Child programme for children from 1½ to 2½ years.

CHATSWORTH INTERNATIONAL SCHOOL
✉ Sector 53

Language of instruction
English

Curriculum
Offers an international curriculum leading to American and British qualifications.

Subjects
Maths
Science
History
PE
PSE
ESL
Asian Studies
Geography
Business Studies
English language/English literature
Other languages: Mandarin
                                    French
Art
Music
Computer classes

Swimming
Field trips
Elective programme in high school
Extensive ECA programme

Age
3 to 18 years

Cost
For 3 to 10 years: $10,000 per year
For 11 to 18 years: $13,500 per year

Teacher-to-child ratio
1:20 maximum

Notes
370 pupils
International teaching staff
Close to Somerset MRT station and Orchard Road

DOVER COURT PREPARATORY SCHOOL
✉ Sector 13

Language of instruction
English

Subjects
Maths
English language and literature
Other language: French
Art
Music
Computer classes
Science
PSE
Social studies/humanities
PE

Swimming
Drama

Age
3 to 14 years
(Special needs: 2½ to 18 years)

Cost
Call Admissions Officer ☎775 7664 for details.

Teacher-to-child ratio
1:28
(Special needs 1:6)

Notes
900 pupils
Predominance of British teachers
ESL assistance and Speech and Language therapy are available.
The school has its own swimming pool.

ETONHOUSE INTERNATIONAL SCHOOL
✉ Sector 43

Language of instruction
English

Curriculum
UK National Curriculum

Subjects
English
Other language: Mandarin
Maths

Science
Technology
Humanities (History and Geography)
Creative Arts (Art and Craft, Music and Drama)
PE
Personal, Social and Moral Education

Age
6 to 11 years

Cost
$10,000 per year
Refundable deposit: $5,000
Registration fee: $1,500
Meals: $100 per month (optional)

Teacher-to-child ratio
1:25

Notes
International teaching staff

INTERNATIONAL COMMUNITY SCHOOL
✉ Sector 9

Language of instruction
English

Subjects
Maths
English language
Art
Music

Age
Preschool: 4 to 5 years
Kindergarten: 5 to 6 years
Elementary: 6 to 12 years
Secondary: from 12 years

Cost
Preschool: $3500 per semester
Kindergarten: $5500 per semester
Elementary: $6500 per semester
Secondary: $7500 per semester
There are two semesters per year.
Non-refundable capital fee: $1000 per year

Teacher-to-child ratio
1:10

Notes
73 pupils
American teaching staff
Christian international school

INTERNATIONAL SCHOOL OF SINGAPORE (ISS)
✉ Sectors 10 and 23

Language of instruction
English

Subjects
Maths
English language
Other languages: Mandarin
French
Japanese
Humanities
Science

PE
Drama
Health education
Art
Music
Computer classes
Field trips

Age
3 to 19 years

Cost
Call Enrollment Manager
☎470 0113 for details.

Teacher-to-child ratio
1:10

Notes
600 pupils
International teaching staff
EFL assistance is available, including a summer school.
Arts summer school for all primary grades

OVERSEAS FAMILY SCHOOL
✉ Sector 23

Language of instruction
English

Subjects
Maths
English language
Other languages: Mandarin
                 French
                 Japanese
                 Spanish

Art
Music
Computer classes
Humanities
Science
Field trips

Age
4 to 18 years

Cost
Varies with grade level.
Contact Soma Matthews
☎738 0211 for details.

Teacher-to-child ratio
1:12

Notes
1600 pupils
International teaching staff
ESL assistance is available.
Accredited by Western Association of Schools and Colleges (WASC)

SINGAPORE AMERICAN SCHOOL
✉ Sector 73

Language of instruction
English

Subjects
Maths
Reading/Language Arts
Art
Music
Computer education
Social studies

Science
PE/Swimming
After-school activities

Age
3 years to grade 12

Cost
Call Admissions ☎360 6309 ext. 301 for details.

Teacher-to-child ratio
Preschool: max 1:18
Pre-kindergarten: max 1:18
Kindergarten to grade 5: max 1:22
Grades 6 to 12: max 1:25

Notes
2780 pupils
Mainly American teachers
ESL assistance is available.
Accredited by Western Association of Schools and Colleges (WASC)

SCHOOLS OFFERING TUITION IN OTHER LANGUAGES

DEUTSCHE SCHULE SINGAPUR
✉ Sector 28

Language of instruction
German

Curriculum
As in Germany

Subjects
Maths
German language
Other language: English (from P1)
                 French (Sec 1)
Science
Art
Music
Field trips
Extra-curricular activities

Age
$3\frac{1}{2}$ to 18 years

Cost
Kindergarten & Preschool ($3\frac{1}{2}$ to 6 years): $6660 per annum
Primary: $7380 to $9160 per annum
Secondary: $10,960 per annum
Additional charges include entrance fee, membership fee, refundable deposit and cost of teaching materials. A loan certificate must be purchased for each child.

Teacher-to-child ratio
1:22

Notes
650 pupils
German teaching staff

HOLLANDSE SCHOOL
✉ Sector 28

Language of instruction
Dutch

Curriculum
Dutch

Subjects
Maths
Dutch language
Other language: English
(from age 6)
Art
Music
Computer classes
Tests
Field trips

Age
4 to 12 years

Cost
$10,500 per annum

Teacher-to-child ratio
Average 1:18

Notes
230 pupils
Dutch teaching staff

SWISS SCHOOL ASSOCIATION
✉ Sector 28

Language of instruction
High German

Subjects
Maths
German language
Other languages: English
French (from P5)
Art
Music

Religious instruction
Field trips

Age
3 years 4 months to 16 years

Cost
Play group: $2210 per term
Kindergarten: $2590 per term
Primary (grades 1 through 4): $2850 per term
Primary (grades 5 and 6): $3480 per term
Secondary (grades 7 through 9): $3900 per term
Deposit: one term's fees
Registration fee: $500 per child
Building fund: $1000 per school year
SSA membership: $100 per school year

Teacher-to-child ratio
Average 1:20

Notes
120 pupils
Swiss teaching staff
Priority given to Swiss citizens. Others must speak German.

OTHER SCHOOLS
The following schools declined to participate:
Tanglin Trust School
Lycée Francais de Singapour
The Japanese School

PLAY CENTRES

Several indoor centres offer play/ gymnastics facilities and structured activity sessions for children. Some also offer preschool and other classes. Sessions for younger children are generally intended for the child to attend with a parent or carer.

Some play centres have three-dimensional play mazes: systems of tunnels, slides, ball pools and other physical challenges. The play mazes are theoretically suitable for children of all ages, but those under four years certainly need to be accompanied by an adult (that means *you* will have to crawl through the tunnels too!). Some play centres also have smaller play areas that are more suitable for toddlers.

FORUM GALLERIA HIP KIDS CLUB

✉ Sector

Activities

Use of indoor children's playground, including track, ride-on cars, tunnel, climbing frame and slides.

Age

Up to 8 years (height limit 120 cm)

Cost

$10 and two passport photos to join Hip Kids Club. Cardholders can accumulate bonus points from selected stores.

Timings

Open Monday to Friday from 11 a.m. to 1.30 p.m. and from 4 p.m. to 9 p.m. and Saturday and Sunday from 10.30 a.m. to 9 p.m.

GYMBOREE
✉ Sectors 24 and 76

Activities
Age-appropriate developmental movement/play programme for parents and their children
"Playgym" facility for children from newborn to 4 years. Call centre for Playgym timings.

Age
Newborn to 4 years
Classes cover the following age bands: Newborn to 6 months, 6 to 12 months, 10 to 18 months, 14 to 28 months, 28 months to 3 years, 3 to 4 years.

Cost
$220 per eight-week term of weekly classes
Annual membership: $50
Playgym: $8 per hour ($15 for non-members)
Trial class: $30

Class timings
Daily 9 a.m. to 6 p.m.
Classes last 45 minutes.

See also
Preschool Survey, Drama Classes, Toys and Games, Party Organisers

JAN & ELLY – THE LEARNING PLACE
✉ Sector 67

Activities
Toddler & Parent play groups

Age
From 18 months

Cost
$180 to $480 per month
Registration fee: $25

Teacher-to-child ratio
1:5 to 10

Class timings
2-hour sessions, Monday to Saturday
Call centre for details.

See also
Preschool Survey, Enrichment Classes

JULIA GABRIEL COMMUNICATIONS
✉ Sector 23

Activities
The "Play Club" offers a range of activities, including Art and Craft, free play, outdoor play, and preschool language and pre-number work.

"Parent and Toddler" classes are similar but have an emphasis on music and movement activities.

Age

Play Club: 1 1/2 to 3 1/2 years. Children must be accompanied by a parent or carer until the teaching team feel that they are ready to attend on their own.
Parent and Toddler: 2 1/2 to early 3 years

Cost

Play Club: $790 per term of 10 weeks
Parent and Toddler: $298.70 per term of 10 weeks
Registration fee: $25
Refundable deposit: $200

Teacher-to-child ratio

1:4

Class timings

Monday to Friday and Sundays, 9 a.m. to 6.30 p.m.
Play Club sessions are for 2 hours, twice a week, and are available in the mornings and afternoons.
Parent and Toddler sessions are for 1 hour per week.

See also

Preschool Survey, Drama Classes

PRIME GYMNASTICS CLUB

✉ Sector 27

Activities

Structured play and gymnastic activities and competitive gymnastics for older children

Age

From 9 months
Classes cover the following age bands: 9 to 17 months, 1 1/2 to 3 years, 3 to 5 years, 5 years and over.

Cost

1 hour per week: $230 per term of 11 weeks
2 hours per week: $375 per term of 11 weeks
Registration fee: $40
Free trial class
Discounts are available for early payment and termly payment, and a 10% discount is given to additional family members.

Teacher-to-child ratio

1:8 maximum

Class timings

Monday to Saturday 9 a.m. to 8 p.m.
Call club for current schedule of classes.

✍ Author's note

A full-sized gymnasium with a good range of equipment. If you have an active child and think he/she would enjoy gymnastics, this is a good place to try.

QUESTXONE (KINDERWORLD EDUTAINMENT CONCEPTS)

✉ Sector 3

Activities

Use of the play maze and play equipment, including a small toddler play area and computers with educational software. Due to re-open May 2000 in new location.

Age

1 to 16 years, but see note on play mazes above.

Cost

$13.50 for a 2-hour package, $10 for 1 hour

Opening hours

Daily 10 a.m. to 10 p.m.

See also

Preschool Survey, Party Organisers

THE FAMILY PLACE

✉ Sector 17

Activities

Drop-in use of the Adventure Boat play area and the Toy and Book Corner
Kindergym classes
Infant play classes

Age

Infant play: 8 to 18 months
Drop-in: 18 months to 7 years
Kindergym: 3 to 6 years

Cost

Drop-in rates:
$6.50 for first hour
$5.50 for subsequent hours
Members get discount
Infant play: $180 for 12 sessions
Kindergym: $180 for 10 sessions
Annual membership is available for $120 (gold) or $80 (green) per family.

Class timings

Call centre for schedule.
Classes last 1 to 2 hours.

See also

Preschool Survey, Art Classes, Drama Classes, Enrichment Classes, Shop 'n' Drop Facilities, Party Organisers, Help for Parents

TUMBLE TOTS

✉ Sectors 12, 23, 25, 44, 51, 52, 53, 57, 60 and 73

Activities

Structured physical play classes which aim to develop motor skills and build self confidence and social skills

Age

6 months to 7 years

Gifts of Joy

One of the best things about being a parent is the surprises—
discovering new things about my children. When my elder son
presented me with a computer printout of a poem he'd written at
school I was delighted! My gawky 5'6" son had been hiding such a
romantic spirit!

The poem now hangs in my office, reminding me to take a break
from the paperwork now and then and let my mind wander out far
across the sea to the ends of the earth. Reading his poem I come
alive with renewed energy. At 13, my son turned out to be my best
de-stress mentor!

I was so proud, having nurtured his development through many
hours of reading and sharing during his growing up years. Who
says children cannot be teachers to parents? As adults and parents
we should always be open to these simple gifts of joy.

Excerpt from Ho Ren Hua's poem:

> "Visions by the seaside,
> Enchantment by the shore.
> The monstrous sea never rests,
> The waves responding, fuming with zest.
> So never will the far off horizon,
> Ever come to a drawn line,
> For it will be us next time,
> Exploring through the seas for all mankind."

– Claire Chiang

*Claire Chiang is director of Banyan Tree Gallery and president of
the Society Against Family Violence. She has two sons—Ho Ren
Hua, 17, and Ho Ren Chun, 5—and a daughter, Ho Ren Yung, 14.*

Classes cover the following age bands: 6 months to walking, walking to 2 years, 2 to 3 years, 3 to 5 years, 5 to 7 years.

Cost

$55 to $60 per month
Registration fee: $10
Annual membership is available for $60 and includes personal accident insurance, a pack for the child and a free T-shirt.
Free trial class

Teacher-to-child ratio

1:6.

Class timings

Call centre for schedule.
Classes last 45 minutes.

CREATIVE CLASSES

Creative and performing arts activities have an increasingly important part to play in Singapore life. Enthused and encouraged by national efforts and events such as the biennial Festival of Arts, there are a growing number of excellent schools where children can nurture and develop their creative talents.

In addition to those listed here, many other organisations offer creative classes. These include schools, which offer creative activities as part of their holiday programmes, and community centres, which generally offer children's activities such as Chinese and Malay dance classes.

ART CLASSES

CHILDREN'S ART SOCIETY

✉ Sector 16

Activities

Children's art classes
The society also organises art competitions, exhibitions, overseas exchange programmes and outdoor painting.

Age

From 2 years

Cost

From $55 per month

Teacher-to-child ratio

1:6

Class timings

Weekdays and weekends, daytime and evening. Call for details.
Classes last 1 to 1½ hours.

CRESTAR LEARNING CENTRE

✉ Sector 44

Activities

Children's art classes

Age

4 to 12 years
Classes are organised for children of similar ages within this range.

41

Cost
From $30.90 per month
Registration fee: $20.60

Teacher-to-child ratio
1:15

Class timings
Monday 1 p.m. to 9 p.m.
Tuesday to Friday 9 a.m. to 9 p.m.
Saturday 9 a.m. to 7 p.m.
Sunday 9 a.m. to 6 p.m.
Classes last 1 to 1½ hours.

See also
Dance Classes, Drama Classes

LA SALLE – SIA COLLEGE OF THE ARTS
✉ Sector 43

★ SFK award
To La Salle – SIA College of the Arts for its innovative and wide ranging programmes for young children, in art, dance, drama and music

Activities
Junior visual art workshops

Age
3 to 12 years

Cost
$190.55 per term of 10 weeks.
Free trial class.

Teacher-to-child ratio
1:8

Class timings
Classes run Friday evenings, all day Saturday, and Sunday mornings. Call centre for class schedule.

See also
Dance Classes, Drama Classes, Music Classes

RADIANCE TRAINING CENTRE
✉ Sector 64

Activities
Art (watercolour, crayon and craft)

Age
From 4 years

Cost
$6.50 to $15 per session

Teacher-to-child ratio
1:10 to 15

Class timings
Monday to Friday 9 a.m. to 9.30 p.m.
Saturday 9 a.m. to 6 p.m.
Sunday 9.30 a.m. to 2 p.m.
Classes last 1 to 1½ hours.

See also
Enrichment Classes

SCHOOL OF YOUNG TALENTS
✉ Sector 18 (2 locations), 22

Activities
Kinderart, Children's art

Age
5 to 6 years, 6 to 8 years, 8 to 10 years and 10 to 12 years

Cost
$247.20 per semester of 20 sessions plus registration fee

Teacher-to-child ratio
1:12 to 1:20

Class timings
Saturday and Sunday only

THE FAMILY PLACE
✉ Sector 17

Activities
Creative Art

Age
Junior class: 3 to 4 years
Advanced class: 4 to 7 years

Cost
$190 for 12 sessions (for members)
Annual membership is available for $120 (gold) and $80 (green) per family

Teacher-to-child ratio
Varies with age group

Class timings
Classes last 1 hour.

See also

Preschool Survey, Play Centres, Drama Classes, Enrichment Classes, Shop 'n' Drop Facilities, Party Organisers, Help for Parents

DANCE CLASSES

5678

✉ Sector 6

Activities

Ballet, jazz dance, Chinese dance, hip-hop

Age

Ballet: 3 to 12 years
Chinese dance: 4 to 15 years
Jazz dance: 6 to 12 years
Hip-hop dance: 6 to 15 years

Cost

$120 for 3 months

Teacher-to-child ratio

Call school for details.

Class timings

Call school for class schedule.
Classes last 45 minutes to 1 hour, depending on age.

CECILIA HON BALLET THEATRE

✉ Sector 28

Activity

Ballet

Age

Pre-primary: 3½ to 6 years
Primary to Advanced: from 6 years

Cost

$100 to $240 per term
Registration fee: $10

Teacher-to-child ratio

1:10

Class timings

Weekday evenings after 6 p.m., Saturdays and Sundays
Classes last 45 minutes to 1 hour, depending on age.

CRESTAR LEARNING CENTRE

✉ Sector 44

Activities

Bébé Ballet and Classical Ballet

Age

From 3 years

Cost

From $36.05 per month

Teacher-to-child ratio

1:10 for Bébé Ballet
1:15 for Classical Ballet

Class timings

Call school for class schedule.

See also

Art Classes

DANCE ARTS
✉ Sector 23

Activities
Ballet, jazz dance, tap dance, hip-hop and funk

Age
3 to 18 years

Cost
$150 to $230 per term of 12 lessons, or pay for individual classes.
Registration fee: $10

Teacher-to-child ratio
1:15

Class timings
Daily 10.30 a.m. to 8.30 p.m.
Classes last 45 minutes to 1½ hours.

FORMS BALLET AND DANCE CENTRE
✉ Sector 12

Activities
Ballet, tap dance
Staging of dance performances

Age
From 4 years

Cost
$90 to $225 per term of three months
Registration fee: $20
Trial class: $10

Teacher-to-child ratio
1:10 to 30

Class timings
Monday to Friday from 3 p.m.
Saturday from 9 a.m.
Sunday from 1 p.m. (November to March only)
Classes last 45 minutes to 1½ hours.

LA SALLE – SIA COLLEGE OF THE ARTS
✉ Sector 43

Activities
Pre-dance and Young Dancers' Theatre (ballet and modern dance with theatre production elements)

Age
Pre-dance: 3 to 6 years
Young Dancers' Theatre: 7 to 14 years

Cost
Pre-dance: $118.45 per term of 10 weeks
Young Dancers' Theatre: $159.65 per term of 10 weeks
Free trial class

Teacher-to-child ratio
1:8

Class timings
Classes run Wednesday evenings, all day Saturdays, and Sunday mornings. Call centre for class schedule.

See also
Art Classes, Drama Classes, Music Classes

TRIGG.

PALAIS DANCE STUDIO
✉ Sector 26

Activities
Ballet, modern theatre dance and tap dance. Performance opportunities

Age
Ballet from 4 years
Modern and tap dance from 7 years

Cost
From $90 per term

Teacher-to-child ratio
1:20

Class timings
Monday to Thursday 4 p.m. to 8.30 p.m.
Weekends 9.30 a.m. to 6 p.m.

Classes last 45 minutes to 2 hours, depending on level.

SINGAPORE BALLET ACADEMY
✉ Sector 17

Activity
Ballet

Age
From 4 years

Cost
From $90 per term of three months

Teacher-to-child ratio
Call school for details.

Class timings
Call school for class schedule.

Classes last 45 minutes to 1½ hours, depending on age and level.

✍ Author's note

This is the school for the serious would-be ballet dancer. Established in 1958, this is the oldest ballet school in Singapore and has built an excellent reputation for classical ballet.

DRAMA CLASSES

ACT 3 DRAMA ACADEMY

✉ Sectors 22, 52 and 59

Activities

Drama courses in English, where children learn to:
speak confidently and communicate effectively,
develop team spirit and cooperation,
develop their imagination.
The academy also runs workshops and programmes at clubs and schools.

Age

18 months to 15 years

Cost

$250 per term
A "module package" discount is also available.

Teacher-to-child ratio

Up to 4 years 1:10
Over 4 years 1:15

Class timings

Classes are held on Fridays or on weekends, depending on the age group.
All classes last 1 hour.

See also

Party Entertainers (ACT 3 Theatrics)

✍ Author's note

Look out for ACT 3's children's theatre activities. These now include international acts as part of "Young Series @ ACT 3 Theatre". Performances are at the Studio theatre, in schools and other community locations.

CRESTAR LEARNING CENTRE

✉ Sector 44

Activities

Speech and drama in English and Chinese

Age

From 4 years

Cost

From $61.80 per month
Registration fee: $20.50

Teacher-to-child ratio

1:12

Class timings

Monday 1 p.m. to 9 p.m.
Tuesday to Friday 9 a.m. to 9 p.m.
Saturday 9 a.m. to 7 p.m.

Sunday 9 a.m. to 6 p.m.
Classes last 1 hour

CRISTOFORI SCHOOL OF FINE ARTS
✉ Sector 17

Activity
Drama in Mandarin

Age
Tiny Tots: 3 to 5 years
Children: from 6 years

Cost
$50 to $200 per month

Teacher-to-child ratio
1:5

Class timings
Call school for class schedule.
Classes last 1 hour.

See also
Music Classes

GYMBOREE
✉ Sectors 24 and 76

Activity
"Gymkids Drama" in English

Age
$4^{1}/_{2}$ to 6 years

Cost
$220 for 8 sessions
Annual membership: $50

Teacher-to-child ratio
2:20

Class timings
Call centre for class schedule.
Classes last 1 hour.

See also
Preschool Survey, Play Centres, Toys and Games, Party Organisers

JULIA GABRIEL COMMUNICATIONS
✉ Sector 22

Activities
Speech and Drama classes in English

Age
$3^{1}/_{2}$ to 18 years

Cost
$260 per term of 10 weeks
Registration fee: $25
Refundable deposit: $50

Teacher-to-child ratio
1:4 to 12, depending on age

Class timings
Tuesday to Saturday and Sundays 9 a.m. to 6.30 p.m.
Classes last 1 to $1^{1}/_{2}$ hours, depending on age.

See also
Preschool Survey, Play Centres

JULIET MCCULLY SCHOOL OF LANGUAGE AND COMMUNICATIONS
✉ Sector 23

Activities
Speech and Drama classes in English

Age
4 to 12 years

Cost
$275 per three-month term
Registration fee: $30
Refundable administration fee: $68

Teacher-to-child ratio
1:4 to 12, depending on age

Class timings
Call centre for class schedule.
Classes last 1 hour.

See also
Enrichment Classes

LA SALLE – SIA COLLEGE OF THE ARTS
✉ Sector 43

Activities
Young Wayang Players (includes role play, improvisation, mime and movement, voice training and puppetry)

Age
7 to 14 years

Cost
$211.15 per term of 10 weeks
Free trial class

Teacher-to-child ratio
1:8

Class timings
Classes run Saturday morning and afternoon. Call centre for class schedule.

See also
Art Classes, Dance Classes, Music Classes

SINGAPORE REPERTORY THEATRE
✉ Sector 6

Activities
Drama classes in English:
poetry, games, scriptwriting, songs, improvisation, mime, reading and acting techniques

Age
2 to 12 years

Cost
$257.50 per term
Registration fee: $30 per child
10% discount for DBS card holders

Teacher-to-child ratio
1:10

Class timings
Daily 9.15 a.m. to 6 p.m.
Classes last 45 minutes to 1 hour.

THE FAMILY PLACE
✉ Sector 17

Activities and ages
"Creative Performance", dance/drama in Mandarin: 4 to 6 years
Drama in English (run by ACT 3): 18 months to 15 years

Cost
Creative Performance: $230 for 12 sessions
Drama in English: $230 for 10 sessions
Annual membership is available for $120 (gold) or $80 (green) per family.

Teacher-to-child ratio
Call centre for details.

Class timings
Saturday and Sunday only
Call centre for class schedule.
Classes last 1 hour.

See also
Preschool Survey, Play Centres, Art Classes, Enrichment Classes, Shop 'n' Drop Facilities, Party Organisers

MUSIC CLASSES

CORONATION MUSIC SCHOOL
✉ Sector 26

Activities
Lessons in classical singing, guitar, violin, clarinet, flute, piano and saxophone

Age
From 5 years

Cost
From $240 per term

Teacher-to-child ratio
1:1

Class timings
Weekdays 9.30 a.m. to 9.30 p.m.
Weekends 9 a.m. to 6 p.m.
Classes last 30 to 45 minutes.

CRISTOFORI SCHOOL OF FINE ARTS
✉ Sector 17

Activities
Children's choir
Group and individual lessons in piano, organ, violin and guitar

Cost
$60 to $250 per month

Teacher-to-child ratio
1:1 or 8

Class timings
Daily 10 a.m. to 9 p.m.
Classes last 30 minutes to 1 hour.

See also
Drama Classes

CRISTOFORI MUSIC SCHOOL
✉ Call school for details of classes in 10 HDB locations.

Activities
Lessons in piano, violin, organ and guitar

Cost
$60 to $220 per month

Teacher-to-child ratio
1:1 or 8

Class timings
Daily 10 a.m. to 9 p.m.
Classes last 30 minutes to 1 hour.

KINDERMUSIK
✉ Sector 27. Classes are also available at The Family Place, Edutots (Bishan), Tampines Arcadia R.C., The American Club and Juliet McCully School of Language and Communications. Call Kindermusik for details.

Activities
Children learn to make music through playing simple instruments, singing, movement, dance and playing games.

Age
Newborn to 7 years
Classes cover the following age bands: Newborn to 18 months, 18 months to $3^1/_2$ years, $3^1/_2$ to $4^1/_2$ years, $4^1/_2$ to 7 years.

Cost
$12.30 per 30-minute class
$19.50 per 45-minute class
$27 per 75-minute class

Teacher-to-child ratio
1:10

Class timings
Call centre for class schedule.
Classes last 30 to 75 minutes, depending on age.

LA SALLE – SIA COLLEGE OF THE ARTS
✉ Sector 43

Activities and ages
Junior Musical Kids (games, musical instruments and singing): 4 to 6 years
Rhythm Lab (the fundamentals of rhythm, sound and composing): 5 to 7 years
Youth Gamelan (games, stories, drills and group playing): 7 to 12 years
Young voices (training choir, experienced choir): 7 to 14 years

Cost
$128.75 to $206 per term of 10 weeks
One-time registration fee: $20.60

Teacher-to-child ratio
1:8

Class timings
Classes run Friday evenings and all day Saturday. Call centre for class schedule.

See also
Art Classes, Dance Classes, Drama Classes

MANDEVILLE MUSIC SCHOOL
✉ Sector 23

Activities and ages
Preschool Music Exploration Class: 3 to 4 years
Individual lessons in –
* piano, violin, cello, voice training: from 3 years
* drums: from 5 years
* guitar (classical or pop), pop/ jazz
  piano: from 6 years
* flute, clarinet: from 8 years
* saxophone: from 10 years
Music theory classes
Studio rental

Cost
Call school for details.
Registration fee: $20

Teacher-to-child ratio
1:1 to 8

Class timings
Monday and Saturday 9 a.m. to 9 p.m.
Call school for class schedule.

SCHOOL OF YOUNG TALENTS
✉ Sectors 18 and 22

Activities
Gifted Young Pianists Course
Gifted Young Violinists Course

Age
4 to 14 years

Cost
From $82.40 per month, depending on age and level.

Class timings
Call centre for class schedule

VICTOR DOGGETT MUSIC STUDIOS
✉ Sector 43

Activities and ages
Preparatory piano course (PPC): 4 to 6 years
Piano lessons: from 7 years
Theory of music, music appreciation and aural training

Cost
$200 per term of 3 months for PPC
$100 to $300 per month for individual lessons

Registration fee: $20

Teacher-to-child ratio
1:3 or 4 for PPC
1:1 for piano lessons

Class timings
Daily 9 a.m. to 7 p.m.
Classes last 30 minutes to 1 hour, depending on age and grade.

ENRICHMENT CLASSES

WHAT IS ENRICHMENT?

Enrichment is a popular concept in Singapore, as parents look to give their children a good educational start in life. Increasingly, parents are seeking extra classes for their children outside the preschool or primary school curriculum, either in the evenings or on weekends.

With the current emphasis on the importance of preschool education, enrichment classes are available for children of all ages—even babies can attend structured play sessions "designed to improve their gross and fine motor skills"!

The term is often misused, so be sure your child is being "enriched" and not just crammed with facts in highly structured classes!

Patricia Koh, who runs Pat's SchoolHouse, says, "A child is normally active, playful, curious and creative. Most of the time he is engrossed with and is fascinated by the world he sees around him, which is very different from how an adult sees it. Knowing this and knowing how to take advantage of this is one of my highest priorities and that of all of my teachers."

These words are applicable to child development as a whole but are particularly relevant to the area of enrichment classes. Classes that seek to exploit a child's natural curiosity and creativity, and teach through play activities, games and songs, are likely to be the most effective. The approach should be one of encouraging, enthusing and inspiring children rather than concentrating on rote learning and filling in worksheets. The end result of this approach should be a confident and happy child who is ready to take on new challenges.

WHY REGISTER MY CHILD?

Any child can benefit from extra classes, but there are two main groups:

1. Children who are struggling and who need to reinforce basic skills in order to keep up with the school curriculum
2. Children of above average ability who are getting bored and

need to be stretched with a new challenge

Be careful not to overload your child with extracurricular activities, as that could just make matters worse.

CHOOSING THE RIGHT SCHOOL

The schools and centres listed in this section are those that offer enrichment classes in Maths and language development. This is a very narrow focus. Creative classes (see previous section) also help in the development of these core skills. Music classes are believed to help in the development of mathematical skills, and Drama classes are good for developing language skills and confidence in speaking. If a child enjoys or excels in a craft or sport, encourage it—the confidence and enjoyment he or she derives from this activity is likely to have a beneficial effect on school studies too.

Preschools and play centres, such as FunDazzle, also offer before- and after-school care (BASC) and enrichment activities. In addition, structured play has a gymnastic element, which in itself has a very "enriching" effect on a child's self-confidence.

Also, don't forget your local community centre. Most centres offer a range of creative and sporting activities for children and are likely to offer better value than a private school.

CENTRES OFFERING MORE THAN ONE SUBJECT

JAN & ELLY – THE LEARNING PLACE
✉ Sector 67

Subjects and Ages
English (Phonics): 3 to 7 years
English (Creative writing and grammar): P1 to P4
Mandarin: 3 to 7 years

Cost
$200 to $380 per term of 10 lessons

Teacher-to-child ratio
1:9

Class timings
Weekday evenings and Saturdays
Call centre for details.

See also
Preschool Survey, Play Centres

RADIANCE TRAINING CENTRE
✉ Sector 64

Subjects and ages
Children's English: 4 to 5 years
Fun with Reading/Mathsboard: 4 to 6 years

Pre-Primary English and Maths: 6 years
Fun with Phonics: 6 to 10 years
International Phonics: from 11 years
English Enrichment: 4 to 16 years
Chinese Enrichment : 4 to 16 years
Tuition classes (English, Maths and Science): Primary and Secondary levels

Cost
$15 per session

Teacher-to-child ratio
1:10 to 15

Class timings
Monday to Friday 9 a.m. to 9.30 p.m.
Saturday 9 a.m. to 6 p.m.
Sunday 9.30 a.m. to 2 p.m.
Classes last 1½ hours.

See also
Art Classes

THE FAMILY PLACE
✉ Sector 17

Subjects and ages
Play and Learn (English or Mandarin): 2 to 4 years
Hanyu Pinyin Experiential Mandarin: 4 to 6 years
Fun with Phonics (English): 4 to 6 years
Mad Science: 5 to 12 years
Creative Writing (English): 7 to 9 years

Cost
Costs for members:
Play and Learn: $230 for 12 sessions
Hanyu Pinyin: $360 per module of 16 sessions
Fun with Phonics: $230 for 12 sessions
Mad Science: $98 for four sessions
Creative Writing: $230 for 10 sessions
Annual membership is available for $120 (gold) or $80 (green) per family.

Teacher-to-child ratio
1:6 to 7

Class timings
Classes last 1 hour.

Notes
Holiday programmes available

See also
Preschool Survey, Art Classes, Drama Classes, Play Centres, Shop 'n' Drop Facilities, Party Organisers

CENTRES OFFERING LANGUAGE CLASSES

ATT LANGUAGE CENTRE
✉ Sector 24

Subjects
Preparatory Language Courses for

55

entry into Singapore, US and UK schools, including SAT, PSLE and 'O' levels

Enrichment classes for primary students

Intensive classes

Speech and drama classes

Age
Singaporeans: from 4 years
Expatriates: 9 to 15 years

Cost
Preparatory courses: $395 per term (3 hours per week)

Intensive classes: $1350 for five weeks

Call centre for further details. Discounts available.

Teacher-to-child ratio
1:10 to 12

Class timings
Monday to Friday 8.30 a.m. to 9 p.m.
Saturday 9 a.m. to 5.30 p.m.

CORRINE PRIVATE SCHOOL
✉ Sector 18

Subjects
English (Phonics, Enrichment)
EFL (English as a Foreign Language)
Mandarin Enrichment

Age
From 5 years

Cost
English (Phonics): from $75 for four lessons of 90 minutes each
English or Mandarin Enrichment: average $150 per month
EFL: average $300 per month

Teacher-to-child ratio
1:10

Class timings
Monday to Friday 9 a.m. to 9 p.m.
Saturday 9 a.m. to 4.30 p.m.
Classes last 1$\frac{1}{2}$ to 3 hours, depending on age and subject.

EXCEL-WORLD LANGUAGE SCHOOL
✉ Sector 18 (main branch)

Subjects
Mandarin
English

Age
Toddlers to 12 years

Cost
$165 to $210 per term

Teacher-to-child ratio
1:14

Class timings
Call main school for class schedule.

INLINGUA SCHOOL OF LANGUAGES

✉ Sectors 23 and 59

Subjects
English
Mandarin
Japanese
Malay
French
German
Spanish
Russian

Age
From 6 years

Cost
General Skills Development (English or Mandarin): $27 to $59 per week for a 10-week term
Junior Intensive English Plus (25 lessons per week): $275 to $410 per week

Teacher-to-child ratio
1:5 or 10

Class timings
Monday to Friday 8.30 a.m. to 9.30 p.m.
Saturday 8.30 a.m. to 1 p.m.

Notes
Budget holiday study programmes are available in June and December. Inlingua also offers a range of classes for adults.

JULIET MCCULLY SCHOOL OF LANGUAGE AND COMMUNICATIONS

✉ Sector 23

Subjects and ages
English Creative Writing: 6 to 14 years
English Reading and Language Arts: 4 to 11 years
English Pre-Readers Programme: 4 years
English Enrichment: 7 to 12 years
Oral Communication: 8 to 18 years

Cost
Creative Writing: $275 per term
Reading and Language Arts: $480 per term
Pre-Readers: $300 per term
Enrichment: $340 per term
Oral Communication: from $250 per term
Registration fee: $30
Refundable deposit: $68

Teacher-to-child ratio
1:8 to 9

Class timings
All classes last 1 hour, except Reading and Language Arts, which lasts 2 hours.

See also
Drama Classes

MORRIS ALLEN STUDY CENTRE

✉ Sectors 30, 42 and 52

Subject
English (including creative writing, phonics, reading and opral practice)

Age
4 to 16 years

Cost
Primary levels: $36.05 to $43.26 per two-hour session
Secondary levels: $40.17 to $45.32 per two-hour session
Fees are paid monthly.

Teacher-to-child ratio
1:8

Class timings
Monday to Friday 9 a.m. to 6.30 p.m.
Weekends 9 a.m. to 4 p.m.
The class schedule follows the school term timetable, but holiday programmes are also offered.

Notes
2300 children are enrolled at the three centres.
All teachers are expatriate native speakers.

THE LEARNING CONNECTION

✉ Sector 57

Subjects and Ages
English language programmes:

Writers' Workshop (P2 to P6)
Beginning Readers (N to K2)
Literacy Skills (P1)
Speech and Drama (N to K2)
Holiday programmes (P1 to P3)

Cost
$200 to $315 per term, depending on duration of programme

Teacher-to-child ratio
Call centre for details.

Class timings
Call centre for class schedule.
Classes last 1 to 1 1/2 hours.

CENTRES OFFERING MATHEMATICS

FORMATION CENTRE

✉ Sectors 27, 28 and 30

Subject
Maths
Science

Age
2 1/2 to 12 years

Cost
Up to 6 years: $455 per 20-week term
Over 6 years: $345 to $380 per 10-week term
Registration/assessment fee: $50

Teacher-to-child ratio
1:8 maximum

Class timings
Tuesday to Saturday 9 a.m. tó 6 p.m. Classes last 1 hour to 1 hour 45 minutes, depending on age.

THE MONTESSORI WORKGROUP
✉ Sector 23

Subject
Mortensen Maths

Age
4 to 12 years

Cost
4 years: $200 per 10-session programme
5 to 8 years: $300 per 10-session module (10 modules)
9 to 12 years: $300 per 10-session topic (five topics)
Registration fee: $40
Additional fees for materials

Teacher-to-child ratio
Call centre for details.

Class timings
Monday to Saturday 10 a.m., 11.30 a.m., 2 p.m., 3.30 p.m.
Classes for 4-year-olds last 1 hour; thereafter, they last 1½ hours.

See also
Preschool Survey, Toys and Games
(The Montessori Shop)

SPORTS ACTIVITIES AND FACILITIES

ARCHERY

ARCHERY CLUB OF SINGAPORE
✉ Sector 57

Activities
Archery lessons

Age
From 10 years

Cost
$65 for 6 group lessons
$85 for six individual lessons

Monthly membership fee: $15
Registration fee: $100

Teacher-to-child ratio
1:5 maximum

Class timings
Weekday evenings and Saturday and
Sunday afternoons
Call club for schedule.
Each class lasts 2 hours maximum.
All equipment provided.

BADMINTON

BEDOK SPORTS HALL
✉ Sector 46

Facilities
Four badminton courts

TRIGG

CLEMENTI SPORTS HALL
✉ Sector 12

Facilities
Twelve badminton courts

DELTA SPORTS HALL
✉ Sector 15

Facilities
Four badminton courts

HOUGANG SPORTS HALL
✉ Sector 53

Facilities
Twelve badminton courts

SINGAPORE BADMINTON HALL
✉ Sector 39

Facilities
Seven badminton courts

BASKETBALL

BEDOK SPORTS HALL
✉ Sector 46

Facilities
One basketball court

HOUGANG SPORTS HALL
✉ Sector 53

Facilities
One basketball court

SACAC
✉ Sector 73 (The Singapore American School)

Activities
Basketball practice and games

Age
8 to 17 years

Cost
SACAC annual family membership: $100
Contact SACAC for fee details.

Class timings
Call SACAC for details.

BEACH VOLLEYBALL

SENTOSA, SILOSO BEACH
✉ Sector 9

Facilities
Beach volleyball nets for public use

Age
Great fun for all the family

Cost
Free

Opening hours
Open daily but busy on weekends

CYCLING
Try the cycling/roller-skating tracks in the East Coast Park, Pasir Ris

Park and West Coast Park. Bikes and in-line skates can be hired from kiosks.

GYMNASTICS
See also "Play Centres".

SACAC
✉ Sector 73 (The Singapore American School)

Activities
Gymnastics classes

Age
Beginner and Intermediate: 3 to 9 years

Cost
SACAC annual family membership: $100
Contact SACAC for fee details.

Class timings
Monday to Friday 3.15 p.m. and 4.15 p.m.

ICE-SKATING

FUJI ICE PALACE
✉ Sector 60

Activities
Ice-skating lessons, use of ice rink

Age
From 3 years

Cost
Classes:
$115 to $180 for five lessons of 30 minutes each, depending on size of group
Use of rink only (including skate rental):
Adults: $12 for 2 hours
Children (3 to 12 years): $10 for 2 hours

Teacher-to-child ratio
1:1 to 10

Class timings
Daily 10 a.m. to 10 p.m.
Call centre for class schedule.

ICE WORLD KALLANG
✉ Sector 39

Activities
Ice-skating lessons, use of ice-skating rink

Age
From 4 years

Cost
Classes (including entrance fee and skate rental):
$88 to $180 for five 30-minute lessons, depending on size of group
Registration: $10
Leisure skating:

$12 (adults)
$10 (children)
for two hours, including skate rental.

Class timings
Classes available:
Monday 10.30 a.m. and 12.30 p.m.
Tuesday 5 p.m. and 7.30 p.m.
Saturday 11 a.m. and 12 noon
Sunday 11 a.m.

See also
Party Organisers

JUDO

SINGAPORE JUDO CLUB
✉ Sector 13

Activity
Judo lessons

Age
From 6 years, depending on size and maturity

Cost
$10 per month
Registration fee: $55 (includes three months' subscription)

Teacher-to-child ratio
1:10

Class timings
Beginners: Sunday 9 a.m. to 10 a.m.
Advanced: Sunday 10 a.m. to 11 a.m.

NETBALL

AUSTRALIAN AND NEW ZEALAND ASSOCIATION (ANZA)
✉ Sector 24

Activity
Netball League

Age
Girls 8 to 15 years

Cost
Annual fee of $30 per player, plus ANZA membership, plus uniform
Sports membership is available for $40 per family.

Class timings
Season runs from late September to May.
Call ANZA for details.

ROLLER-SKATING

KALLANG ROLLER DISCO
✉ Sector 39

Facilities
Roller-skating rink

Age
All ages

Cost
$10 for 2 hours
Discount card available to students.

Opening hours
Daily 10 a.m. to 11 p.m.; to 1 a.m.
on Saturday

RUGBY

SINGAPORE RUGBY UNION
✉ Sector 25

Activities
Singa Rugby programme, a minimal
contact form of rugby
Mini Rugby programme, contact
rugby for boys under 12 years
Touch Rugby, a minimal contact
form of rugby for boys and girls
under 14, under 17 and under 20

Age
From 7 years

Cost
Club membership fees only.

Teacher-to-child ratio
1:25

Class timings
Singa/Mini season runs from March
to July
Touch season runs from July to August

SOCCER

ANZA
✉ Sector 24

Activities
Junior Soccer Leagues involving
over 600 boys and girls

Age
5 to 15 years

Cost
Annual fee of $85 per player (includes kit), plus ANZA membership Sports membership is available for $40 per family.

Class timings
Season runs from late September to May. Practice sessions are held on Wednesday evening and games on Saturday afternoon.
Call ANZA for details.

SWIMMING CLASSES

Enquire at your local public swimming complex for details of their courses. Nearly all offer Learn-to-Swim courses. In addition, the following private organisations offer swimming classes for children.

AQUADUCKS
✉ Sector 57 (classes held at Bishan Swimming Complex)

Activities
Infant and preschool swimming lessons

Age
6 months to 3 years.
Stroke perfection 4 years and up.

Cost
$100 for four lessons
Registration fee: $25
Deposit: $100

Class timings
Monday to Friday 10 a.m. to 6 p.m.
Classes last 30 minutes.

SACAC
✉ Sector 30 (Anglo-Chinese School, Barker Road)

Activity
"Fighting Fish" competitive swimming

Age
5 to 18 years

Cost
Membership: $100, plus $70 per month for one swimmer, discount for second swimmer

Class timings
4.15 p.m. to 6 p.m. at least three times per week. Season runs from September to May.

SWIMFAST AQUATIC SCHOOL
✉ Call or check web site for class locations

Activities and ages
Parent-Infant Swim: 5 months to 2 years

Toddler Swim: 2 to 4 years
Beginner Swim: from 4 years

Cost
$202 for 10 lessons
Registration: $100

Class timings
Call school for schedule.
Classes last 45 to 60 minutes, depending on age.

SWIMMING POOLS (PUBLIC)

Public swimming complexes offer very good value for money and, except on weekends and public holidays, are not crowded unless school groups are having lessons there.

Consult the Singapore Sports Council web site (www.ssc.gov.sg) for current information on all public sports facilities.

Most complexes include a wading pool with a maximum depth of 45 centimetres, which is ideal for teaching young children to swim in. Teaching pools have a maximum depth of 1 metre. An additional fee is payable for use of the diving pool.

Many of the pools have cafés serving snacks and refreshments and selling swimming accessories such as goggles.

The entrance fees for public swimming complexes are:

	Adults	Children, senior citizens
Weekdays	$1	$0.50
Weekends	$1.30	$0.70

Facilities of Public Pools

Name	Sector	Opening hours	Facilities
Ang Mo Kio	56	Daily 8 a.m. -9.30 p.m.	Wading pool, teaching pool, competition pool
Bedok	46	Daily 8 a.m.-9.30 p.m.	Wading pool, teaching pool, learner pool, competition pool
Bishan	57	Daily 8 a.m.-9.30 p.m. 6.30 a.m.-8 a.m. Morning swim	Wading pool, teaching pool, competition pool
Boon Lay	64	Closed Wed., otherwise: Mon.-Fri. 1 p.m.-8.45 p.m. Sat., Sun., public holidays 9 a.m.-8.45 p.m.	Wading pool, competition pool
Bukit Batok	65	Daily 8 a.m.-9.30 p.m.	Wading pool, teaching pool, competition pool
Bukit Merah	15	Daily 8 a.m.-9.30 p.m.	Wading pool, teaching pool, competition pool
Buona Vista	27	Daily 8 a.m.-9.30 p.m.	Wading pool, teaching pool, competition pool
Clementi	12	Daily 8 a.m.-9.30 p.m. Tues, Thurs. and Sat., 6.30 a.m.-8 a.m. Morning swim	Wading pool, teaching pool, competition pool
Delta	15	Daily 8 a.m. -9.30 p.m. Mon., Wed., Fri. 6.30 a.m. -8.30 a.m. Morning Swim	Teaching pool, competition pool
Farrer Park	21	Daily 8 a.m.-9.30 p.m.	Teaching pool, competition pool
Geylang East	38	Daily 8 a.m.-9.30 p.m.	Wading pool, teaching pool, competition pool
Hougang	53	Daily 8 a.m.-9.30 p.m.	Wading pool, teaching pool, competition pool

Name	Sector	Opening hours	Facilities
Jurong Town	61	Closed Mon., otherwise daily 8 a.m.-8.45 p.m.	Wading pool, competition pool
Kallang Basin	33	Daily 8 a.m.-9.30 p.m.	Wading pool, teaching pool, competition pool
Katong	43	Daily 8 a.m.-9.30 p.m.	Wading pool, teaching pool, competition pool
Pandan Garden	60	Closed Tues., otherwise Mon.-Fri. 1 p.m.-8.45 p.m. Sat./Sun. 10 a.m.-8.45 p.m.	Wading pool, competition pool
Paya Lebar	53	Daily 8 a.m.-9.30 pm	Wading pool, teaching pool, competition pool
Queenstown	14	Daily 8 a.m.-9.30 p.m. Tues., Thur., Sat. 6.30 a.m.-8.30 a.m. Morning Swim	Wading pool, teaching pool, diving pool, competition pool
River Valley	17	Daily 8 a.m.-9.30 p.m.	Teaching pool, competition pool
School of Physical Education	25	Mon.-Fri. 6 p.m.-9 p.m. Sat. 2 p.m.-9 p.m. Sun., public/school holidays 8 a.m.-9 p.m.	Teaching pool, competition pool
Serangoon	54	Daily 8 a.m.-9.30 p.m.	Wading pool, competition pool
Tampines	52	Daily 8 a.m.-9.30 p.m.	Wading pool, learner pool, teaching pool, competition pool
Toa Payoh	31	Daily 8 a.m.-9.30 p.m. Also daily 6.30 a.m.-8.30 a.m. Morning Swim	Wading pool, teaching pool, training pool, diving pool, competition pool
Woodlands	73	Daily 8 a.m.-9.30 p.m.	Wading pool, teaching pool, competition pool

Name	Sector	Opening hours	Facilities
Yan Kit	8	Daily 8 a.m.-9.30 p.m.	Wading pool, teaching pool, competition pool
Yio Chu Kang	56	Daily 8 a.m.-9.30 p.m.	Wading pool, teaching pool, competition pool
Yishun	76	Daily 8 a.m.-9.30 p.m.	Wading pool, teaching pool, competition pool

LIBRARIES

Why not visit your local library and help your children get the reading bug? Even very young children are catered for, as all libraries stock picture and concept books for preschoolers. It's also a fun and cheap outing on a rainy day!

The National Library Board runs 15 community libraries, all of which have children's sections. It has also set up 40 community children's libraries (CCLs) in a joint project with the PAP Community Foundation, and has even more planned for the future.

COMMUNITY LIBRARIES

Community Library services are free to all Singapore citizens and Permanent Residents. Others have to pay an annual fee of only $10. Additional fees are payable for various services, including reserving books and, of course, if borrowed items are overdue for return.

The children's section of each library is open until 9 p.m. once a week on different days, so if one evening your child has an urgent need for books to help with homework you should be able to find them somewhere! The opening hours for the children's sections of the libraries are listed here. The adult sections generally have different opening hours.

Children can become members of a library at any age (even babies can be registered) and, in most libraries, are allowed to borrow up to eight books for 21 days.

A leaflet called "Beginning with Books", which is available at libraries, lists books available for parents on the topic of selecting books for children. For further information on the resources available in libraries call the Automated Enquiry Service ☎ 1800 332 3188.

✍ Author's note

Look out for the storytelling (in English, Mandarin and Malay) and art and craft sessions offered by many libraries, which are either free or for a nominal charge.

ANG MO KIO COMMUNITY LIBRARY
✉ Sector 56

What's available

Concept books for preschoolers
Children's books and magazines in English, Mandarin, Malay and Tamil
Encyclopaedias for reference
Resource lists for school students on popular topics
Other media, such as videos and CDs, for children

Activities

Regular storytelling (free of charge) and school holiday programmes ($2 per session)

Children's section opening hours

Monday 11 a.m. to 5 p.m.
Tuesday and Thursday 10 a.m. to 5 p.m.
Wednesday and Friday 10 a.m. to 9 p.m.

Saturday 10 a.m. to 5 p.m.
Sunday 1 p.m. to 5 p.m.

BEDOK COMMUNITY LIBRARY
✉ Sector 46

What's available

Concept books for preschoolers
Children's books and magazines in English, Mandarin, Malay and Tamil
Encyclopaedias for reference
Resource lists for school students on popular topics
Other media, such as videos, CDs, CD-Roms, LDs and audiotapes, for children
Reading corner

Activities

Weekly storytelling sessions are held. The current schedule is as follows:
Tuesday 7.30 p.m. in English
Wednesday 2.30 p.m. in Mandarin
Wednesday 3 p.m. in English
Wednesday 3.30 p.m. in Malay

Children's section opening hours

Monday 11 a.m. to 5 p.m.
Tuesday and Thursday 10 a.m. to 5 p.m.
Wednesday and Friday 10 a.m. to 9 p.m.
Saturday 10 a.m. to 5 p.m.
Sunday 1 p.m. to 5 p.m.

BUKIT BATOK COMMUNITY LIBRARY
✉ Sector 65

Children's section opening hours
Monday to Friday 11 a.m. to 9 p.m.
Saturday and Sunday 11 a.m. to 8 p.m.

BUKIT MERAH COMMUNITY LIBRARY
✉ Sector 15

What's available
Concept books for preschoolers
Children's books and magazines in English, Mandarin, Malay and Tamil
Encyclopaedias for reference
Resource lists for school students on popular topics

Other media, such as CDs and videos, for children
Reading corner

Activities
Storytelling session—"Tales 'n' Things"—on Wednesday night
Movie shows, seminars and workshops

Children's section opening hours
Monday 11 a.m. to 5 p.m.
Tuesday and Thursday 10 a.m. to 5 p.m.
Wednesday and Friday 10 a.m. to 9 p.m.
Saturday 10 a.m. to 5 p.m.
Sunday 1 p.m. to 5 p.m.
Closed on public holidays

BUKIT PANJANG COMMUNITY LIBRARY
✉ Sector 67

Children's section opening hours
Monday to Friday 11 a.m. to 9 p.m.
Saturday and Sunday 11 a.m. to 8 p.m.

CENTRAL COMMUNITY LIBRARY
✉ Sector 17

What's available
Concept books for preschoolers
Children's books and magazines in English, Mandarin, Malay and Tamil
Encyclopaedias for reference
Resource lists for school students on popular topics
Other media, such as CD-Roms, for children
Fairy tales collection
Reading corner

Activities
Storytelling and craft activities during school holidays

Children's section opening hours
Monday 11a.m. to 9 p.m.
Tuesday to Friday 10 a.m. to 9 p.m.
Saturday 10 a.m. to 5 p.m.
Sunday 1 p.m. to 5 p.m.
Closed on public holidays

CHENG SAN COMMUNITY LIBRARY
✉ Sector 53

Children's section opening hours
Monday to Friday 11a.m. to 9 p.m.
Saturday and Sunday 11 a.m. to 8 p.m.

CHOA CHU KANG COMMUNITY LIBRARY
✉ Sector 68

Children's section opening hours
Monday to Sunday 11 a.m. to 9 p.m.

GEYLANG EAST COMMUNITY LIBRARY
✉ Sector 38

What's available
Concept books for preschoolers
Children's books and magazines in English, Mandarin, Malay and Tamil
Encyclopaedias and other books for reference
Resource lists for school students on popular topics
Other media, such as videos, CDIs and CD-Roms, for children
Fairy tales collection
Preschool reading "pool"
Students' corner in the reading room

Activities
The library organises storytelling, parenting talks, parent reading

workshops and activities for 4- to 6- and 8- to 12-year-olds. The usual charge is $1 to $2 per event.

Children's section opening hours
Monday 11 a.m. to 5 p.m.
Tuesday and Thursday 10 a.m. to 5 p.m.
Wednesday and Friday 10 a.m. to 9 p.m.
Saturday 10 a.m. to 5 p.m.
Sunday 1 p.m. to 5 p.m.
Closed on public holidays

JURONG EAST COMMUNITY LIBRARY
✉ Sector 60

What's available
Concept books for preschoolers
Children's books and magazines in English, Mandarin, Malay and Tamil
Encyclopaedias for reference
Resource lists for school students on popular topics
Other media, such as videos, CDs, CD-Roms, LDs, CDIs and PC Tutorials, for children
Reading corner

Activities
Storytelling, art and craft sessions and children's holiday programmes are organised on a regular basis. A fee of $2 per session is charged for some activities; others are free of charge.

Workshops, seminars and talks for parents are organised on an occasional basis.

Children's section opening hours
Monday 11 a.m. to 5 p.m.
Tuesday and Thursday 10 a.m. to 5 p.m.
Wednesday and Friday 10 a.m. to 9 p.m.
Saturday 10 a.m. to 5 p.m.
Sunday 1 p.m. to 5 p.m.
Closed on public holidays

JURONG WEST COMMUNITY LIBRARY
✉ Sector 64

What's available
Concept books for preschoolers
Children's books and magazines in English and Mandarin
Resource lists for school students on popular topics
Other media, such as videos and CDs, for children
Reading corner

Activities
Storytelling sessions in English and Mandarin, craft sessions and video shows are organised on a regular basis. All are free except for the craft sessions ($2 per session).

Children's section opening hours
Monday to Friday 11 a.m. to 9 p.m.

Saturday and Sunday 11 a..m. to 8 p.m.
Closed on public holidays

MARINE PARADE COMMUNITY LIBRARY
✉ Sector 44

What's available
Concept books for preschoolers
Children's books and magazines in English, Mandarin and Malay
Resource lists for school students on popular topics
Encyclopaedias for reference
Other media, such as videos, LDs, audiotapes, CDIs and CDs, for children
Storytelling room

Activities
Weekly storytelling sessions are held according to the following schedule.

Day	Time	Language
Wed.	7.30 p.m. -8.30 p.m.	English
Sat.	4 p.m.	Mandarin

The library also organises programmes for children, especially during the school holidays, including puppet shows, storytelling-cum-art and craft sessions, magic shows, video shows and reading competitions. Some of these involve a nominal charge of $1 to $2; others are free.

Talks and workshops are organised for parents on a regular basis, for a charge of $2 per session. Topics include encouraging children to read, effective parenting and selecting books for children.

Children's section opening hours
Monday 11 a.m. to 5 p.m.
Tuesday and Thursday 10 a.m. to 5 p.m.
Wednesday and Friday 10 a.m. to 9 p.m.
Saturday 10 a.m. to 5 p.m.
Sunday 1 p.m. to 5 p.m.

QUEENSTOWN COMMUNITY LIBRARY
✉ Sector 14

What's available
Concept books for preschoolers
Children's books and magazines in English, Mandarin, Tamil and Malay
Resource lists for school students on popular topics
Encyclopaedias for reference
Other media, such as videos and CDs, for children
Reading corner
Storytelling room
The auditorium and the storytelling room can be booked for events. The

charges are $50 and $20 respectively.

Activities

Weekly storytelling sessions are held as follows:

Monday 7.30 p.m. to 8 p.m. in English

Saturday 10.30 a.m. to 11 a.m. in English and 11 a.m. to 11.30 a.m. in Mandarin.

School holiday programmes are organised, including art and craft sessions and puppet shows.

Children's section opening hours

Monday 11 a.m. to 5 p.m.
Tuesday and Thursday 10 a.m. to 5 p.m.
Wednesday and Friday 10 a.m. to 9 p.m.
Saturday 10 a.m. to 5 p.m.
Sunday 1 p.m. to 5 p.m.
Closed on public holidays

TAMPINES REGIONAL LIBRARY

✉ Sector 52

What's available

Concept books for preschoolers
Children's books and magazines in English, Mandarin, Tamil and Malay
Resource lists for school students on popular topics
Encyclopaedias for reference
Other media, such as videos, LDs, CD-Roms and CDs, for children
Reading corner

Children's section opening hours

Monday 11 a.m. to 5 p.m.
Tuesday to Saturday 10 a.m. to 9 p.m.
Sunday 1 p.m. to 5 p.m.

TOA PAYOH COMMUNITY LIBRARY

✉ Sector 31

What's available

Concept books for preschoolers
Children's books and magazines in English, Mandarin and Malay
Encyclopaedias for reference
Other media, such as videos and CDs, for children
Reading corner

Activities

Regular storytelling sessions are held, and special programmes are organised during school holidays. Some of these activities involve a nominal charge of $1 to $2; others are free.

Children's section opening hours

Monday 11 a.m. to 5 p.m.
Tuesday to Friday 10 a.m. to 9 p.m.
Saturday 10 a.m. to 5 p.m.
Sunday 1 p.m. to 5 p.m.
Closed on public holidays

YISHUN COMMUNITY LIBRARY

✉ Sector 76

Children's section opening hours
Monday to Friday 11a.m. to 9 p.m. Saturday and Sunday 11 a.m. to 8 p.m.

COMMUNITY CHILDREN'S LIBRARIES (CCLs)

The community children's libraries are a collaboration between the National Library Board and the PAP Community Foundation (PCF). The idea was first mooted by Prime Minister Goh Chok Tong to bring libraries closer to neighbourhood children.

CCLs are aimed at children up to the age of 10 years, and each has a unique theme, such as Prehistoric, Planetarium, Ocean or Treasure Land. See the NLB's website (www.lib.gov.sg) for more information.

Locations

CCLs are located in HDB void decks in the following areas. See the List of Addresses for full addresses and telephone numbers.

- Aljunied (Sector 53)
- Ang Mo Kio (Sector 56)
- Bishan East (Sector 57)
- Bishan-Toa Payoh North (Sector 57)
- Braddell Heights (Sector 55)
- Bukit Batok (Sector 65)
- Bukit Panjang (Sector 67)
- Bukit Timah (Sector 59)
- Changi Simei (Sector 52)
- Changkat (Sector 52)
- Clementi (Sector 12)
- Eunos (Sector 47)
- Hong Kah East (Sector 60)
- Hong Kah North (Sector 65)
- Hong Kah West (Sector 64)
- Jalan Besar (Sector 32)
- Jurong (Sector 61)
- Kaki Bukit (Sector 46)
- Marsiling (Sector 73)
- Mountbatten (Sector 43)
- Nanyang (Sector 64)
- Nee Soon Central (Sector 76)
- Nee Soon East (Sector 76)
- Nee Soon South (Sector 76)
- Pasir Ris Central (Sector 51)
- Pasir Ris Elias (Sector 51)
- Pasir Ris South (Sector 52)
- Paya Lebar (Sector 53)
- Punggol Central (Sector 54)
- Punggol South (Sector 54)
- Sembawang (Sector 73)
- Serangoon (Sector 55)
- Tampines Central (Sector 52)
- Tampines East (Sector 52)
- Tampines West (Sector 52)
- Thomson (Sector 57)
- Toa Payoh East (Sector 31)
- Whampoa (Sector 32)

- Yew Tee (Sector 68)
- Yio Chu Kang (Sector 56)
- Yuhua (Sector 60)

What's available

Each CCL stocks more than 7,000 books and resources, including:
Picture books
Fairy tales collection
Concept books
Rhymes
Finger plays
Poetry
Simple fiction and informational books in English, Malay, Mandarin and Tamil
CD-Roms and educational videos
At least one multimedia PC (most have four)

Activities

Talks, video shows, storytelling sessions, library visits and user education programmes are organised regularly.

Opening hours

Monday to Friday 4 p.m. to 9 p.m.
Weekends 1 p.m. to 6 p.m.
Closed on public holidays

Cost

Membership fee: $12 for six months or $24 for a year
One-off registration fee: $5

— Chapter Two —

Out and About

This chapter contains a range of information to help you get out and about in Singapore with your children. Many of the activities suggested are good for all ages, whereas with others I have tried to indicate the ideal age range of children to participate. This doesn't mean that there are any age restrictions, or that if one child is outside that age range you shouldn't go—it is only a guide.

Getting Around Singapore with Kids

Some practical tips on using the various forms of transport available

A Guide to Events and Festivals

A quick guide to some of the more child-friendly events and some activities to look out for

Ten Great Family Outings

A selection of the best places in Singapore to take children for a day out

Places to Go When it's Raining

Guaranteed fun whatever the weather—an essential guide to attractions under cover

Green Spaces

A look at Singapore's green places—some are parks, some are on the wilder side. All are safe, and great fun for active kids.

Singapore's Top Kid-Friendly Restaurants

A guide to restaurants that make a special effort to welcome children

GETTING AROUND SINGAPORE WITH KIDS

BY BUS

Singapore has an extensive bus network that serves all the major attractions. A Singapore Explorer ticket is great value—you can use the buses all day for $5 (a standard fare for all ages).

Children up to 0.9 metres in height travel free on all public transport. Children over 0.9 metres pay a child fare of 30 to 45 cents, and those over 1.2 metres need to carry a concession card to be eligible for this child fare. All full-time students are eligible for concession fares.

Using the bus with a stroller is not easy, especially at peak times, as there is no space allocated for storage of bulky items. Ideally, take a stroller that is compact and easy to fold and take small babies in a baby carrier or sling.

BY MRT

For many children, especially the younger ones, travelling on the MRT is an adventure by itself. Once you get out of the city centre and above ground there is a lot to see. The MRT also has the advantage that it starts early (before 6 a.m. from most stations), so you can catch the sunrise!

Again, travelling with a stroller can be difficult. Not all MRT stations have escalators down to the platforms, so you may have to negotiate a long flight of steps in one or both directions. Once on the platform, however, pushing a stroller on and off the train is easy.

You can buy single-trip tickets, but if you use the MRT a lot it's more efficient to buy a TransitLink Farecard, which is a stored-value card usable on the MRT and buses.

For further information on the MRT, call the MRT Information Centre ☎ 1800 336 8900.

BY TAXI

You can either hail a taxi on the street or book one by telephone. All the major taxi operators now have a satellite link service, which speeds up the process of booking by telephone. However, during peak hours it is sometimes very difficult to get a taxi by either method.

Taxi drivers may not know how to find the place you're going to. Check the address and exact location (in the *Singapore Street Directory*) before you travel. Some taxi drivers are not as helpful as they might be with pushchairs/strollers/heavy bags. Don't be afraid to ask for help if you need it!

Taxi fares in Singapore are cheap compared to many countries. There are surcharges to the standard fare during peak hours, after midnight, for journeys booked by telephone, for journeys starting in the CBD and for journeys from Changi Airport.

ON FOOT

When the streets are jammed with traffic during peak hours, getting from A to B can sometimes be considerably quicker on foot. Make allowances for children, however, who often walk more slowly in the heat.

I hate to repeat myself, but again there are problems for those with strollers! Most modern areas such as Orchard Road have lovely wide open walkways with slopes down to road level, which make life easy. Older areas such as Chinatown still have the "five foot ways", where ledges and steps abound. In back streets, where there is not much traffic, I usually take to the road, but this may not be a safe option if you have children walking alongside the stroller.

Air pollution is generally not a problem here, even in the city centre. Most important, remember your umbrella in case it rains!

RECOMMENDED SOURCES OF INFORMATION

For further information on the public transport network (the MRT and bus services), buy the *TransitLink Guide,* which provides bus timetables and lists bus services by streets, famous buildings and MRT stops. The *Singapore Street Directory* includes detailed maps of the whole island and indexes in English and Chinese. It's very useful, especially if travelling by car. Both books are updated annually and available from all major bookstores.

A GUIDE TO EVENTS AND FESTIVALS

This is not a comprehensive list but is intended as a guide to events and festivals that may be of interest to children. To find out more about local festivals and events call the STPB Information Centre ☎1800 334 1335.

Festival or event	Time of year	Notes for children
Singapore River Raft Race	January	Colourful rafts race down the historic Singapore River along Clarke Quay.
Lunar New Year	January or February	Once Christmas is over, it's not long before the lights are switched on again for the Chinese celebration of the Lunar New Year, the most important public holiday of the year. "Chingay" is a procession of floats and entertainers, lion and dragon dancers, stilt walkers, acrobats and big-headed "dolls". Kids either love or hate the sights and sounds of the Lion Dance, performed regularly in various locations during the Chinese New Year period.
Hari Raya Puasa	Varies each year. In 1996 and 1997 it coincided with Chinese New Year.	The Muslim festivities that follow the monthlong fasting of Ramadan are a special family time. A feast of special cakes and delicacies is prepared, and the young ask forgiveness from their elders for their wrongdoings.
Thaipusam	January or February	Singapore's most colourful festival, where Hindu devotees who have entered a trance pierce their bodies with skewers and carry a *kavadi* supported by spikes driven into the skin. This is suitable only for older children— younger ones might find it frightening or upsetting. Dress appropriately and remove your shoes if you want to enter the temple.

Festival or event	Time of year	Notes for children
Vesak Day	May	Monks commemorate the Lord Buddha's entry into Nirvana by chanting holy sutras and releasing captive birds. Good locations to watch the festivities include the Buddhist Lodge on River Valley Road, the Thai Buddhist Temple on Jalan Bukit Merah and the Buddha Sasna Temple on Jalan Toa Payoh. Visitors should dress appropriately.
Festival of Arts	June	Every year, Singapore plays host to an international arts festival offering a taste of dance, drama, theatre and other art forms from around the world. Many events are organised specifically for children.
The Great Singapore Sale and the Singapore Food Festival	July	Two great reasons to get out and about, although I don't recommend taking the kids along on the first day of the sale—it can be hellish in there!
National Day	9 August	The National Day Parade is a great spectacle, with displays from community and cultural groups, bands and military personnel.
Festival of the Hungry Ghosts	August to September	Outdoor concerts and colourful *wayangs* (Chinese street operas) can be seen at street corners in Chinatown and at other venues throughout the island.

Festival or event	Time of year	Notes for children
Lantern Festival	September	Tang Dynasty City and the Chinese and Japanese Gardens are the places to go during this event, when each night there are lantern displays, night bazaars and dance and acrobatic performances.
Deepavali	October or November	Deepavali, or the Festival of Lights, is a joyous Hindu celebration that marks the victory of light over darkness and good over evil. The Little India area, around Serangoon Road, is decorated with lights and garlands. Visit the street markets selling clothes, jewellery and Indian delicacies.
Christmas	December	The third of the three "light-ups" that keep Singapore looking festive for months. Competition amongst hotels and shopping centres for the most beautifully decorated building means that you'll see huge constructions depicting various Christmas themes and even (fake) snow! A trip with the kids to see this array is a must. Some department stores also have a "Santa's grotto".

TEN GREAT FAMILY OUTINGS

These are my recommendations for fun-filled family outings. All entries include the following information:

Age guide
The age at which children are likely to enjoy the attraction the most

Access with stroller
Tips on visiting with a stroller

Highlights
Some suggestions on the best activities available for children

Facilities
Facilities provided for changing babies and feeding infants (e.g., high chairs)

Nearby
Some places to visit nearby if you have more time and energy

SINGAPORE ZOOLOGICAL GARDENS

✉ Sector 72

✶ **SFK award**
For the best children's attraction in Singapore—provides baby changing facilities, children's toilets and play facilities for all ages.

Age guide
All ages

Opening hours
Daily 8.30 a.m. to 6 p.m., including public holidays
Very few places in Singapore open

After-School Getaway

When I first came to live in Singapore 20 years ago, we didn't even have a TV. I used to pick up the boys from school, pack up a picnic and some wine and drive to the World Trade Centre, where we'd hop on a boat to Pulau Hantu, Kusu or St. John's Island. The children did their homework there, and my husband would join us after work. It was and still is a great getaway.

– Jenny Hulton-Smith

Jenny Hulton-Smith, health officer and counsellor at Tanglin Trust School, set up and runs Professional Nursing Services. She has two adult sons.

this early! Perfect for early rising children, with cooler temperatures for walking around.

Access with stroller

Access is excellent, and the car park is close to the zoo entrance. Strollers are available for rental at $5.15 per stroller per day.

Cost

You are recommended to get Friends of the Zoo (FOZ) membership, which costs between $40 and $70, depending on the size of your family and your children's ages. This gives you unlimited access to the zoo for a year as well as free car parking, various discounts (for example to the Night Safari) and a regular newsletter.

The standard daily entrance fees for nonmembers are –
Adults: $10.30
Children (3 to 12 years): $4.60

The tram costs $2.50 for adults and $1.50 for children. The mini-train costs $1.50 for adults and $1 for children. Or you can save money by buying a combined ticket for the two—adults $3.50, children $2.50.

Highlights

Children's World, at the far end of the zoo (but the tram will take you there in five minutes), has something for all ages. The new play pool is equipped with fountains and a water gun. **Play Land** has two sets of swings—one suitable for children under two and the other for those up to 12 years—climbing frames and a bubble bowl (for younger children only). A ride on the **Mini Train,** or a short walk, takes you to **Animal Land,** with farm animals to stroke, birds, and a **splash pool** to play in. Older children can attempt the **Space Walk** nearby. **Fragile Forest,** the zoo's latest attraction, teaches kids about ecosystems and features "creepy-crawlies", butterflies, birds and lemurs ranging freely.

The **animal shows,** at 10.30 a.m., 11.30 a.m., 2.30 p.m. and 3.30 p.m. daily, are ideal for children aged two and above.

Pony and elephant rides are available daily—call the zoo for the full schedule. They cost $3 for adults and $2 for children.

There are regular feeding times for all the animals—ask at the zoo for details. You can also have your photograph taken with various animals (including snakes and orangutans) for $4.50.

Facilities

There is a fold-down baby changing table next to a sink outside the toilets at the zoo entrance. A tiled area next to a sink is available at the entrance to the toilets in Play Land. Both can be used by fathers!

There are small toilets and low sinks for children in Play Land and Animal Land.

High chairs are available at both KFC outlets.

Food and drink

Various local foods are available at Makan Terrace, next to the orangutan enclosure, and fast food is available from the KFC outlets at the entrance and in Play Land. Drinks are also available from machines in the air-conditioned shelters around the zoo.

If wet

Rain shelters are found throughout the zoo, and many of the animal enclosures are covered, but it's not a great place to be in a thunderstorm!

Nearby
Night Safari

Cost –
Adults: $15.45
Children (3 to 12 years): $10.30
A discount of 33% on these fees is available to FOZ members.
The tram costs $3 for adults and $2 for children (3 to 12 years).

The fun starts here at 7.30 p.m. and the Creatures of the Night show at 8 p.m. and 9 p.m. includes animal contact opportunities. Older children will appreciate the spookiness of wandering along trails in the half-light looking for leopards, tigers and hyaenas. Of course it is all perfectly safe, but thanks to the excellent "open zoo" concept it is real enough to send a few chills up the spine!

You can eat here at the Prima Safari Restaurant or Bongo Bongo Burger Bar. Both have high chairs, and there are baby changing facilities both at the entrance and at the East Lodge.

TANG DYNASTY CITY

✉ Sector 61

Age guide

From 18 months

Opening hours

Daily 10 a.m. to 4 p.m.

Access with stroller

Perhaps because Tang Dynasty City is such a realistic replica of an ancient city, there are lots of steps and uneven walkways to be negotiated. It's not at all easy with a stroller, although we found a friendly security guard who looked after ours for an hour or so while we walked around.

Cost

Adults: $15.45
Children (3 to 12 years): $10.30

Highlights

The free tram ride around the city is a good starting point.

Various **craft activities** are displayed in the shophouses, some of which will interest older children, including Chinese knot-knitting, flour doll making and glass etching.

There are also **music performances** and **kung-fu d**isplays.

The buffet lunch and **acrobatic display** are a great treat for kids (see "Food and drink").

Facilities

There are no baby changing facilities. Tang Palace Restaurant and Tai He Lou Theatre Restaurant both provide high chairs.

Food and drink

There's an excellent local buffet lunch at Tai He Lou Theatre Res-taurant, which includes a Chinese acrobatic display. The only problem may be that the kids enjoy the display so much they forget to eat!

Alternatively, you could eat Cantonese food at Tang Palace Restaurant or buy snacks and drinks in Food Street.

If wet

The wax museum (featuring heroes from 15 Chinese dynasties with some beautiful costumes) is likely to keep kids amused for a while. There is also a life-size replica of the terra-cotta army. Otherwise, it's a question of hopping from one shop or temple to another!

Nearby

Jurong BirdPark
Chinese and Japanese Gardens
Jurong Town Swimming Complex
Jurong Lake

JURONG BIRDPARK

✉ Sector 62

Age guide

All ages

Opening hours

Monday to Friday 9 a.m. to 6 p.m. Weekends and public holidays 8 a.m. to 6 p.m.

Access with stroller

Getting into the park is easy. Look out for the lift available to the

Panorail (you can even wheel your stroller onto the train).

Cost

Entrance fee –
Adults: $10.30
Children (3 to 12 years): $4.12
Panorail –
Adults: $2.50
Children: $1.00
Family Package (parents and up to three children, includes Panorail): $28.50
3-Tier Family Package (parents, grandparents and up to three children, includes Panorail): $43.90
Friends of the Birds annual family membership is available for $51.50 (includes parents and up to three children). This gives you unlimited access to the bird park, a 50% discount on the Panorail and various other discounts.

Highlights

The **Panorail** is a good place to start, as it gives you a good view of the park and takes you to the **waterfall** enclosure.

There is a large **children's playground** next to the picnic grounds; consult the free map for directions. It includes Little Tikes equipment suitable for toddlers. However, this is not ideal when it's sunny, as there is very little shade.

The **penguin enclosure** is always a hit with children and is a good place to cool off!

You could also try the **Thunderstorm** at the Southeast Asian Birds exhibit, which takes place every day at 12 noon, and the **All Star Bird Show** at 11 a.m. and 3 p.m. daily.

You can watch birds being fed throughout the day.

Facilities

Fold-down baby changing tables are available in the ladies' toilet next to the playground and in the main foyer. High chairs are available at McDonald's.

Food and drink

McDonald's is near the main entrance, and there are kiosks around the park selling snacks and drinks, where you can sit in more scenic surroundings. There's also a picnic area.

If wet

Most of the park is inaccessible if it's raining heavily, as there are only a few shelters. However, the **Penguin Parade** enclosure and **Macaw Courtyard** are under cover and will entertain most children for a while.

There are audiovisual shows at 12 noon, 1 p.m. and 2 p.m.

Nearby
Tang Dynasty City
Chinese and Japanese Gardens
Jurong Town Swimming Complex
Jurong Lake

SENTOSA
✉ Sector 9

Age guide
All ages

Access with stroller
Options to get onto the island –
On foot: easy, via the Causeway bridge
By bus: more difficult with a stroller
By cable car or ferry: easy—there is a lift to the cable car, and the ferry is "walk on, walk off".

Cost
Island admission –
Adults: $5

Children (3 to 12 years): $3
By bus from Orchard Road –
Adults: $7
Children (3 to 12 years): $5
By ferry from World Trade Centre (not including admission) – $2.30 round trip
By Cable Car (not including admission) –
Adults: $6.90
Children (3 to 12 years): $3.90

The island has a lot to offer free of charge, once you've paid to get onto it. Entrance fees for paying attractions are indicated below.

Highlights and opening hours
Free with entrance –
Nature Walk
Cycling and roller-skating track
Central, Siloso and Tanjong Beaches
Musical fountain (shows between 5 p.m. and 9.30 p.m.)
Maritime Museum
Enchanted Grove of Tembusu
Flower Terrace
Fountain Gardens
Monkey Show at Central Beach (11.30 a.m. and 2.30 p.m.)
Bird Show at Ferry Terminal (1.30 p.m. and 3 p.m.)
Lost Civilisation and Ruined City
All internal transportation, including the monorail
For additional charge –

For all ages:

Fantasy Island (see separate entry)

Butterfly Park and Insect Kingdom Museum
Open: 9 a.m. to 6.30 p.m. daily
Cost: $6 for adults, $7 for children (3 to 12 years)

Underwater World
Open: 9 a.m. to 9 p.m.
Cost: $13 for adults, $7 for children (3 to 12 years)

For ages 6 to 12:

Cinemania
Open: 11 a.m. to 8 p.m.
Cost: $10 for adults, $6 for children (3 to 12 years)

VolcanoLand
Open: 10 a.m. to 7 p.m.
Cost: $10 for adults, $6 for children (3 to 12 years)

Fort Siloso
Open: 9 a.m. to 7 p.m.
Cost: $3 for adults, $2 for children (3 to 12 years)

Images of Singapore (Pioneers of Singapore, The Surrender Chambers and Festivals of Singapore)
Open: 9 a.m. to 9 p.m.
Cost: $5 for adults, $3 for children (3 to 12 years)

Sijori Wondergolf Sentosa
Open: 9 a.m. to 9 p.m.
Cost: $8 for adults, $4 for children (3 to 12 years)

Facilities

Baby changing facilities are available in the toilets at the ferry terminal. Otherwise, it's best to find a quiet spot in the open air! Most eating places on the island provide high chairs, with the exception of the Sentosa Food Centre.

Food and drink

Fast-food restaurants include:
Burger King (at ferry terminal)
Sentosa Food Centre provides reasonably priced local foods, freshly squeezed fruit juices and other hot and cold drinks.

Other eateries include the cafés along the beach, and restaurants and bars at the hotels. Several of the attractions also have their own cafés. You won't go hungry here!

If wet

Try any of the following (see "Highlights and opening hours" for details):
Underwater World
VolcanoLand
Cinemania
Images of Singapore
Maritime Museum

Nearby

World Trade Centre
Maritime Showcase

✍ Author's note

It's a little known fact that you can actually stay on Sentosa overnight without spending hundreds of dollars at the resort's beautiful but expensive hotels. The NTUC Sentosa Beach Resort has chalets and attap huts overlooking Siloso Beach. There is also a youth hostel, campsite and holiday chalets. Call ☎279 1777 for reservations.

FANTASY ISLAND (SENTOSA)
✉ Sector 9

Age guide
From 4 years

Opening hours
Friday to Sunday, school and public holidays 10 a.m. to 6.30 p.m.

Access with stroller
Easy access—just walk in—but see also note on getting onto Sentosa.

Cost
Adults: $16
Children (3 to 12 years): $10

Highlights
Fantasy Island is one of the best paying attractions on Sentosa for lively and adventurous older kids and is ideal for anyone who loves the water. They organise kids' parties on request.

A few rides are suitable for supervised toddlers (from 2 years), including:
Pygmy puddle—toddler-sized slides and pool

Eye of the Storm—gentle ride around the resort on big floats

Additionally, only for children over 1.07 metres (from approximately 4 to 5 years) there are two rides called Double Trouble and Flashflood. Clearly parents need to judge on the basis of age, not height, whether or not these rides are suitable for their children!

There are also some more dramatic rides for older children and adults who are strong swimmers, including flumes, raft rides and fast water slides.

Facilities
None

Food and drink
Tex-Mex Restaurant
Sweetimes Café
Soft drinks and beer are available from the poolside bar.

If wet
Well, you'll be wet anyway! Rides will continue unless it's a very heavy storm.

Nearby
On Sentosa:
Musical Fountain
Maritime Museum
Cinemania
Via the Causeway:
World Trade Centre
Singapore Maritime Showcase

CLARKE QUAY AND THE SINGAPORE RIVER

✉ Sector 17

Age guide
4 to 12 years

Access with stroller
You can stroll around Clarke Quay easily (there are no steps). When using the River Taxi or taking a River Cruise you will need to fold up your stroller and ask for help to get it on and off the boat.

Highlights
Cruises along the river are organised by Singapore River Cruises (☎227 6863/336 6119). They depart hourly from Parliament House from 9 a.m. to 8 p.m. and offer great views of the colonial district as well as the restored godowns (warehouses) of Boat Quay and Clarke Quay—now one of the island's biggest and brightest entertainment districts. Alternatively, you can board at Clarke Quay and do the trip in reverse. Adults pay $7; children two years and over pay $4.

There is also a **River Taxi** that runs between Boat Quay (near Raffles Place) and Clarke Quay. It operates Monday to Friday from 11 a.m. to 10.45 p.m. and on weekends and public holidays from 9 a.m. to 10.45 p.m. Boats depart every 10 to 15 minutes. They charge only $1 before 2.30 p.m. and $2 after, for adults and children two years and over.

Please note that both cruise and River Taxi schedules are subject to tidal and weather conditions.

Facilities
There is a baby changing room (accessible to dads too!) with two fold-down baby changing stations, a sink and a chair, next to the toilets between the car park and the landing site for the River Taxi on North Boat Quay. The toilets are clearly signposted.

Food and drink
There's too much choice to mention, although many of the best restaurants open only in the evening. Children may enjoy eating on board one of the boats moored here.

Nearby
Cross River Valley Road via the pedestrian walkway and climb the countless steps to **Fort Canning Park.** It's worth the climb and a good picnic spot (see "Green Spaces").

You could cross the bridge over the Singapore River to the newly opened **Riverside Point** shopping centre, which has a cinema, yet more restaurants and shops.

In the neighbouring Liang Court shopping centre, **Daimaru** department store has a good children's department (see "Guide to Department Stores").

CHINESE AND JAPANESE GARDENS

✉ Sector 61

Age guide
All ages

Opening hours
Weekdays 9 a.m. to 7 p.m.
Sundays and public holidays 8.30 a.m. to 7 p.m.
Last admission is at 6 p.m.

Access with stroller
There are a few steps to negotiate, but generally access is good.

Cost
Adults: $4.50
Children (under 12 years): $2
Concessions for groups of 30 or more

Highlights
The Chinese and Japanese Gardens offer wonderful hide-and-seek and make-believe possibilities, with their various features such as bridges, gateways and fountains. This place really comes alive during the Lantern Festival in September (see "A Guide to Events and Festivals" for details).

Active children may be keen to climb up the seven-storey pagoda.

Facilities
None

Food and drink
A mini cafeteria serves lunch, snacks and canned and hot drinks. Drinks are also available from vending machines.

If wet
Shelter is available in the pagoda, the Bonsai Garden, the Stone Boat and the Tea House. The gardens are not recommended for very hot days, as there is no escape from the heat.

Nearby
Jurong Lake
Jurong Town Swimming Complex
Tang Dynasty City
Jurong BirdPark

SINGAPORE DISCOVERY CENTRE

✉ Sector 63

Age guide
From 18 months

Opening hours
Tuesday to Friday 9 a.m. to 7 p.m.
Weekends and public holidays 9 a.m. to 8 p.m.
Last admission is one hour before closing time.
Closed on Mondays except public holidays.

Access with stroller

There is excellent access into and within the centre, as it has been designed for use by the disabled. Access to the Adventure Playground is more difficult, though, as there is a long flight of steps and no alternative route.

Cost

Entrance fee –
Adults: $9
Children (3 to 12 years): $5
Optional extras –
Motion Simulator: $4
Shooting Gallery: $3

Highlights

Three galleries feature discoveries of the past, present and future of Singapore. They include exhibits of jungle and urban survival and weapons. There is also an excellent walk-through history of Singapore, which includes the history of the HDB and Changi Airport. Older children may be interested in the touch screen computers, which provide further information and old film clips. Grandparents will no doubt supplement these with their own stories of the past.

The **IWERKS Theatre** features a "day in the life of Singapore" film show on a large format screen, which blends different aspects of Singapore life into a mix that is certainly no ordinary day. A fun experience for children of all ages—and adults too.

Outdoor Exhibits include military aircraft, a helicopter and a boat, some of which you can climb into and press the buttons!

Children's Adventureland is an imaginatively designed series of wooden structures, including a "castle", a "boat" and a rope bridge. This is not suitable for toddlers but is ideal for children around four years and over.

Older children may prefer to experience the thrills of the **Motion Simulator** or give it their best shot in the **Shooting Gallery.** These involve an extra fee; see "Cost".

Facilities

There is a toilet for the disabled and baby changing facilities. High chairs are available at McDonald's and the food court.

Food and drink

The centre has a McDonald's restaurant and a small food court. There is a landscaped area outside, with a small lake and fountain, which is suitable for picnics.

If wet

There is enough inside to keep most children amused for hours.

SINGAPORE SCIENCE CENTRE AND OMNI-THEATRE

✉ Sector 60

Age guide
From 18 months

Opening hours
Tuesday to Sunday and public holidays 10 a.m. to 6 p.m.
The Omni-Theatre is open until 8 p.m.
Closed on Mondays except public holidays

Do not attempt to visit during Youth Science Fortnight, held at the end of May, as 100,000 school students attend! Weekday afternoons are generally the quietest times, but if in doubt call the centre to check whether any school groups are visiting that day.

Access with stroller
There are five steps up to the main entrance of the centre. After that, most exhibits are on the same level and there is a lift to other floors.

There are several sets of steps along the walkway from the centre to the Omni-Theatre. You'd need to make a major detour to avoid them.

Cost
Science Centre standard entrance fees–
Adults: $3
Children (3 to 16): $1.50

Extra charges are generally payable for special exhibitions.

There are also a number of special deals, including the following:
Family membership, for up to five people, costs $25 for a year;
Young Scientist membership, open to all students, costs $15 for a year.

Both these types of membership include a free subscription to the *Singapore Scientist* magazine, access to the centre's library and invitations to special talks and functions.

Omni-Theatre entrance fees:
Adults: $3
Children (3 to 16 years): $1.50
Senior Citizens: $2.50

Highlights
There's a lot here to entertain and interest children of all ages. Using the concept of "edutainment", most exhibits are interactive, and many, especially in the **Main Atrium** near the entrance, make noises and have flashing lights—fascinating for toddlers.

A new, larger **Discovery Centre** is due to open in 2000, to provide a creative introduction to science for young children. It will include a water play area and construction site, a rock wall, puppet theatre and more.

The **Hall of IT** features information technology in learning, at home, on the move and at play—an interactive exhibition with plenty to interest children. **Energy** covers the fundamentals and more complex topics in a fun way, including regular lightning demonstrations.

In the **Life Sciences Gallery**, there are two computer quizzes—"How green is your home?" and "Are you a green consumer?"—which older children might find interesting.

The big-screen **Omni-Theatre** is obviously a big attraction for older children. There is a film show every hour. Call first to check on films showing and timings, as they change every four to six months.

Call the centre's 24-hour information service ☎568 9100 for up-to-date details of film showings and exhibitions.

Facilities

There is a baby changing station in the ladies' toilets near the main entrance.

Food and drink

The Seattle Café on the second floor of the Science Centre has a Little Tikes play area. The E-Meals Café at the Omni Theatre also serves drinks and snacks.

If wet

It's perfect. The walkway between the Science Centre and the Omni-Theatre is partially covered.

Nearby
Chinese and Japanese Gardens
Tang Dynasty City
Jurong Lake

SUNGEI BULOH NATURE PARK
✉ Sector 71

Age guide
6 to 12 years

Opening hours
Monday to Friday 7.30 a.m. to 7 p.m.
Weekends 7 a.m. to 7 p.m.

Access with stroller

It's slightly rough terrain in places, but otherwise it's stroller-accessible throughout.

Car parking is available at the entrance. If you're travelling by public transport get the MRT to Kranji, then TIBS bus 925, which runs to the park entrance on Sundays and public holidays, and nearby on weekdays.

Cost
Adults: $1
Children, students and senior citizens: $0.50
$2 per hour for hire of binoculars

Highlights
The park was designated a wild bird reserve and nature park for mangrove flora and fauna in 1989. It was

opened to the public in 1993. Over 180 species of bird live in or visit Sungei Buloh, including herons, egrets and kingfishers. The best time to visit is when the migratory birds are around, between September and March. Bird Identification Charts are available from the souvenir shop.

There are plenty of other inhabitants that are resident all year round. You can spot some beautiful mangrove flowers and fruits, insects such as dragonflies, damselflies and butterflies, snakes (leave them alone and they won't bother you) or even a rather large monitor lizard!

A visit to the park makes an ideal excursion for children aged six and above; younger children need to be supervised carefully as there are pools of water that they could fall into, and snakes. It makes an ideal early morning trip, when you're likely to see more birds.

More than anything else, the park is a quiet, peaceful backwater of Singapore, where all you can hear is the hum of insects and the occasional bird cry. I loved it!

Food and drink

Bring a picnic. There is a small cafeteria, but only the drinks are worth having. There's also a vending machine for canned drinks.

If wet

The bird observation hides around the park offer reasonable temporary shelter, and the Visitors' Centre

97

could keep you occupied for a little longer. There's also a Theatrette showing a 10-minute audiovisual programme on the park.

Nearby

Opposite the park is **Tropical Aeroponics,** a vegetable farm using a high-tech approach developed by the Nanyang Technological University (NTU). Aeroponics involves suspending plants in air and spraying their roots with nutrient solution. You can look around free of charge, and buy ultra-fresh, pesticide-free green vegetables such as kai lan and lettuce.

It's only a short walk to **Kranji Dam,** with a children's playground and picnic tables, and great views across the causeway to Malaysia. A good spot for lunch.

If travelling by car, take Lim Chu Kang Road, either north to the coast where you may see fish being brought ashore in the early morning and there is a customs post, or south past the cemeteries. You may notice the road is very straight—in fact, it is designated as Singapore's third runway!

Staying overnight would be a great adventure for older children. Guides and scouts camp nearby, and their camps are available for hire to the public during school term time. You stay in *pondoks* that sleep six.

Call the Girl Guides Association ☎235 3001 and ask about "Camp Christine".

PLACES TO GO WHEN IT'S RAINING

Since it rains so much in Singapore, here are some suggestions for good places to visit that are under cover. They're also much more fun than touring the shopping centres, really! These places are also ideal for very hot, humid days, as they all have air conditioning. Many of the "Ten Great Family Outings" are also suitable; see the "If wet" sections for details.

All entries include the following information:

Age guide
The age at which children are likely to enjoy the attraction the most

Access with stroller
Tips on visiting with a stroller

Highlights
Some suggestions on the best activities available for children

Facilities
Facilities provided for changing babies and feeding infants (e.g., high chairs)

Nearby
Some places to visit nearby if you have more time and energy

ASIAN CIVILISATIONS MUSEUM

✉ Sector 17

Age guide
All ages

Opening hours
Tuesday to Sunday 9 a.m. to 5.30 p.m.
Wednesday 9 a.m. to 9 p.m.
Closed on Mondays

Access with stroller
Easy access via lift to all levels in the museum.

Cost
Adults: $3
Students/Senior citizens: $1.50
Free admission for children up to 6 years.

Highlights
Two-thirds of the galleries are devoted to the Chinese cultural heritage and include multimedia kiosks exploring subjects such as the Chinese dynasties and ceramics authentication. Temporary exhibitions explore civilisations both close to home and further afield. Children's workshops and on-site demonstrations are organised."pool";

Facilities
Visitors can rest on antique furniture found throughout the museum.

Food and drink
The museum has a café and there is also a café at The Substation next door.

Nearby
The museum is within walking distance of the Singapore Philatelic Museum, the National Library and MPH's largest book store with a whole floor devoted to children's books.

SINGAPORE MARITIME SHOWCASE AND WORLD TRADE CENTRE

✉ Sector 9

Age guide
All ages

Opening hours
Tuesday to Friday 10.30 a.m. to 6.30 p.m.
Weekends and public holidays 10.30 a.m. to 8.30 p.m.
Closed on Monday

Access with stroller
The World Trade Centre (WTC) is well designed, with ramps close to most stairways and plenty of lifts and escalators. However, the Maritime Showcase has several flights of stairs, and the exit is different from the entrance, so you need to take your stroller with you. Try asking one of the friendly staff for help.

Cost

Entrance to the World Trade Centre is free, but there may be a charge for individual exhibitions.

Entrance to Maritime Showcase –

Adults: $4

Children (over 4 years): $2

Highlights

On arrival you are whisked away on the **Maritime Odyssey** ride. As the aim of the place is to educate you about the workings of a modern port, not surprisingly you travel inside an actual ship container and the ride is authentically bumpy and grindy! Great lights, action and noise for kids, although babies and toddlers could be frightened (mine, at nearly two, was just mesmerised).

The best of the rest are:

Lego exhibit and play area, which has five play tables and a big Lego "pool";

Computer games with lots of terminals so you shouldn't have to queue—great for six years upwards. You can take on Cargo Joe's Challenge or pilot a Seek and Destroy Vessel;

A replica of a **Ship's Bridge** called Neptune Topaz, with state-of-the-art equipment, where you're allowed to press all the buttons and pretend to steer the ship.

The whole of the World Trade Centre complex is under cover, with the exhibition halls linked by covered walkways, offering excellent "running around" opportunities for children on a wet or hot day.

Facilities

None

Food and drink

Plenty of choice. The usual children's favourites are all represented (Swensen's, McDonald's and Kentucky Fried Chicken), but there are "real" restaurants too!

Nearby

The **World Trade Centre** hosts regular shows, fairs and exhibitions, many of which are of interest to children. Call the main information desk ☎321 1972 for details of current events.

The **Pirate Ship** children's playground is a short walk away, outside the Kentucky Fried Chicken by the Causeway Bridge.

Sentosa's myriad attractions are just a walk across the bridge, or can be reached by bus from the WTC.

SINGAPORE HISTORY MUSEUM

✉ Sector 17

Age guide

6 to 12 years

Opening hours
Tuesday to Sunday (except Wednesday) 9 a.m. to 5.30 p.m.
Wednesday 9 a.m. to 9 p.m.
Closed on Monday
Busy on weekends

Access with stroller
There are steps at the entrance and to the upper galleries, but the staff are friendly so just ask for help.

Cost
Adults: $3
Children (6 to 16 years): $1.50
Children under 6 go free.

Highlights
The **Children's Discovery Gallery** is open from 12 noon to 2 p.m. on weekdays and until 4 p.m. on weekends. It is used for school activities during the week. Exhibits can often be touched and examined (carefully!), and there are activity worksheets and art and craft materials too. Great for provoking interesting parent-child discussions. When I visited, the theme was festivals, with corners of the room devoted to Christmas, Chinese New Year, Deepavali and Ramadan. The theme changes every six months.

The **History of Singapore Gallery** features 20 dioramas (cases with models depicting various historical scenes). Very helpfully, there are little steps in front of each case, so that small children can see inside more easily. Guaranteed to provoke lots of "what's that?" and "but *why*, Mummy?"

A **3-D audio-visual show**, *The Singapore Story,* is shown daily, every hour from 9.30 a.m. to 4.30 p.m. Cost: $2 for adults and $1 for children, students and senior citizens. You can save money with combined museum and show tickets.

Some of the temporary exhibitions may also be of interest to children. Call ☎375 2510 and follow the recorded instructions for current information.

Facilities
None

Food and drink
There's a drinks machine in the courtyard, or try the nearby Stamford Road Food Centre, which is open 24 hours.

If wet
It's all under cover, except for a short walk from the main museum building to the Children's Discovery Gallery. Note that only the individual galleries are air conditioned.

Nearby
If you're yearning for more learning, try the **Singapore Art Museum, MPH Bookstore** or **Central**

Community Library, all of which are only a short walk away.

Alternatively, try more sporting endeavours such as climbing the steps to **Fort Canning Park** and swimming at the **River Valley Swimming Complex.**

SINGAPORE ART MUSEUM
✉ Sector 18

Age guide
6 to 12 years

Opening hours
Tuesday to Sunday (except Wednesday) 9 a.m. to 5.30 p.m.
Wednesday 9 a.m. to 9 p.m.
Closed on Monday

Access with stroller
Access is easy to the ground floor level, and a lift is available to the upper galleries.

Cost
Adults: $3
Children (6 to 16 years): $1.50

Highlights
Older children who are fond of art are likely to enjoy visiting the main galleries, and the **E-mage Gallery**, a computerised audiovisual gallery with touch screen controls and musical accompaniment, may lure the more technologically inclined!

In addition, the museum sometimes organises hands-on art activities for children on weekends. See newspapers for details.

Facilities
A baby changing table is available in the ladies' toilet. There are no high chairs in the café.

Food and drink
Dome Café in the courtyard serves hot and cold drinks and light meals.

Nearby
See the previous entry for suggestions.

CHANGI AIRPORT
✉ Sector 81

Age guide
Newborn to 4 years

Opening hours
As you would expect, the airport is open 24 hours a day, seven days a week. Avoid visiting on peak travelling days, such as around Chinese New Year, unless you have to.

Access with stroller
There is good access to all parts of the airport, although some of the lifts are difficult to find.

Cost
Free

Highlights
This is an ideal trip for lively children on rainy or very hot days. Take

them to the **Viewing Mall** on level three of either terminal, where there is plenty of space for running around, especially midweek, and they can watch the planes taking off.

Terminal 2 has a **Science Discovery Centre** with interactive exhibits on level three, and a small **Aquarium** in the Arrivals hall on level one.

The high-speed **Skytrain**, which links the airport's two terminals, is free and is open from 6 a.m. daily.

Facilities

Terminal 2 has a nursery on level three (the viewing mall), which you can use on the land side.

If you're flying out, Terminal 1 has a nursery and children's play area on the air side on level three (the viewing mall) near the business centre.

Many of the restaurants have high chairs.

Food and drink

There are many restaurants here, including:

Swensen's (Terminal 1, level three, and Terminal 2, level three)

McDonald's (Terminal 1, level one)

Terminal 2 also has a supermarket in the basement, which sells baby supplies, biscuits, juice, etc.

Nearby

Changi Village and **Changi Beach Park** are within easy reach by car.

✍ Author's note

Check out the luxury Airbus—it's the easiest way to get to the airport and takes only 30 minutes from the city.

INDOOR PLAYGROUNDS

Some indoor playgrounds are free, provided by shopping centres or fast-food restaurants such as McDonald's. Others involve a fee but are also larger and therefore likely to provide entertainment for longer! They include the following (see "Play Centres" for further details):

Forum Galleria Hip Kids Club (sector 23)

Gymboree ("Playgym" at selected times only, sector 24)

QuestXone (Kinderworld Edutainment Concepts) (sector 3) Due to re-open in May 2000 at a new location.

FIRE STATIONS

Most kids, and more than a few adults if they dared admit it, would love to see the inside of a fire station. Most fire stations are open on Saturday mornings for tours where you and the kids can see the contents of the fire engine, slide down the pole and even try on the uniform. Call the following numbers for details.

Alexandra Fire Station will put on a fire fighting display for groups of more than 10 people. If you're bringing a large group, call a few days in advance:
☎474 1166

Ang Mo Kio Fire Station:
☎482 2733
Bukit Timah Fire Station:
☎466 2128
Central Fire Station (Hill Street)—closed for renovation until 2001:
☎337 4441
Changi Fire Station:
☎542 4988
Geylang Fire Station:
☎743 1500
Clementi Fire Station:
☎776 0655
Jurong Fire Station:
☎265 5666
Sembawang Fire Station:
☎257 1221
Serangoon Fire Station:
☎291 3111

GREEN SPACES

We all need to get away from the bustle of the city sometimes, and children especially need open spaces to run around in. Visiting Singapore's nature reserves and parks offers a great opportunity for children and adults alike to explore and learn about the local flora and fauna. Don sun protection and mosquito repellent and get out there and discover Singapore's wilder side.

Close Call

I'll never forget the day we made an early evening trip to the nature reserve with our children (then aged seven, six and four years), our Great Dane and two Dachshunds. We parked near the McRitchie Reservoir and walked into the reserve, only to find on our return that the boom was down and our car was trapped! With visions of the chicken I'd left roasting at home for dinner turning to cinders, I reviewed our options. Could I ask a neighbour to break into our house and turn off the gas? Would we camp in the reserve overnight? Luckily my husband succeeded in contacting the neighbouring Singapore Island Country Club, and we drove out in style, across the golf courses.

– Rosalyn Tay

Rosalyn Tay has three adult children and is a counsellor at Barker Road Methodist Church. She works with adults, children and families who are experiencing difficulties.

BUKIT TIMAH NATURE RESERVE
✉ Sector 58

Opening hours
Open all hours, but it's best to visit in the early morning or late afternoon, as the local wildlife is more lively then.

Access with stroller
Access is good, but most of the walks, including from the entrance to the Visitors' Centre, are steep uphill slopes. Providing you're not heavily pregnant and have the stamina, though, it's well worth the effort.

Cost
Free

Highlights
There are four marked trails through the reserve. Route 1 follows the main road to the Summit Hut, where you have spectacular views of the jungle and reservoirs below. This is the only route that is negotiable with a stroller. Routes 2 to 4 are of varying length and difficulty; consult the

105

free leaflet and map (available from the Visitors' Centre) for details.

Depending on the time of day, you are likely to see long-tailed macaques and squirrels, and you will hear lots of birds and insects (don't forget your insect repellent).

Who knows, if you're really lucky you might even see other residents, such as anteaters, mouse deer, geckoes, lizards, snakes (don't worry, they are shy of humans) and terrapins.

Facilities
There are no organised baby changing facilities, but the benches at the Visitors' Centre and the Summit Hut are serviceable.

Food and drink
There's a water cooler and drinks outlet at the Visitors' Centre. Bring your own supplies too, as the walk will make you thirsty!

If wet
Give it a miss.

✍ Author's note
Many taxi and bus drivers do not know this place exists, so check your map before you leave.

PASIR RIS PARK
✉ Sector 51

Opening hours
All day

Access with stroller
There are no steps to negotiate, and the free car park is nearby.

Cost
Free

Highlights
The huge and imaginative **playground** (the largest in Singapore) includes equipment for different age groups, although there's not much for toddlers.

Also look out for:
Cycling and roller-skating track
Beach with a view
Bird-watching tower
Maze garden

Food and drink
Drinks are available from stalls or vending machines during the day. In the evening there are three food centres offering seafood and other local favourites.

Barbecue pits are available for you to cook your own food.

If wet
Give it a miss.

BOTANIC GARDENS
✉ Sector 25

Opening hours
Weekdays 5 a.m. to 11 p.m.; to midnight on weekends and public holidays

Access with stroller
Good access throughout

Cost
Free, except for the Orchid Centre, which has an entrance fee of $2 for adults and $1 for children (3 to 12 years) and senior citizens.

Highlights
Children's Garden
Swan Lake—real swans!
Palm Valley—cooler and a nice walk
Orchid Centre—a beautifully designed orchid garden
   Call the School of Horticulture ☎471 9940 or 471 9963 for details of holiday workshops for children.

Food and drink
Refreshments are sold at the souvenir kiosk at the entrance to the Orchid Centre. You can eat at the café next to the Visitors' Centre.

If wet
Give it a miss.

Nearby
Tanglin Mall, for shopping, and **Gymboree** (see "Play Centres")

EAST COAST PARK
✉ The park borders on sectors 43, 44, 46 and 48.

Opening hours
All day

Access with stroller
There are no steps to negotiate and several car parks nearby.

Cost
Free

Highlights
There is a **cycling and roller-skating track** that runs practically the whole length of the park, and kiosks rent out adults' and children's bicycles, child seats and in-line skates.
Other attractions include:
Landscaped ponds—where you can see turtles
Bedok jetty—popular for fishing
Swimming in the lagoon
Wet and wild fun at Big Splash
Bowling

Food and drink
Some of the best seafood restaurants on the island are at the East Coast Seafood Centre. Most restaurants

have high chairs. There's also a Food Centre near the Sailing Club.

McDonald's and Kentucky Fried Chicken are available next to the bowling alley.

Drinks and snacks are available at kiosks and vending machines throughout the park.

If you want to bring your own food, there are picnic areas and barbecue pits.

If wet
You have the choice of eating or bowling—I'd go for eating!

MARINA CITY PARK
✉ Sector 1

Opening hours
All day

Access with stroller
There is a car park close to the playground. The nearest MRT (Marina Bay) is a long walk, but you could take a bus.

Cost
Free

Highlights
Despite the constant hum of the traffic on the nearby ECP, this park doesn't have a city feel. Full of small flowering trees and wide expanses of green, it's a relaxing place to retreat to and is within easy reach of the financial district.

A **children's playground** provides plenty of climbing challenges for children aged four and above, including a "rope walk". There are no swings or toddler play equipment.

Small hills and sea breezes make this a good place for **kite flying.** There's also a **pond** with a miniature island in the middle, which is home to a variety of plant, insect and bird life.

Food and drink
Unfortunately, no refreshments are available in the park itself. The nearest possibilities are the Superbowl Golf and Country Club (which has several restaurants) and the Marina South Food Centre. However, the park makes a good picnic spot.

If wet
There are shelters throughout the park, but if there's a serious downpour head for home.

FORT CANNING PARK
✉ Sector 17

Opening hours
All day

Access with stroller
Virtually impossible, as you need to negotiate several long flights of steps to get into the park, one of the highest points on the island. Until

the 22nd century, that is, by which time lifts may be installed!

Cost
Free

Highlights
Fort Canning Park has an interesting history, remains of which can still be seen. The reservoir at the top of the hill was originally built by the British when they had a military base here (see "The Battle Box"). An eclectic mix of sculpture is on display in the park gardens, and regular signposts give further snippets of historical information on the park.

The Fort Canning Centre houses the local drama group TheatreWorks, and performances are held at the studio theatre (Black Box Theatre). The Singapore Ballet Academy is also based here.

The Battle Box
Cost –
Adults: $8
Children (3 to 12 years): $5
Opening hours –
Tuesday to Sunday and public holidays 10 a.m. to 6 p.m.
Closed on Monday
Last admission is at 5.50 p.m.
Enquiries ☎ 333 0510

This underground hideaway is a genuine war relic. Used by the British Army as part of the Malaya Command Headquarters during World War Two, it was reopened to the public in 1997. Air conditioning has been installed, making the place pleasantly cool, unlike the sweaty conditions of the past. Hi-tech audio, video and animation effects take you back in time to the day the decision was taken to surrender to the Japanese. Realistic details—many copied from photographs of the time, some original (like the graffiti!)—make this a fascinating historical visit for adults and children around eight years and over. Younger children will probably get bored—this place was not designed with them in mind.

Food and drink
There is a drinks machine at the Battle Box ticket counter, and the park is a good place for a picnic.

If wet
Try **The Battle Box.**

Nearby
You can see the water rippling in the **River Valley Swimming Complex** from the park high above. Once on River Valley Road you're also close to **Clarke Quay.**

MORE PARKS

Practically all neighbourhoods have a park. Some of the larger ones include:

Bishan Park has cycling and roller-skating tracks, a pond and several playgrounds (though unfortunately little tree cover);

Bukit Batok Nature Park has nice forested areas with tall trees and wildlife, including two kinds of squirrels. A good spot for bird watching. A disused quarry is now a scenic pond;

Changi Beach Park has a good children's playground (if the noise of the neighbouring airport gets too much you can always go inside to the Meridien Changi Hotel, or hop on a boat to Pulau Ubin).

RESERVOIRS

Don't forget the reservoirs! To get a good view of at least two of them, go to **Bukit Timah Nature Reserve** and climb to the summit. You can also visit —all the reservoirs have parks with benches to sit on and, even on weekends, are usually extremely quiet and peaceful. You'll need to take along your own food and drink, and sun protection and insect repellent are also recommended.

The **Lower Peirce Reservoir** is one of the most accessible if you don't have a car. You can take a bus or taxi along Upper Thomson Road as far as Bishan Park, then walk along Old Upper Thomson Road to the entrance.

MacRitchie Reservoir Park has trails winding through mature rainforest.

The **Kranji Reservoir,** accessible by bus from Kranji MRT, has a children's playground next to Kranji Dam. You get good views across the Johor Straits, and there's a food centre a short walk along the coast on Kranji Road. **Sungei Buloh Nature Park** is also close by.

Upper Seletar Reservoir can be seen from the **zoo, a**nd there's a park on the opposite side, just off Mandai Road.

THE NATURE SOCIETY

☎ 741 2036

If you're interested in finding out more about the natural world and protecting the remaining 3% of wilderness left in Singapore, why not join The Nature Society? Annual family membership (including up to three children) costs only $75 and includes a bimonthly newsletter, *Nature Watch* magazine, entry to nature appreciation outings both in Singapore and abroad, conservation projects that kids can get involved in and a children's playgroup with fun nature activities for children up to 11 years.

SINGAPORE'S TOP KID-FRIENDLY RESTAURANTS

How to begin? Anyone writing a guide to eating out in Singapore has a tough job—there is just so much choice! Dining out is generally a relaxed occasion here: parents are lucky in that children are welcomed nearly everywhere, at any time of day. Even Prego, realm of the island's wheeler-dealers and power dressers, has high chairs and smaller portions for kids.

This book focuses on restaurants that go out of their way to look after families by providing children's menus, high chairs, baby changing facilities and something to keep the kids occupied while you finish your meal or enjoy a cup of coffee. Let's hope it encourages more restaurants to follow their lead.

Other good places to eat with your kids that are not listed here include the open-air hawker centres (sadly declining in number) and shopping centre basement food courts. If you're looking for a relaxed and casual family meal, they are hard to beat. Seating and cutlery may be basic, but the food is tasty and inexpensive. Indoor food courts often have high chairs.

All entries include the following information:

Access with stroller
Tips on visiting the restaurant with a stroller

Cost
Restaurants are rated either "Expensive", "Moderate" or "Good Value" for adult and child meals according to these criteria:

	Child's main meal	Adult's main meal
Expensive	over $10	over $25
Moderate	$6-10	$10-25
Good Value	under $6	under $10

Facilities
Facilities provided for changing babies and feeding young children (e.g., high chairs or booster seats)

Kids' food
The range of items available on the kids' menu and their cost

Distractions
Anything that will keep children entertained while you eat!

Quality of service
The quality of service observed (only those restaurants visited personally by the author)

Nearby

Some places to visit before or after your meal

STAMFORD CAFÉ, WESTIN STAMFORD HOTEL

✉ Sector 17

☎ 338 8585

Types of food

East/West fusion

Opening hours

Daily 7 a.m. to 10 a.m. for breakfast and 12 noon to 10 p.m. for lunch and light meals

Access with stroller

The hotel and adjoining Raffles City shopping centre and car park are well served with both lifts and escalators, and there are no steps at the entrance.

Cost

Adult meals: Good value

Child meals: Good value

Facilities

High chairs with trays are available in the restaurant. Baby changing facilities are available nearby, in the nursery room on level two of Raffles City near the ladies' toilet (but accessible to fathers!).

Kids' food

Children under six eat free at the breakfast buffet—so long as their parents are eating there too, of course!

The kids' menu has main meals such as sandwiches, spaghetti with tomato sauce and fish fingers at $6 including juice or soft drinks, and desserts at $2.50.

Distractions

Top-class service here: at one end of the café is a play area equipped with Duplo and a play table, so you can watch the children from a nearby table and continue your meal in peace. The staff also provide colouring sheets and crayons.

Quality of service

Cheerful if slightly slow. The staff will provide children's cutlery on request.

Nearby

The newly renovated **Plaza Café** at the Westin Plaza offers a buffet for breakfast, lunch, high tea and dinner and lets children under six dine free. It's a good place to go for an early breakfast, as it opens at 6 a.m.

After you've eaten, it's all shopping, but some of the best in Singapore for kids. **Raffles City** has a Sogo store, with a large kids' clothes and toy department, and nearby **Marina Square** has a FunDazzle (see "Play Centres") and the Mothercare and Metro stores. If you

Balancing Act

I arrived home on the eve of Chinese New Year. My son Sean, who is seven (but tells people he will soon be nine) said he wanted Kentucky Fried Chicken for dinner. As our maid was already cooking fried chicken, it didn't sound like a great idea.

"But Daddy, if you buy a feast (eight pieces of chicken, mashed potato, coleslaw and four mango desserts) you get to buy a money box for eight dollars which plays music when you drop in a coin."

Hmm. If Sean got a money box, Sharda would want one too. That meant 16 pieces of chicken, mashed potato, etc., etc. . . . No way! An hour later, Sean was still crying. He was testing me. Suddenly he changed his mind and wanted french fries, and they had to be from McDonald's. Then, as soon as I'd agreed, he decided he didn't want to eat anything at all.

I snapped. "If you don't come with me to get those fries now, I'll pour this mug of water over your head". No reaction. Still wailing. I poured the ice water over his head, and it seeped through his long hair, T-shirt and shorts to form a large puddle on the floor.

We soon made up, and five minutes later Sean was asleep. The next morning, after 11 hours' sleep that he'd clearly needed desperately, I asked him if he remembered what had happened the night before. He recounted every detail and claimed he'd found the water quite refreshing.

The moral of this story? Well, if you constantly give in to your children's demands, they'll hold you ransom for your whole life, but you do have to strike a balance between the books' theories of parenting and the reality of raising high-spirited kids. I hope we've got the balance about right.

– Bernard Harrison

Bernard Harrison is chief executive of the Singapore Zoological Gardens and father of Sharda, 13, and Sean, 10.

really want more, you can then cross the covered walkway to **Suntec City Mall,** which houses QuestXone (see "Play Centres") and the Warner Bros. Studio Store.

HARD ROCK CAFÉ

✉ Sector 24
☎ 235 5232

Type of food
American

Opening hours
Sunday to Thursday 11 a.m. to 2 a.m.
Friday, Saturday and eve of public holidays 11 a.m. to 3 a.m.

Access with stroller
Access is the one major problem with this place: there is a long flight of steps up to the entrance.

Cost
Child meals: Moderate
Adult meals: Moderate

Facilities
High chairs and booster seats are available. A fold-down baby changing station is available in the ladies' toilet.

Kids' food
The kids' menu has five main meal choices, including mini hamburger and chick 'n' chunk at $7.30, des-serts at $7.30 and free, refillable Coke or 7UP.

Distractions
Crayons and a picture to colour are provided, plus a free balloon and badge.

Quality of service
The staff are generally very friendly and seem to love children—certainly a bonus!

Nearby
Next door is **Forum Galleria,** which houses Toys R Us and other shops selling children's goods.

SPAGEDDIES ITALIAN KITCHEN

✉ Sector 24
☎ 339 9062/733 5519

Types of food
American Italian

Opening hours
12 noon to 3 p.m. and 6 p.m. to 9.30 p.m., until 10.30 p.m. on Fridays, Saturdays and public holidays.

Cost
Adult meals: Moderate
Child meals: Moderate

Facilities
High chairs and booster seats are available.

Kids' food

The kids' menu is all Italian, featuring four kinds of spaghetti as well as ravioli, macaroni cheese and kid-sized pizza. All these main meals are $6.50 and include a choice of soft drink. A glass of milk is $1.95, but there are no kids' desserts (although no doubt the kids will go for one of the "adult" alternatives if they're hungry enough).

Distractions

An activity/colouring sheet and crayons are handed to every child.

Quality of service

This restaurant is clearly aimed at families, and staff are generally friendly and helpful.

Nearby

Tanglin Mall offers a range of shops catering to families and children. Close to the **Botanic Gardens.**

MÖVENPICK MARCHÉ RESTAURANT

✉ Sector 23
☎ 737 6996

Type of food

Local and Swiss specialities

Opening hours

Daily 11 a.m. to 11 p.m.

Access with stroller

If you have a stroller, you can avoid the steps by using the escalator or ask to use the lift.

Cost

Adult meals: Good value
Child meals: Good value

Facilities

In the "Safari" theme section of the restaurant, there are child-sized tables and chairs and high chairs for the tinies. There is a baby changing station in the adies' toilets.

Kids' food

Children get pizza or pasta for $2.90 including a free Ribena drink, and they get to pick their own pizza topping. The selection of fresh fruit includes bananas sold at $0.80 per piece, or there's ice cream in various tempting flavours at $2.80.

Distractions

There's a small playground with a slide and ride-on toys to keep toddlers amused while you sit and eat close by.

Nearby

Toddlers can go and see the fountain just outside the restaurant. Older children may be keen to visit the bead shop upstairs, where you can buy all the stuff you need to make your own jewellery. The Heeren is also a good place to buy computer games and music CDs.

CAPERS, THE REGENT HOTEL

✉ Sector 24
☎ 739 3019

Type of food
Sunday brunch buffet includes a variety of international cuisine.

Opening hours
Sundays from 11.30 a.m. to 2.30 p.m.

Access with stroller
No steps, just take the lift to the second floor.

Cost
Adult meals: Moderate to expensive
Child meals: Expensive (but free for children under 5)

Facilities
High chairs and booster seats are provided, but there are no baby changing facilities.

Kids' food
The Sunday Brunch for children from 5 to 12 years costs $18 and includes pasta, waffles, mini croissants and desserts. Children under 5 can share their parents' meals for free.

Distractions
Video shows, soft toys and balloons are provided to amuse the children. Child care will be provided free of charge if there are enough children.

Quality of service
The staff are generally attentive and charming to guests of all ages.

Nearby
The Regent is close to Tanglin Mall and the Botanic Gardens.

CHAPTER THREE

MATERNITY AND FAMILY HEALTH

CHOOSING A DOCTOR

You can get a list of practising doctors from the Singapore Medical Association (SMA)—although the list does not give specialisations. Alternatively, you may look up "Medical Practitioners—Registered" in the Yellow Pages Buying Guide.

Expatriates from Australia and the UK, especially, may be tempted to go straight to a specialist (such as a paediatrician) simply because in their home country it was impossible to do so without a referral and they believe a specialist is giving

them better care. It is true that the specialist may have the latest knowledge, but he is also likely to be very busy, and all specialists' fees are set higher than those of a general practitioner. For this reason, a general practitioner is recommended for day-to-day care, coughs and colds, etc. He/she will refer you to a specialist if needed.

Finding a doctor you're happy with is partly a matter of personality. You may want to try more than one doctor before you find one who is "on your wavelength". If you are

117

an expatriate whose company specifies a doctor, and having tried him you are not happy, contact the company's personnel department and advise them of the problem immediately.

Some expatriates find that doctors here prescribe more medicine for their children than they would like. As in all medical matters, if you are unhappy with what your doctor is prescribing or if you are unsure whether certain drugs are strictly necessary, ask your doctor to explain why he is prescribing them.

EMERGENCY CARE

THE SINGAPORE CIVIL DEFENCE FORCE

☎ 995

The Singapore Civil Defence Force (SCDF) operates a 24-hour fire and emergency service—the Emergency Ambulance Service (EAS)—which is ready at all times to rush to any part of Singapore to respond to an emergency. The ambulances are manned by qualified medical personnel who are well equipped to handle most emergencies. They are always there to deal with life-threatening situations.

In order to stabilise patients within the shortest time possible, the ambulances take them to the nearest designated hospital. Patients and their relatives should not insist on being sent to the hospital of their choice.

In a fire or medical emergency, call 995.

WHAT IS AN EMERGENCY?

The SCDF gives the following guide to cases generally classified as emergencies:

1. Drowsiness
2. Unconsciousness
3. Difficulty in breathing, choking
4. Sudden and severe chest pains
5. Sudden, severe abdominal pain that won't go away
6. Dislocated or broken bones
7. Deep cuts or wounds with profuse bleeding
8. Head injuries that are followed by drowsiness, vomiting, bleeding from the ear, nose or mouth or unusual behaviour
9. Fall from a height
10. Poisoning, e.g., inhalation of toxic gases or drug overdose resulting in unconsciousness and respiratory distress
11. Crush injuries
12. Severe allergy
13. Drowning

14. Burns and scalds—deep, with white or charred skin, or covering an area bigger than the size of a hand, or covering the face
15. Any burn caused by electric shock or by lightning

NON-EMERGENCY CASES

Many people abuse the EAS by calling them in non-emergency situations (over 30% of calls to the EAS in 1996 were to do with non-emergency cases), thereby impeding their ability to respond to real emergencies. Some of the calls are "crank calls" from children. Teach your children never to call 995 or 999 (police) unless it is a real emergency.

In the following cases, do not call 995. If you need to come to hospital call either a private ambulance service or a taxi. In addition, many doctors offer a home visiting service for needful cases.

1. Toothache
2. Slight abdominal pain
3. Fever, coughs and colds
4. Aches and pains that have been present for a long time
5. Minor bruises, slight cuts or broken skin
6. Slight burns or scalds
7. Drunkenness with no serious injury or excessive vomiting
8. Mild vomiting, diarrhoea or constipation
9. A traffic accident where victims sustain only light injuries
10. Other similar injuries where victims can seek medical attention on their own at the nearest outpatient clinic or private practitioner
11. Labour pains

MATERNITY HEALTH

ANTENATAL CARE AND ADVICE

There is a high tendency towards medical intervention in childbirth in Singapore, and pain relief drugs, including epidurals, are widely used. There are also a high number of elective caesarean births, principally as working mothers can then plan their maternity leave and get back to work more quickly.

Having said this, it is perfectly possible to have a drug-free natural birth, but expect to have to explain this to your obstetrician, as it is not the rule. In any case, you should discuss any concerns you have about childbirth with your obstetrician.

Both Singaporean and foreign obstetricians practice here, although

Diet For Mothers-to-Be

When I found out during the fifth month of pregnancy that I was expecting a girl, my husband rushed out to buy bird's nest for me. This is because, according to Chinese custom, eating foods such as bird's nest, bean curd and soft-boiled egg during pregnancy ensures that the baby has beautiful skin. This is just one of the many Chinese practices handed down through the generations, which all modern Chinese Singaporean mothers still follow.

After the delivery, most Chinese and Malay new mothers stay at home for at least the first month. My mother told me to avoid fish, yam and cucumbers during this time, and eat "heaty" foods cooked with sesame oil and ginger as they help to eliminate wind. Rather than washing my hair as I normally would, I used water boiled with ginger and lemongrass.

Some of these practices may sound strange to others, but experience often shows them to be correct, so why not try them and see!

– Caroline Wong

Caroline Wong is a trained systems analyst working with her husband in a civil and structural engineering company. She has two daughters—Krystie, 8, and Juliette, 3.

foreign doctors often charge higher rates. All obstetricians are linked to particular hospitals; check with your doctor first if you want to be cared for by him/her at an alternative hospital. Although Singapore is a comparatively small place, it probably still makes sense to pick an obstetrician and hospital close to your home, just in case you hit the rush hour or have a very short labour! Through the "Partners in Pregnancy Care" scheme, women can be seen by their family doctor for some of the pregnancy checkups.

Singapore citizens and others paying into the CPF can claim part of the maternity expenses from Medisave for the births of up to three children. This can be done directly from the hospital. A booklet called "Using your Medisave", produced by the CPF, describes what to do. For expatriates, it is important to find out whether your medical insurance or the company will cover the cost.

Antenatal classes run by maternity hospitals and private companies are detailed in the following section. Support groups for breastfeeding mothers are listed in chapter 5.

POSTNATAL CARE AND PAEDIATRIC SERVICES

All maternity hospitals provide a range of postnatal services, including physiotherapy, breastfeeding advice and help in the immediate postnatal period. Once you're discharged from hospital, you may want to contact one of the support groups for new mothers listed in chapter 5, as they are a good way of meeting others in the same situation.

For paediatric medical services you can go to a government clinic (where many of the routine vaccinations are given free of charge), a private general practitioner or a private paediatrician. Your decision will depend on what you can afford and your personal preference. The private clinics below are a good choice if you want general health advice. They are run by foreign midwives and nurses who are not permitted to give vaccinations but can perform health checks on your baby, record the baby's weight and height and give advice on breastfeeding, introducing solids and so on. They are also a good place to meet other new mothers.

GOVERNMENT CLINICS (MATERNAL AND CHILD HEALTH SERVICES)

The government provides antenatal and postnatal services to women through its network of clinics. For addresses and telephone numbers, see the Ministry of Health listing of "Primary Health Clinics/Institutions" in the phone book (Business).

PRIVATE CLINICS

The following organisations are run by expatriates, although they are certainly open to all.

CHILDBIRTH EDUCATION & PARENTCRAFT
✉ Sector 24

Opening hours
Monday to Friday 10 a.m. to 6 p.m.
Saturday 10 a.m. to 5 p.m.

Notes
Childbirth and baby care classes are available in Japanese and English, provided there is sufficient demand.

Services Offered by Childbirth Education and Parentcraft

Antenatal services	Cost
Prepared Childbirth class	$320 per couple for six 2-hour sessions
Refresher Workshop	$120 per couple for one 4-hour session
Watercise class	$120 for six 1-hour classes
Yoga-based Stretch and Tone Exercise class	$120 for six 1-hr. classes
Babycare class	$90 per couple for one 3-our session
Breastfeeding Workshop	$80 per couple for one 3-hour session

Postnatal services	
Mother and Baby Exercise class	$120 for six 1-hour sessions
Infant Massage	$115 for four 1-hour sessions
Home visits by midwife	$80 per visit or $225 for three visits
Baby's Clinic (measuring and weighing)	$10 per visit
Baby's Clinic and New Mum's Circle	$25 per visit
Parenting Workshop	$30 per visit

MATERNITY SUPPORT SERVICES

✉ Sector 26
☎ 463 4285 or 9817 1010 (h/p)

Opening hours
By appointment.

Notes
Mhairi Higgins is a Scottish midwife with several years' experience as a senior midwife. She has worked in Singapore for four years and has three children.

Services
Early antenatal classes
Antenatal classes—six classes held over three weeks: $330 including one postnatal visit
Postnatal visits: package of four visits at $300 or one-off visits for $80 per visit
Breastfeeding advice and support: $80 per visit
Babycare for maids classes: $100 for two classes

Services Offered by Professional Nursing Services

Antenatal services
Antenatal Education classes

Private refresher classes

Postnatal services
Home visits

Breastfeeding service

Training courses for maids

Well baby clinic (babies and children up to 6 years), which includes:
- weight and growth checks
- advice for weaning
- toilet training
- sleep problems
- behavioural difficulties

Other services
Emergency Aid and CPR, for maids and others, including children counselling services

PROFESSIONAL NURSING SERVICES
✉ Sector 13
☎ 479 1044, 463 6678, 9604 1530 (pgr) or 9833 7470 (h/p)

THE MOTHER AND CHILD CENTRE
✉ Sector 23
☎ 836 0063
The Mother and Child Centre is based in Forum Galleria amd run by Glenys Quayle.

HOSPITALS: MATERNITY AND PAEDIATRIC CARE
All hospitals in Singapore provide excellent nursing care and modern facilities. Some are newer than others—KK Hospital recently moved to a new site and has a new name, and the Singapore General Hospital just opened a new O&G Centre. The main advantage of these new facilities is that all maternity and paediatric medical services are under one roof, but then nothing is ever far away in Singapore.

Services Offered by The Mother and Child Centre

Antenatal services

Antenatal/Childbirth classes: a course of five weekly classes

Refresher class

Yoga for pregnancy

Postnatal services

Well baby drop-in clinic: Monday, Wednesday and Thursday from 9.30 a.m. to 1 p.m.

New Mothers Get Together: Friday 10.30 a.m. to 12 noon

Home visits

Developmental assessment: appointment necessary

Other services

Health education classes: weaning massage, first aid

Education for helpers in the home

The government-funded Singapore General Hospital and KK Women's and Children's Hospital provide the best value care; nonprofit Mount Alvernia Hospital also offers excellent value for money. Of course, location is also important when choosing a maternity hospital. If you live on the East Coast, for instance, you may prefer to register with the East Shore Hospital.

EAST SHORE HOSPITAL

✉ Sector 42

☎ 344 7588

Antenatal programme

A programme of six two-hour sessions for expectant women and their partners

Cost: $154.50 for those registered for delivery at East Shore Hospital, $206 for others. Call ☎340 8658 or 340 8610 to register.

Estimated maternity costs

	Normal delivery	Caesarean delivery
2-bed room	$1380 for 2-day stay	$2358 for 3-day stay
Private room	$1636 for 2-day stay	$2722 for 3-day stay
Extra charges	Specialists' fees	Specialists' fees

Paediatric care

East Shore's paediatric ward offers a full range of subspecialty services in paediatric, medical and surgical care, including neonatal intensive and high-dependency care. Volunteers hold activities for patients in the paediatric ward. Paediatric outpatient services are also available.

Emergency care

Ambulance Service
☎ 345 1516

Accident and Emergency
☎ 340 8666

GLENEAGLES HOSPITAL
✉ Sector 25
☎ 473 7222

Antenatal programme
Four practical lessons and two lectures, each lasting one hour
Cost: $144.20 per couple. Those registered for delivery at Gleneagles get two complimentary postnatal classes. To register, call ☎ 470 5715 or 471 2222.

Maternity facilities
- Ten delivery suites and one first stage room with four beds. Each delivery suite has a TV, radio, telephone and recliner chair for the accompanying husband!
- Central monitors (including infant resuscitator)
- An 18-bed neonatal intensive care unit (NICU) from level 2A to level 3 NICU intensity

Estimated maternity costs

	Normal delivery
2-bed	Approx. $1600 room for 2-day stay
Extra charges	Specialists' fees

Postnatal programme
Parentcraft lessons, breastfeeding programme, bath demonstration, sterilisation of feeding utensils, care of the newborn, etc.

Paediatric care
Gleneagles' paediatric ward offers a full range of subspecialty services in paediatric, medical and surgical care, including paediatric cardiac surgery and neonatal intensive and

high-dependency care. The paediatric ward has a playroom and baby changing room, and volunteers conduct art and craft and play sessions.

Gleneagles Medical Centre, which adjoins the hospital, has about 20 paediatric clinics.

Emergency care

Ambulance Service
☎ 473 2222

Accident and Emergency
☎ 470 5688

KK WOMEN'S AND CHILDREN'S HOSPITAL
✉ Sector 22
☎ 293 4044
This is a specialist hospital providing obstetric, gynaecological, paediatric medical and surgical services, including paediatric cardiac surgery, children's and neonatal intensive care. It operates Singapore's only Children's Emergency department, dedicated specifically to the care of children up to 16 years.

Antenatal programme
Covers pregnancy topics and tips on baby care.
Call the Patient Education Centre
☎ 394 1268 for programme details.

MOUNT ALVERNIA HOSPITAL
✉ Sector 57
☎ 359 7923/359 7810
Mount Alvernia is a 303-bed private acute general, maternity and paediatric hospital. It is a non-profit hospital and finances the Assisi Home and Hospice, which takes care of terminally ill cancer patients, and the Villa Francis Home for the Aged.

Estimated maternity costs

	Normal delivery	Caesarean delivery
4-bed room	$990 for 2-day stay	$1780 for 3-day stay
2-bed room	$1130 for 2-day stay	$2000 for 3-day stay
Private room	$1780 for 2-day stay	$2880 for 3-day stay
Includes	BCG and first Hepatitis injection for baby. reduction of $250 applies to elective Caesarean section using epidural.	
Extras	Specialists' fees, antibiotics, pessaries, phototherapy, any complications.	

Other "packages" available. All charges are subject to annual review.

Maternity facilities
• Eleven delivery suites. Individual, double and four-bed rooms

are available, with TV, telephone, music and attached bathroom.

- A four-bed observation room
- Operating theatres are easily accessible should a Caesarean operation be required.
- Central fetal monitoring system

Postnatal and paediatric facilities

- Neonatal Intensive Care Unit on the same floor as the delivery suites
- Team of parentcraft and lactation nurses and physiotherapists offer support on breastfeeding techniques, baby care and postnatal exercises.
- Outpatient clinics with specialty services in paediatrics, neonatology and paediatric surgery.
- Paediatric wards are located on the second level, each with its own play area.

Emergency care

Outpatient and Emergency Centre
☎ 359 7910

MOUNT ELIZABETH HOSPITAL

✉ Sector 22
☎ 737 2666

Antenatal programme

Six weekly sessions, each 1½ hours, from 6.30 p.m. to 8 p.m.

Cost: $240. A $90 rebate is available to women who deliver at MEH. To register, call ☎731 2133 or 731 2132.

Maternity tour

Free tours of the maternity facilities every Tuesday and Thrusday. Call ☎731 2891 for booking and enquiries.

Maternity facilities

- Eight delivery suites and one first stage room with six beds. Each delivery suite has a TV, radio, telephone and recliner chair.
- A 26-bed neonatal intensive care unit (NICU) from level 1 to level 3 intensity

Estimated maternity costs

Between $2000 and $4000 for a normal delivery, depending on length of stay. This excludes specialists' fees, which may vary.

Postnatal and paediatric facilities

- Postnatal programme with breastfeeding counselling and parentcraft classes: sessions on breastfeeding, bottle-feeding, bathing and care of the newborn
- Outpatient clinics include specialty services in paediatrics.

Mount Elizabeth's paediatric ward offers a full range of subspecialty services in paediatric, medical and surgical care, including paediatric cardiac surgery. A separate unit provides neonatal intensive and high-dependency care. The paediatric ward has a playroom and baby changing room.

Mount Elizabeth Medical Centre, which adjoins the hospital, has about 15 paediatric clinics.

Emergency care
Ambulance service
☎ 731 2218/731 2259/731 4444

Accident and Emergency
☎ 737 2666 (24 hours)

NATIONAL UNIVERSITY HOSPITAL (NUH)
✉ Sector 11
☎ 779 5555

The National University Hospital's O&G department is supported by consultants and doctors from other disciplines such as Anaesthesia, General Medicine, Paediatrics, Orthopaedics, Surgery and Cardiology. This is its strength as a university hospital.

Antenatal programme
Conducted by nurse educators in English on Tuesday and Saturday. The package of six weekly two-hour sessions costs $130.

To register call the O&G Clinic ☎772 5503/772 5403.

Emergency care
There is a walk-in clinic for all unexpected obstetric and gynaecological problems during clinic hours. After clinic hours, the same service is provided in the emergency department. Call ☎ 772 5000.

Estimated maternity costs

Delivery	Type of fee	4-bed room	Private room
Normal or assisted (2-day stay)	Hospital charges	$1100	$1370
Caesarean (5-day stay)	Hospital charges	$2046	$2510

N.B.: Excludes doctors' professionsl fees.

Packages cover facility charges, hospital stay and professional fees for antenatal, delivery and postnatal care. Prices include GST. Additional fees are payable for any procedures not included in the package. CSC card holders, employees and dependents of Statutory Boards and SIA are entitled to special rates.

Paediatric care
☎ 772 5002

The NUH Children's Medical Centre (CMC) provides tertiary medical service. It offers a full range of subspecialty services in paediatric medical and surgical care in the outpatient and inpatient areas, including neonatal intensive care.

The CMC has a creativity room and a baby changing room. Volunteers conduct art and craft and storytelling sessions both at the outpatient clinics and in the inpatient paediatric wards.

SINGAPORE GENERAL HOSPITAL (SGH)

✉ Sector 16
☎ 222 3322 (Main)
☎ 326 5605 (O&G Centre)
Singapore General Hospital recently opened a new Obstetrics and Gynaecology (O&G) Centre. The centre offers a number of specialisations under one roof and extended opening hours, from 7 a.m. to 7 p.m. daily.

Ante- and postnatal programmes

- Antenatal classes: Eight weekly classes, including four practical sessions, are held after office hours. This package is very popular, and places are limited. Register with the O&G Centre.
- Hospital tours: Free tours of the labour ward and inpatient facilities are conducted on Saturday afternoons.

- Parentcraft lessons: These are held every morning in the ward after delivery.
- Breastfeeding talks and postnatal exercise programme: Lessons are held every afternoon in the ward after delivery.

Maternity facilities

- Eight delivery suites. Private and two-bed rooms are equipped with a television and telephone. Private and four-bed rooms are air conditioned with attached bathrooms. They are equipped with a television and telephone. Six-bed rooms are also available.
- A neonatal ward equipped with an eight-bed intensive care unit.

Estimated maternity costs

	Normal delivery
Private or 2-bed room	$1640
4-bed room	$1330
6-bed room	$710

Estimates are based on statistical averages of past admissions for a first child and a three-day stay.

Pampered Mums

Jacqueline was born in a private hospital in Singapore. From the moment I registered at the Admissions desk, I was cosseted. It was a great feeling, and the "wrapped-in-cotton-wool" treatment lasted right until the time I was discharged. Nice.

In stark contrast, Samantha was delivered in Ontario, Canada, where I would describe the health system as "socialist". Everyone receives the same standard of health care, and money won't buy you any extras. Cultural differences compounded my misery. In the East, new mothers are persuaded to rest as much as possible. In Canada, I was expected to care for my baby entirely by myself. The nurses didn't help to bathe or change her.

My advice is, for an easier childbirth, plan to have your baby in Singapore. Compared to some facilities in the West, hospitals in Singapore are a luxury!

– Sandra Chua

Sandra Chua is a freelance writer and mother of two girls— Jacqueline, 6, and Samantha, 5.

THOMSON MEDICAL CENTRE

✉ Sector 30
☎ 256 9494
No information supplied. Call the hospital for details.

FAMILY HEALTH

RECOMMENDED VACCINATIONS FOR BABIES AND CHILDREN

Immunisation against all diseases except hepatitis B is available free at government Maternal and Child Health clinics.

POLIO

Everyone should receive a primary series of vaccinations against polio. These are routinely administered in Singapore and most other developed countries during infancy and childhood. They are usually given in the form of a syrup to babies at 3 months, 4 months, 5 months and 18 months.

HEPATITIS B

Vaccines against hepatitis B are widely available. Anyone living in Asia is well advised to be vaccinated. Adults who grew up in endemic areas should have a blood test prior to vaccination to preclude existing natural immunity to the virus, in which case vaccination is not necessary. Babies are usually given the injection at birth, at one month and at five months.

DIPHTHERIA, PERTUSSIS AND TETANUS (DPT)

The diphtheria, pertussis and tetanus vaccine is routinely administered in Singapore and most other developed countries during infancy and childhood. Babies are usually given the injection at 3 months, 4 months and 5 months, with a booster at 15 to 18 months.

BCG INJECTION AGAINST TUBERCULOSIS

Tuberculosis (TB) is endemic in impoverished countries, and as international travel is on the increase, the incidence of TB in developed countries is on the rise. The most common mode of transmission of the disease is by inhalation of droplets from the cough of an infected person. The BCG vaccination against TB is safe and is given at birth in Singapore.

MEASLES, MUMPS AND RUBELLA (MMR)

Immunisation against measles, mumps and rubella involves a single injection, usually given to babies once they reach one year. A second booster injection is recommended at 4 to 6 years.

HEPATITIS A

An effective vaccine against hepatitis A has recently been developed. Hepatitis A is contracted as a result of consuming contaminated food or drink. Although there is some risk of contracting the disease in Singapore, it is probably more important for those who intend to travel to remote and rural areas to be immunised. The new vaccine is safe and is approved by the World Health Organisation. For adults, a single injection provides protection for at least one year. For children (over 2 years), two paediatric doses given six months apart will provide immunity against the disease for up to 10 years.

VACCINATIONS DURING PREGNANCY

Some vaccines pose a theoretical risk to the foetus during the early stages of life. For this reason, women who are pregnant or who think they may be pregnant should defer vaccination with live-attenuated virus vaccines (such as the polio, oral typhoid and MMR vaccines) until the second or third trimester, unless they have to travel to highly endemic regions. Other vaccines, made of inactivated bacteria or virus or toxoids, can be safely administered during pregnancy. If in doubt, ask your doctor.

CLIMATE CONSIDERATIONS

HIGH TEMPERATURES, HIGH HUMIDITY

Newcomers to Singapore, be aware that your body acclimatises to the heat within a few days. In some cases, as your blood vessels dilate to aid heat loss, some swelling o your feet and ankles may occur, bu this usually disappears within a cou ple of weeks.

High temperatures mean we sweat more. It is therefore impor tant to have adequate fluids before during and after exercise. Children particularly, who spend time outdoors running around, need to consume plenty of fluids.

Prickly heat rash

Excessive heat and humidity commonly cause a prickly heat rash in those who are not acclimatised. Treatment consists of keeping cool, wearing cotton clothes and drying the body carefully after washing. Calamine lotion or antihistamine creams can also be applied.

Be safe in the sun

If you have a dark skin, you are lucky to have natural protection from the damaging effects of the sun. For those with pale skin, and for babies and children (who have particularly sensitive skin), additional protection is necessary to

avoid both short-term (sunburn) and long-term (skin cancer) problems.

- Wear protective clothing. Sun-safe swimwear and legionnaire hats (which protect the back of the neck and have deeper brims) have been developed for children in Australia and are available here (see chapter 4).

- Use sunscreen creams. These are rated for their photoprotection effect by their skin protection factor or SPF. The higher the SPF the higher the protection. Para-aminobenzoic acid (PABA) in sunscreen creams can cause severe skin irritation in children and adults with sensitive skin; look for PABA-free products.

- Limit exposure to sunlight, especially around midday. Research shows that it takes less time for skin to burn in Singapore than it does in most parts of the US and Europe.

SOIL-BORNE DISEASES

CUTANEOUS LARVA MIGRENS

The cutaneous larva migrens is a skin-burrowing parasite that may be found in sand or earth contaminated with dog faeces. It can be easily avoided by wearing shoes and avoiding skin-to-soil contact.

It is, therefore, recommended that children wear shoes when playing in playgrounds and gardens frequented by dogs, and that they avoid playing with soil and sand unless it is known to be safe.

If in doubt, see your doctor.

MELIODOSIS

Meliodosis is a tropical soil disease that is endemic in southeast Asia. The bacteria grows in wet soil, ponds and rice paddies. It is primarily contracted by soil contamination of skin wounds and abrasions. Although the disease is not common in Singapore, it is best to take commonsense precautions, such as ensuring cuts and grazes are kept clean, applying antiseptic cream on them and covering them with a plaster or bandage.

EAR INFECTIONS

External otitis, better known as "swimmer's ear", is common in the tropics. Dry your children's ears after swimming or showering (do not put anything inside their ears; simply tip their heads and dry with a towel). People who are prone to this

affliction are advised to wear ear-plugs when swimming. Treatment is by topical antibiotic cream or ear drops.

SKIN PROBLEMS

FUNGAL SKIN INFECTIONS

The heat and humidity can often lead to fungal skin infections. These are best avoided by reducing moisture. Try to keep your feet and skin fold areas, particularly, as dry as possible.

Change babies' nappies regularly, and ideally leave the nappy off or use a terry nappy for part of the day to aid the drying process. A persistent rash, particularly in the nappy area, should always be seen by a doctor.

In most cases, fungal infections can be quickly and easily treated with antifungal creams available from pharmacies.

BACTERIAL INFECTIONS

Bacterial skin infections are also relatively common in Singapore. These are usually caused by excessive sweating and affect the sweat glands, skin and lymph glands, sometimes resulting in boils. They can generally be prevented by washing regularly. Infection can be treated with oral antibiotics. See your doctor.

ALLERGIES

Less commonly, skin allergies can sometimes occur after contact with certain tropical fruits, particularly mangoes and occasionally papaya, pineapple or citrus fruits. Some people are allergic to peanuts. In this region, where peanuts and peanut oil are widely used in local dishes such as satay, parents of children with this allergy need to be particularly vigilant.

TUMMY TROUBLES

Singapore's restaurants, hawker centres and food stalls are all extremely well regulated, and therefore the risk of developing gastrointestinal complaints such as diarrhoea as a result of consuming contaminated food or water is extremely low, especially compared to other countries in the region. However, bacteria do multiply quickly due to the heat and humidity. For this reason, the following precautions should be taken:

- Food, particularly meat, dairy products and seafood, must be adequately cooked and served piping hot.

- Milk and milk products, such as ice cream, should be kept refrigerated and consumed promptly.

- Raw seafood and meat should generally be avoided, although a good Japanese restaurant can probably be relied upon to employ stringent hygiene standards.

For mild diarrhoea, drinking extra fluids and possibly isotonic fluids (containing sodium and potassium salts) may be all that is required. However, symptoms can often be more serious in young children. If in any doubt and if symptoms persist more than a few days, are acute or are associated with high fever, vomiting, dizziness or bleeding, consult a doctor immediately.

POISONOUS PLANTS

It's not something many people are aware of, but several ordinary household or garden plants are poisonous to humans. Many contain skin and respiratory irritants or cyanide, and several can be fatal. Following are the plants to avoid:

Areca Palm (*Areca catecu L.*)

The seeds of the areca palm are poisonous, and ingestion can cause swelling of the tongue and severe diarrhoea.

Butterfly Tree (*Bauhinia tomentosa L.*)

Ingestion of the leaves or fruits of the butterfly tree can cause severe diarrhoea. The symptoms in acute poisoning may be delayed for a few hours.

Candelabra Cactus (*Euphorbia lactea*)

The sap from the candelabra cactus is caustic and internally irritant, causing vomiting, diarrhoea and even death. Severe swelling, blisters or blindness can occur if the sap touches the skin or eyes.

Century Plant (*Agave angustifolia var marinata*)

Contact with the sap of the century plant causes dermatitis, itching and a red rash.

Common Bamboo (*Bambusa vulgaris*)

The outer sheaths of the common bamboo are extremely irritating to the skin and may cause severe damage to the stomach if eaten.

Cycad (*Crotalaria mucronata*)

The cycad seed contains neurotoxic compounds and a carcinogen. The high incidence of Parkinson's disease amongst the people of Guam is linked to consumption of this seed, used in traditional medicine.

Devil's Ivy (*Scindapsus aureus*)

The juice of devil's ivy is an irritant, both externally and internally. Chewing the leaf or stem leads to severe irritation of the lips and tongue as well as diarrhoea. It also causes dermatitis.

Dumb Cane (*Diffenbachia pictal*)

All parts of the dumb cane plant contain an irritating juice, which causes severe irritation and inflammation if swallowed. This may cause difficulty in speaking, breathing and swallowing. Plucking a leaf causes sap to squirt into the eyes, a common cause of child injury. This causes intense pain and abrasions of the corneal surface.

Frangipani (*Plumeria rubra*)

Symptoms produced by eating parts of the frangipani plant include vomiting, diarrhoea, erratic heartbeat, respiratory distress and coma.

Giant Elephant's Ear (*Allocasia macrorrhiza*)

All parts of the giant elephant's ear contain an acrid juice. Biting or chewing the leaf, stem or flowers could lead to convulsion and death.

Glory Lily (*Gloriosa superba*)

All parts of the glory lily are highly toxic, and death has been reported within four hours of ingestion.

Lantana (*Lantana camara*)

The attractive black lantana berries are poisonous; all parts of the plant are toxic. The symptoms in acute poisoning are delayed for a few hours. Symptoms include vomiting, diarrhoea, weakness, lethargy and laboured breathing.

Oleander (*Nerium oleander*)

All parts of the oleander are extremely toxic. A single leaf is potentially lethal, and death can occur if branches are used to barbecue food.

Pencil Plant (*Euphorbia tricucalli*)

The pencil plant's milky latex is extremely caustic and an internal irritant. Ingestion leads to vomiting, diarrhoea and death. It is also very irritating to the eyes, causing conjunctival haemorrhage.

Poinsettia (*Euphorbia pulcherrima*)

The leaves, flowers and sap of the popular poinsettia are toxic and can cause skin irritation, including severe swelling and blistering. Contact with the eyes should be avoided. If any part of the plant is swallowed it can cause severe vomiting and diarrhoea and swelling of the lips, tongue and throat.

Pong Pong (*Cerbera odollam*)

The seeds and sap of the pong pong are poisonous, causing constriction of the heart muscles if swallowed.

Tufted Fishtail Palm (*Caryota mitis*)

The pulp and juice of the mature tufted fishtail palm's fruit contain irritating crystals. Contact with the juice causes painful inflammation and itching.

Yellow Allamanda (*Allamanda carthatica*)

The sap of the yellow allamanda can cause a rapid heartbeat if swallowed.

Yellow Oleander (*Thevetia peruviana*)

Yellow oleander can be fatal if ingested.

Prevention

Learn to identify the poisonous plants that are found in many homes, parks and gardens.

Teach your children never to put leaves, flowers, seeds or berries in their mouths, and never to break the leaves or stems or pick the flowers of growing plants and trees.

Spread the word. Many people wouldn't have poisonous plants in their gardens if they knew how dangerous they were.

Treatment

If you suspect your child has swallowed or chewed a poisonous plant, try to induce vomiting, to eliminate as much of the poison as possible. Then rush to the nearest hospital, if possible with a sample of the plant.

INSECT STINGS AND BITES

Venomous insect stings and bites usually cause allergic reactions. These can range from localised swelling, pain, itching and hives to severe reactions, including breathing difficulties and shock.

Localised skin reactions can be treated with cool compresses, 1 percent hydrocortisone, calamine lotion or anti-itching creams. If more generalised reactions occur, such as breathing difficulties, swelling of the face or eyes, or dizziness, you should see a doctor immediately.

MOSQUITO-BORNE DISEASES

MALARIA

The risk of contracting malaria in Singapore is extremely low, and therefore no prophylactic treatment is necessary. However, malaria is a major worldwide problem and endemic in many rural parts of southeast Asia, including the Malaysian and Indonesian islands, where many of us spend our holidays. Take advice from a doctor before you travel to remote or rural areas in the region. Many antimalarial drugs are unsuitable for young children and pregnant women.

DENGUE FEVER

Dengue fever has reached almost epidemic proportions in Singapore and neighbouring tropical regions. There is no vaccine or drug treatment available for dengue fever. Trials for a vaccine are currently being carried out in southeast Asia under the direction of the World Health Organisation. Preliminary trials have shown it to be safe and effective in developing immunity against all four strains of the dengue virus. The vaccine may be commercially available in five years.

Until it becomes available, prevention is very important.

Symptoms

Dengue occurs about five to eight days after being bitten by an Aedes mosquito infected with the virus. Classic symptoms include splitting headaches, high fever, backache, muscle and joint pains and skin rashes. The symptoms last five to seven days, and complete recovery is the rule.

Treatment

As the symptoms of the virus can be treated, early consultation with your doctor is recommended. Treatment includes oral or intravenous fluid replacement, analgesics, fever medicine and close observation. Aspirin should not be given.

As there are at least four different strains of the dengue virus, recovering from one type of infection does not provide immunity against the others.

Prevention

Keep doors and windows closed from dusk onwards, and use mosquito coils or insecticide sprays to kill any remaining mosquitoes. An electric fan discourages mosquitoes from settling, and mosquito nets can be purchased to protect beds and babies' cribs.

Adults and children should wear clothes with long sleeves and long trousers or skirts when outside during the evening and at night. Avoid wearing dark-coloured clothing and using perfume or cologne, as this will attract mosquitoes.

Use mosquito repellents that contain at least 30% DEET (diethyltoluamide) on exposed skin and clothing. However, use them sparingly as they can cause severe reactions, especially in children. Also, young children cannot be relied upon to avoid touching their mouth or eyes with an arm that has been sprayed with repellent. Wash the repellent off once you are indoors and protection is no longer required.

Most important, check your home and garden regularly for standing water. Plant pots and stands are a major risk area. These are potential breeding habitats of mosquitoes. Don't assume your maid will do it. If it is one of her duties, make sure she knows it, and take the time to check yourself as well.

Regular fogging is recommended to kill resting mosquitoes in dwellings. If you live in a private house this is your responsibility. Take out a contract with a pest control company (see listing under "Pest Control" in the Yellow Pages Buying Guide).

TRAVELLING IN THE REGION

BEFORE YOU PACK

Here are some of the health issues you might wish to discuss with your doctor before travelling, especially to rural or remote areas:

- Food and drink precautions
- Malaria drug prophylactics suitable for children
- Soil and water precautions
- Any dangers associated with contact with stray dogs, cats or wild animals such as monkeys
- Environmental concerns such as sun exposure and pollution
- What to include in your medical kit

FLYING WITH KIDS

Air travel with children necessitates a certain amount of preparation. By all means contact the airline regarding baby and child meals available, but take along snacks and drinks you know they like as well. Of course, you should also pack all the usual

supplies, such as nappies, bottles, changes of clothes and any medicine.

Infants (over a week old) can easily adjust to changes in air pressure by breast- or bottle-feeding. For older children bring sweets to suck or carton drinks with straws. Take-off and landing may be a problem for children with sinus disorders, ear infections, colds or respiratory infections. In these cases, seek medical attention prior to departure. Your doctor may prescribe oral decongestants or antihistamines.

IF YOU'RE PREGNANT

Travelling when pregnant is generally safe, though most airlines do not allow it during the last month unless it is essential and authorised by a doctor. Bear in mind that you will tire more quickly, and therefore it is a good idea to allow for extra resting time in case you need it. See also the note on vaccinations during pregnancy earlier in this chapter.

YOUR MAID'S HEALTH

If you have a maid looking after your children, you may be concerned about whether you need to take any medical precautions. In fact, the government insists on regular six-monthly health checks that cover all necessary tests, including a chest X-ray for TB every 12 months. As it is possible the maid is a carrier of hepatitis B, you may wish her to have a blood test and, if necessary, a hepatitis B vaccination. This is not part of the government health check. All medical costs, including the doctor's fees for the health check, are payable by the employer. For more information on employing a maid, see chapter 5.

Chapter Four

Good Shopping Guide

No guide to Singapore would be complete without a chapter on shopping. It's something of a national pastime, and one that (as my husband will testify) I fully participate in! I've discovered, however, that finding specific equipment and materials for children can be a challenge. I hope this guide answers a few needs.

EDUCATIONAL TOYS, GAMES AND MATERIALS

ART MATERIALS

THE CONCOURSE SHOPPING CENTRE, BEACH ROAD
✉ Sector 19

Recommended for
Cheap paper products of all kinds

IKEA
✉ Sector 15

Recommended for
A range of art materials, including a huge roll of paper for only $6! Ideal for painting and colouring on.

NURTURE CRAFT
✉ Sectors 3, 23, 30, 52, 53, 57, 58 and 64

Recommended for
Good-quality art materials, including crayons, finger paints and *Galt* craft kits. Also stocks educational toys and puzzles.

SAGACITY ARTS AND CRAFTS CENTRE
✉ Sector 18

Recommended for
Wide range of good-value art materials suitable for all ages from toddlers upwards

TWINKLE THINKERS
✉ Sectors 22, 23, 44 and 57

Recommended for
Good quality art materials, craft kits, wooden puzzles and other educational toys and games.

TOYS AND GAMES

Toys are available everywhere, from the corner store selling toy cars and water pistols to luxurious department stores with electronic amusements and cuddly toys galore. Here are some suggestions on places to go for specialised educational toys that are more difficult to find.

DISCOVERY STATION
✉ Sector 67

Recommended for
Educational materials, books, manipulatives and games for children aged three years and above, including *Ginn New Reading 360* and *Rigby Maths* resources, *Winslow* colour cards and *Unifix* maths manipulatives.

GYMBOREE

✉ Sectors 24

Recommended for

Play equipment, including a play parachute (great for a toddler's birthday party) and balls that have big holes in them, designed so that babies can pick them up easily

IKEA

✉ Sector 15

Recommended for

Wooden puzzles, toys and building blocks at reasonable prices. Also hand puppets, cardboard puppet theatre, play tunnel, play tent and other imaginative play ideas.

THE MONTESSORI SHOP

✉ Sector 23

Recommended for

Books, games and equipment supporting the Montessori teaching techniques

BICYCLES

BIKE HAUS

✉ Sector 26

Recommended for

Children's bicycles, children's helmets, child seats for adult bicycles and adult bicycles

CHILDREN'S WORLD

✉ Sector 21

Recommended for

Battery-powered cars, tricycles and children's bicycles

TOYS R US

✉ Sectors 3, 23, 52 and 76

Recommended for

Ride-on cars, battery-powered cars and children's bicycles

BOOKS, COMICS AND MAGAZINES

BOOKABURRA

Recommended for

Everything from baby board and bath books right up to books for young adults and special interest books for parents and teachers. Includes many titles not available elsewhere in Singapore. Author visits and storytelling sessions are planned. The cushioned reading area makes this a particularly enjoyable shop to visit with your children.

KINOKUNIYA

✉ Sectors 17 (2 outlets), 18 and 23

Recommended for

The new store at Ngee Ann City is reputedly Asia's largest.

Parenting Through Playacting

On the way to Drama class, my 10-year-old asks me how much electrical power it would take to power the whole of Singapore. I'm not an expert in science or mathematics, and so have to plead ignorance, but not wanting to discourage his curiosity, I ask him why he wants to know. He tells me it's for a role he's playing in Drama class—he's playing the electricity expert and has to make proposals at the experts' planning meeting for a development that could be big as the entire island.

Maybe that's not what you thought Drama was all about. In fact, through Drama we often act out real-life situations. "Playacting" is all about thinking creatively, solving problems, being resourceful, being quick on your feet and improvising. It generally involves working with others to make a successful production. All these skills are valuable for our young people.

You can try playacting at home by improvising in the car, at the dinner table, at bedtime, waiting for the bus or walking to the MRT. Ask and answer the "who, what, when, where and why", and make up strange and inventive scenarios. You take it in turns to listen and express your thoughts, learning patience and turn-taking in the process. Best of all, you're communicating with your young person on a topic other than homework, school and making grades.

This is the only method of parenting I know, and luckily for us it is great fun. I also believe that having respect for your young person is very important, and that this needs to be consciously worked at—it's not instinctive. Substitute kindness for sarcasm, encouragement for ridicule, guidance for blame and praise for humiliation.

P.S. And learn to say sorry too!

– Ruby Lim-Yang

Ruby Lim-Yang has been a theatre practitioner for 15 years and a mother for 10 (she has one son, Siew San). She is currently director of ACT 3 Drama Academy.

Parco Bugis Junction and Liang Court outlets are also good for children's books.

MPH
✉ Sectors 6, 17, 23, 44, and 57

Recommended for
The main MPH store on Stamford Road covers three floors. It has a large children's book and video section. The Parkway Parade outlet also has a very good children's book section, the other outlets also stock children's books.

POPULAR BOOK COMPANY
✉ Main stores in sectors 18, 23, 31, 44, 53, 60 and 64

Recommended for
All Popular Book stores stock children's books in English and Mandarin. The bigger stores, listed here, stock a larger range and also stock toys, videos and audiotapes in English and Mandarin.

TIMES THE BOOKSHOP
✉ Sectors 4, 22, 23 (2 outlets), 30, 52 (2 outlets), 76 and 81 (3 outlets)

Recommended for
Children's books, educational toys, videos and audiotapes. The best selection of children's books is at the Centrepoint outlet.

MUSICAL INSTRUMENTS
See also the "Musical Instruments—Dealers" listing in the Yellow Pages.

KINDERMUSIK
✉ Sector 27

Recommended for
Range of unusual instruments, including percussion, many suitable* for young children

PIANO MASTER
✉ Sector 38

Recommended for
Rental of top-quality pianos from $40, sale of used pianos, professional tuning and repair

VIDEOTAPES
See also the bookshops listed in this section: all the bigger outlets stock children's videos.

THE DISNEY STORE
✉ Sector 23

Recommended for
Disney favourites, for children of all ages, are too numerous to mention. New releases and some of the classics are sold here.

What Do Our Children Really Want?

Mary Ann, aged six, is in one of Singapore's grandest restaurants with her proud and indulgent father, who tells her in front of the bowing maitre d':

"Choose your favourite meal—whatever you like."

"Oh Daddy, may I really have whatever I want?"

"Yes dear, choose anything you like."

"Are you sure? Well then, I'll have white rice and peanuts please."

White rice and peanuts arrived (on a silver dish) and were greatly enjoyed.

– Jean Marshall

Jean Marshall, widow of David Marshall, Singapore's first chief minister, is now retired. She has four adult children and two granddaughters, aged 10 and 7.

WARNER BROS. STUDIO STORE

✉ Sectors 3 and 23

Recommended for

Videos of all-action heroes such as Batman, Bugs Bunny, Sylvester and more. They also stock clothes for children and toys for adults and children.

Distractions

The Suntec City store has a play "rocket" with lots of buttons and flashing lights and touch screen games, which will keep most kids amused while you shop.

ORGANISING A KIDS' PARTY

Do you find that the more children you have, the greater the organisational headache associated with planning a birthday party? The following party organisers, entertainers and suppliers will help to make your job easier, and so help ensure that everyone enjoys the party, maybe even you!

PARTY ORGANISERS

MCDONALD'S RESTAURANTS

Forty outlets offer party packages—chances are there is an outlet near you.

Cost

$6.50 per package ($5.50 for takeaway)
Minimum booking: 10 children

Times available

Call restaurant for details.

Age restrictions

None

What's included

Private party room (only at outlets in Bukit Merah, Ginza and King Albert Park) Use of play equipment (only at outlets in Ginza, Jurong East St 24, Seletar and Toa Payoh Central)
Organised games
Party hostess
Food
Invitations
Party novelties and balloons
Gift for birthday child
Gifts for all invited children

Extras

1-kg Ronald McDonald birthday cake: $10

GYMBOREE

✉ Sector 24

Cost

Option A: $245 without food
Option B: $340 with food

148

Package is for up to 12 children. $15 per additional child up to a total of 35 children

Times available
Monday to Thursday from 5.30 p.m.
Friday 12.30 p.m. to 2 p.m.
Saturday 10 a.m. to 1.30 p.m.
Sunday 5 p.m. to 7 p.m.

Age restrictions
1 to 7 years. Children over 2 years are not allowed on the equipment.

What's included
1½ hours of party time
Private party room
Use of play equipment (up to 2 years)
Organised songs/games
Party entertainer
Food (option B only)
Birthday cake
Sandwiches and snacks
Helium balloons
Invitations

Extras
Gymbo the live clown

ICE WORLD KALLANG
✉ Sector 39

Cost
Option A: $160 for 15 children, including cake
Option B: $8 per child and $10 per adult for a party of 10 children (not including cake)

$10 per additional child/adult who wishes to skate
No charge for those not skating

Times available
Any time between 10 a.m. and 10 p.m. daily, but lunchtime is the quietest time.

Age restrictions
Children must be able to skate. Usually from 4 or 5 years.

What's included
Skate rental
Use of ice rink for up to 2 hours
Organised songs and music
Birthday cake (option A only)

Extras
Food is extra and is available from the snack counter.
Games on the ice can be organised for an extra $30.

KANGAROO CREEK GANG ROADSHOW
✉ Sector 32

Cost
$700 for 30 to 40 children

Times available
Call organiser for details.

Age restrictions
Up to 10 years

What's included
1½ to 2 hours of party time

God Will Be So Angry

Rachel had just finished her dessert but refused to finish the two prunes that were left on her plate. Mum tried to persuade her to eat them, but she was quite sure that she did not like them. After much persuasion Mum got really wild and, as a last resort, screamed: "Eat them up or God will be really cross with you!"

But Rachel was not going to eat the prunes because Mum had used God's name to threaten her. So she did not eat the prunes, and Mum sent her off to bed early that evening, feeling cross.

Later that night, lightning struck, thunder bellowed and the wind howled. The rain poured down. Mum started to feel anxious that her precious, darling girl was alone in her room, and was convinced that she must be terrified, so she rushed upstairs to comfort her.

Instead, she found Rachel looking out of her window saying, "Tsk . . . tsk . . . what a fuss over two prunes!"

– Patricia Koh

The above events took place at a friend's house while Patricia was visiting.

Organised shows/games
Party entertainer
Food (no specific menu)
Birthday cake
Invitations
Party novelties
Mascots
Club membership
Discount on STAR
phonics classes

MONKEYS CAFÉ
✉ Sector 23
☎ 735 3707

Cost
$22 per child (minimum 15 children)

Times available
Call for details.

Age restrictions
None

What's included
Games and prizes
Goodie bags
Cake
Food and drinks
Costumed ape appearance

QUESTXONE (KINDERW
EDUTAINMENT CONCEP
✉ Sector 3
Due to re-open in May 200(
location.

Cost
$200 for 10 children
$17.96 per additional child

Times available
Daily 10 a.m. to 8 p.m.

Age restrictions
None

What's included
1 hour 45 minutes of party time
1 hour in playground
Organised games
Party coordinator
Food and drinks
Birthday cake
Invitations
Party novelties
Birthday present, card and photo
Helium balloons

Extras
Magic show
Mascot appearance
Buffet for adults

YOU LOOK SMALLER ON TV

TRIGG.

THE FAMILY PLACE
✉ Sector 17

★ SFK award
For packaged parties with a difference, The Family Place is tops, offering a range of indoor and outdoor activities at an affordable price.

Cost
$8.24 to $25 per child, depending on package chosen

Times available
Call centre for details.

Age restrictions
Programmes can be customised to suit all age groups.

What's included
Indoor Programme: $8.24 to $12.36 per child

151

The Indoor Programme is a customised programme that can include play in the Adventure Boat, games, bumboat rides, a puppet show and high tea. There must be at least 50 children in the group.

Outdoor Programme: $12.36 per child

The Outdoor Programme includes a guided nature walk, a show of historical sights and a treasure hunt. There must be at least 30 children in the group.

Theme Parties: $25 per child

Children can have a "Pirates of Penzance" or "Under the Sea" party. Included are play in the Adventure Boat, refreshments, party games, party goodies, a private party room and a customised programme. There must be at least 25 children in the group.

Birthday Parties: $20 to $25 per child

If you want a pure and simple birthday party, the Birthday Parties package is the one to go for. It includes play in the Adventure Boat, high tea, party games, balloons and gifts, special requests and the all-important birthday cake. There must be at least 15 children in the group.

PARTY ENTERTAINERS

Here are a few ideas for kids' party entertainment. For more ideas, look up "Magicians" or "Entertainers" in the Yellow Pages Buying Guide. For ideas on creating your own entertainment, buy *The Singapore Party Book* (see "Useful Publications" for details).

BOUNCY CASTLES

☎ 469 6409 or 9511 2849 (pgr)

Entertainment

Stick-ups, inflatable castle, truck and fire engine

Age range

Suitable for 2 to 10 years
Stick-ups suitable for 8 years upwards

Cost

From $160, including delivery to most areas

Notes

Inflatables are for hire for parties indoors or outdoors. Stick-ups incorporate inflatable base and Velcro suits with wall for children to throw themselves at.

JANI BABA—SNAKE CHARMER
☎ 742 5625 or 9256 2495 (pgr)

Entertainment
An hour's show at your home with snakes and magic.

Cost
$300 for 1 hour

GICIAN
☎ 744 1945

Entertainment
A fast-paced and visual magic show.

Age range
He prefers to perform for children over 4 years old and likes the parents to join in.

Cost
$300 for 35 to 45 minutes

WANG LENG MAGIC
☎ 259 6595

Entertainment
"If you don't laugh you must be bananas"—offers a programme of cartooning, magic and balloon sculpture. They promise to tailor the show to suit kids of all ages, and keep them laughing all the way through.

Age range
All ages

Cost
$250 for a 45-minute show

INFLATABLE CREATIONS
☎ 252 7363

Entertainment
If you need to cater to a wide range of ages, this could be the answer. Suitable for kids from 2 to 12, the mazing Maze has tunnels to crawl or run through, ideal for hide and seek. The Balloon Typhoon has 100 balloons flying around inside. This company also supplies helium balloons for decoration.

Age range
From 2 to 12

Cost
$200 to $250 for four hours rental, including delivery and setup.

PARTY GOODS
It's not difficult to find balloons, paper plates, napkins and so on. Bargains are to be had in **The Concourse, Beach Road,** and provisioners will deliver plastic cups, cutlery and paper plates. Supermarkets stock them too. Specialist party suppliers include the following:

IN THE STATES

✉ Sectors 23 and 27

A range of party goods and table-ware, including balloons, banners, streamers and funny hats

PARTY LAND

✉ Sector 15

Everything for parties, including balloons, costumes, masks, banners and paper plates

PARTYLINK

✉ Sector 59

☎ 479 6127

Supplies a minimum of 50 helium balloons ($60) and 100 balloons for $1 each.

BALLOON BARON SPECIALITIES

☎ 785 4929

Rubber or foil balloons and balloon columns ($100). Minimum order is $200 ($500 on Sundays).

TOYS R US

✉ Sectors 3, 23, 52 and 76

A range of goods, including balloons, party favours and tableware

PARTY BAGS

Please don't do as I heard one mother did and give out goldfish in plastic bags to take home! Instead, try one of the following, depending on the age of the children:

- Rather than buying lots of small, cheap toys that fall apart the next day, how about giving each child a box of crayons or pencils, a small tub of play dough and cutters, a comic or a book?

- Edible gifts are good, and they don't have to be sweets. Try a combination such as mini biscuits, small boxes of raisins and apples.

- Try gift vouchers, for example to one of the indoor play centres.

- *The Singapore Party Book* is full of more ideas (see "Useful Publications").

KITTING OUT THE KIDS

CLOTHES

The range of children's clothes available in Singapore is vast. There are designer clothes, not just in boutiques but also in many department stores. Boutiques always seem to have the most gorgeous names—HIPOfant, Jacadi and OshKosh B'Gosh, to name but a few. Many adult fashion retailers have also got on the bandwagon and developed children's wear ranges; examples include Guess and Benetton. Clothes from these places don't come cheap. By all means splash out now and then on a special outfit, but for best value try the department stores (see "Guide to Department Stores") or local shops and market stalls.

BABY EQUIPMENT AND TRANSPORT

APRISIN SINGAPORE
✉ Sector 18

Recommended for
Japanese brands of car seats, strollers and baby carriers, mostly Aprica

BIKE HAUS
✉ Sector 26

Recommended for
All-terrain stroller (ideal for family walking and trekking or pushing while Rollerblading!)

CHILDREN'S WORLD
✉ Sector 21

Recommended for
Strollers and baby walkers

IKEA
✉ Sector 15

Recommended for
- Safety equipment (including bath mats, shower mats and cupboard and drawer latches)

- Reasonably priced own-brand equipment, such as high chairs, potties, inflatable change mats, plastic tableware

MOTHERCARE
✉ Sectors 3 (2 outlets), 23 and 44

Recommended for
- Safety equipment (including bath mats, cupboard and drawer latches, video guards and safety film for glass tables)
- Baby equipment
- Cots and high chairs (larger outlets only)
- Own-brand prams and strollers, baby carriers and car seats (larger outlets only)
- Warm clothes for babies and children travelling to colder climates

TOYS R US
✉ Sectors 3, 23, 52 and 76

Recommended for
Range of baby equipment

FURNITURE

IKEA
✉ Sector 15

Recommended for
Cots, children's tables, desks and chairs, and children's beds

TRIGG

HAIRDRESSER

FANTASTIC SAM'S
✉ Sector 23 (2 outlets)

Recommended for
Probably the only hair salon with stylists who specialise in cutting children's hair. $15.90 per cut for children up to 12 years old. Every sixth haircut (for same child) is free.

SWIMWEAR
Swimwear for babies and children is available from many department stores and children's clothes shops. What is more difficult to find is Australian-made swimwear specially designed to protect children's sensitive skin from the sun. Here are some established retailers.

ECO KIDS
✉ Sector 13

Recommended for
Swimwear in new chlorine-resistant fabric, for newborns to adults, legionnaire hats and children's protective sunglasses. This business is run from home, so call first for an appointment. They will visit your home if you get a group of parents together.

SUNSAFE SWIMWEAR

✉ Sector 25

Recommended for

Australian-made swimwear with UPF of 100 wet or dry, for children from 1 year up to adult sizes. Available at Robinson's and other stores. Call for stockist details.

GUIDE TO DEPARTMENT STORES

Being a great fan of doing all my shopping under one roof, I use department stores a lot. For parents of young children, they also have the advantage of having large children's departments and, in some cases, good baby changing and feeding facilities.

★ SFK award

For best baby changing facilities:
1st: Takashimaya
Joint 2nd: Daimaru and Isetan Scotts

C. K. TANG

✉ Sector 23

Access

Access from the car park to the store with a stroller is not good. It's better to park at Scotts on Scotts Road, where access is better. Otherwise, you can get to all floors easily using the lift.

Recommended for

Clothes, shoes (a good selection), toys, books and baby equipment

Facilities

None

DAIMARU, LIANG COURT

✉ Sector 17

Access

No steps to negotiate and scenic lifts to all floors of the shopping centre

Recommended for

Clothes, shoes, strollers, toys and party goods

Facilities

The nursery room in the children's department on level four has five baby changing stations, a curtained-off breastfeeding area with two chairs, and a kettle for boiled water.

ISETAN SCOTTS

✉ Sector 23

Access

Access at ground level is easy, and lifts and escalators serve all floors, including the basement.

Recommended for

Clothes, shoes, strollers, cots and baby equipment. This has the biggest range of all the Isetan stores.

Facilities

The nursery room is nicely decorated and provides cots with sides for babies to play in. They're not so well designed for nappy changing, though! Also provided are a kettle for boiled water and a sink.

ISETAN KATONG

✉ Sector 44

Recommended for

Clothes, shoes, strollers, cots and baby equipment

Facilities

A nursery room is provided.

ISETAN TAMPINES

✉ Sector 52

Recommended for

Clothes, shoes, strollers, cots and baby equipment

Facilities

A nursery room is provided.

JOHN LITTLE

✉ Sectors 23, 51, 73 and 76

Access

There are a few steps that it is impossible to avoid at the front entrance to the Orchard Road store. Once in the shopping centre there are escalators and lifts to all floors.

Recommended for

Cots, strollers, baby equipment, clothes and toys

Facilities

None

METRO FAR EAST

✉ Sector 22

Recommended for

Clothes, shoes, baby equipment and toys

Facilities

None

METRO MARINA

✉ Sector 3

Access

Use the narrow escalator from ground level or go via the car park to the lift, which goes to all floors.

Recommended for

Strollers, high chairs, booster chairs, clothes, shoes, baby equipment and toys

Facilities

None. Try Mothercare instead!

METRO PARAGON

✉ Sector 23

Access

There are no steps at the entrance to the building, and all floors can be accessed by lift or escalator.

Recommended for

Clothes, shoes, baby equipment and toys

Facilities

There are baby changing facilities in the ladies' toilet on the ground floor next to the lifts.

METRO TAMPINES

✉ Sector 52

Recommended for

Strollers, high chairs, booster chairs, clothes, shoes, baby equipment and toys

Facilities

None

ROBINSONS

✉ Sector 23

Access

Using the main entrance involves flights of stairs either up or down. To avoid these, go to the side entrance in Cuppage Terrace (past the car park entrances, near Pizza Hut) and get to the main shopping centre via the escalator.

Recommended for

Clothes, shoes, swimwear, baby equipment, strollers, cots, high chairs and toys

Facilities

A small room near the shoe department has a baby changing table and a chair, so it could be used for breastfeeding—although it's a bit claustrophobic.

SEIYU WING ON

✉ Sector 18

Access

You have the choice of scenic lifts or escalators from ground floor and underground (MRT) level.

Recommended for

Strollers, walkers, ride-on toys, tricycles, travel cots, car seats, baby chairs, clothes, shoes, baby equipment and toys

Facilities

The nursery room is well equipped although a bit gloomy and in need of redecorating. It has several baby changing stations, a small curtained-off breastfeeding area, scales for weighing small babies and a kettle for boiled water.

Distractions

A play area for children under six years is provided in the children's department. This is a great idea, but unfortunately the area is unequipped except for a small Lego table, so bring your own toys (or buy them here, I suppose!).

TAKASHIMAYA

✉ Sector 23

Access

There is a ramp at the main entrance to Takashimaya, making it possible to access the whole of Ngee Ann City with a stroller. This could be why it's my own favourite store. Inside the store there are lifts and escalators to all floors.

Recommended for

Strollers, baby carriers, baby equipment, clothes and toys

Facilities

The bright and cheery nursery room on level 3 has 10 baby changing stations and a curtained-off breast-feeding area with two chairs. It also has a sink and a kettle for boiled water. The store also has specially designed children's toilets for boys and girls.

Notes

Some of the staff are trained in baby care. They are dressed differently from other staff for easy identification. The store's "Little Ones Club" for children from 3 to 12 years organises regular educational activities and parties.

SHOP 'N' DROP FACILITIES

Wouldn't it be great to take the kids out for lunch and then drop them off somewhere to play for an hour or two while you get some "serious" shopping done? A few play centres offer this facility.

Do bear in mind, however, that if your child is suffering from separation anxiety (most common around one to three years) it may be impossible to leave him/her, especially in unfamiliar surroundings.

DROPXONE (KINDERWORLD EDUTAINMENT CONCEPTS)

✉ Sector 3

Due to re-open in May 2000 at a new location.

Opening hours

Daily 10 a.m. to 10 p.m.

Age

From 4 years

Facilities

See entry on QuestXone in "Play Centres" for details.

Carer-to-child ratio

Approximately 1:6 or 7, depending on age

Cost
$10 per hour for first child, $9 per hour for second child in same group, $8 for third and so on
Minimum stay 2 hours

FUNDAZZLE
✉ Sectors 3, 23, 51, 53, 61 and 68

Opening hours
Daily 10 a.m. to 10 p.m.

Age
1 to 12 years

Facilities
See entry in "Play Centres" for details.

Carer-to-child ratio
Depends on age.

Cost
$10 for the first hour (with two Magic Land tokens) and $7.50 for each additional hour

THE FAMILY PLACE
✉ Sector 17

Opening hours
Tuesday to Sunday 9 a.m. to 7 p.m. Closed on Mondays and public holidays

Age

18 months to 6 or 7 years. This is the only "shop 'n' drop" programme designed for toddlers.

Facilities

See entry in "Play Centres" for details.

arer-to-child ratio

Call centre for details.

Cost

$6.50 for the first hour and $5.50 for each additional hour. Discounts for members.

THE KIDZ STATION

✉ Sector 23

Opening hours

Monday to Friday 9 a.m. to 5 p.m. Call for an appointment as availability varies.

Age

18 months to 4 years

Facilities

See entry in Preschool Survey for details.

Carer-to-child ratio

1:6 to 8

Cost

$10 per hour

Chapter Five

Help for Parents

COUNSELLING AND SUPPORT SERVICES

NEW MOTHERS

For some it's a breeze, but for most of us, becoming a mother is a major life upheaval that takes some getting used to.

Planning ahead to ensure you have practical and emotional support in the first few weeks after the birth can help to minimise depression. Avoid major upheavals immediately before and after the birth, and encourage your partner to avoid taking on extra work.

Get to know other women who are having babies around the same time. Friends with older children can also be a big help—they'll know just what you're going through and be able to tell you how it gets much easier over time.

Do you plan to breastfeed your baby? It has been shown that breastfed babies are less prone to allergies, asthma, eczema, colic, constipation and sudden infant death syndrome (also known as cot death) than bottle-fed babies. In my opinion, breastfeeding is also a great way of bonding with your baby and much less fuss than bottles! The organisations listed here will provide you with useful information, advice and support.

NEW MOTHERS' SUPPORT GROUP

This group is for expectant mums and mothers of newborns through to preschoolers and meets at the Hollandse Club. You can meet other mothers and their children, listen to interesting speakers and make use of the library of parenting books, baby scales and other resources. Annual subscription of $10 which includes a bi-monthly newsletter. Meetings are held on the second Monday of every month at 10.30 a.m. ($8, includes speaker) and on the last Friday at 2.30 p.m. ($5, social only). An NMSG Breastfeeding Mothers group meets separately. The group is part of the Australian and New Zealand Association (ANZA) but you do not have to be a member of ANZA or the Hollandse Club to join.

For more information call:

Barbara Bonser ☎ 462 6203
Catherine Trengrove ☎ 468 3727
Nicola Supka ☎ 256 4791

BREASTFEEDING CLUB

Anna Wong ☎ 736 1636
The Breastfeeding Club is a support group of women who are pregnant or already mothers. The group meets on the first Thursday of every month and has video shows and occasional speakers. Anybody interested in breastfeeding is welcome. Admission is free.

BREASTFEEDING MOTHERS SUPPORT GROUP

Helpline ☎ 339 3558
The Breastfeeding Mothers Support Group (BMSG) provides free counselling on breastfeeding problems through its telephone hotline Monday to Friday, from 9 a.m. to 12 noon and from 2 p.m. to 5 p.m. The group also runs regular "Back to work and breastfeeding" workshops at counsellors' homes at a cost of $10 for non-members and $5 for members. Members receive a quarterly newsletter, a monthly update and access to the group's library (containing books on childbirth, child care and breastfeeding). The group also sells breast pumps and breastfeeding accessories at a discounted rate.

PARENTING SKILLS

Bringing up our children is probably the most important thing we do in our lives, but something for which in most cases we receive no training. Reading books on child care and parenting, of which there are a great number, is valuable, but sometimes a seminar or support group can answer your questions more effectively and comprehensively.

Little Girl Lost

It was 8.30 p.m., and I had told Daena to stay with Daddy at the local corner shop while I walked to the other end of the block to another shop. When I returned, she had gone. Ben had thought that she was with me.

I asked everyone around if they had seen a little girl with pigtails, about four and a half years old. I shouted her name and ran up and down the entire block. My worst fears set in: had she been lured away? Knocked down by a car? We spent the next half hour searching to no avail, by which time I went berserk from fear of losing my little girl.

Ben decided that we should retrace our steps to our apartment block, a 10-minute walk. I half walked, half ran, looking all around for Daena, but she was not there. We asked the security guards outside the apartment block if they had seen her, but they shook their heads. My heart sank.

Then we reached the lobby, and there she was! I hugged her tightly as she told me she had tried to get the elevator to our apartment (on the 18th floor) but could not reach the buttons. When she had not been able to find us after having wandered off, she had decided to try to find her way home and had run all the way. How had she crossed at the traffic lights? She had waited for the "green man", as her father and I had taught her.

Six years on, Daena is nearly 11 and leaves me messages like this:

"I wish you not to stress yourself with work. . . . You come first in my heart. That means you come first. Not even my future boyfriend can beat you! Ha ha. Your only daughter, Daena."

I will never forget that night. Such joy would not be mine today if anything terrible had happened to her.

– Diana Ee-Tan

Diana Ee-Tan is vice-president of Raffles International. She has three children—Ansel, 16, Daena, 14, and Darren, 11.

In addition to the organisations listed here, some preschools offer resources for parents, such as parenting seminars and a library of parenting/child development books.

Some of the following organisations have been set up specifically to help parents who are either disadvantaged or who have particular needs.

AMP CENTRE

✉ Sector 43
☎ 346 0911

The AMP Centre, run by the Association of Muslim Professionals, offers support for Muslim families, including:

- A family resource centre with reading and audiovisual materials for parents and study and play areas for children
- Seminars on parenting for Muslim parents or parents-to-be
- "Learn with your child" programmes for parents of preschool and primary school children
- Lists of family organisations, preschools and useful publications
- A preschool teacher training programme

CHILD CARE INFORMATION

☎ 1800 258 5812

Child Care Information is a hot line service sponsored by the Ministry of Community Development giving advice on issues relating to child care and child care centres.

COUNCIL FOR THE DEVELOPMENT OF THE SINGAPORE MUSLIM COMMUNITY

☎ 240 2130/240 2133

The Council for the Development of the Singapore Muslim Community runs parenting programmes for low-income families in collaboration with various Malay organisations. Sessions are held on Saturday afternoons at various locations and are practical workshops aimed at problem solving.

NTUC CHILDCARE CO-OPERATIVE PUBLICATIONS UNIT

☎ 293 9161

The NTUC publishes books for children and parents with content that is relevant to Singaporean children. For example, it has published two books on wildlife for young children.

SINGAPORE CHILDREN'S SOCIETY

☎ 272 3229

Founded in 1952, the Singapore Children's Society provides help for needy parents and children through a range of activities. It runs two social work service centres, in Bukit Merah and Toa Payoh, and a family service centre in Yishun. It also organises the Tinkle Friend hot line, a play group and holiday programmes for children, and workshops for parents. It works to prevent child abuse and neglect. The society welcomes volunteers and financial support for its work.

SINGAPORE MALAY YOUTH LIBRARY ASSOCIATION

☎ 741 7977

The Singapore Malay Youth Library Association provides child care and before- and after-school care (BASC) at subsidised rates, runs a halfway house and family service centre, and organises talks and workshops for single parents.

ADOPTIVE FAMILIES OF SINGAPORE

☎ 462 1237 (Jane)

The group meets at the Mother and Child Centre (see List of Addresses).

THE FAMILY PLACE

✉ Sector 17

☎ 334 3937

The Family Place is an exclusive enrichment centre and a subsidiary of NTUC Childcare Co-operative. It organises seminars, interactive workshops and classes on parenting skills. The first organisation of its kind in Singapore, it was developed with the aim of improving the amount of quality time for families by offering a range of activities under one roof. Annual membership is available for $120 (gold) or $80 (green) per family. Members receive discounts, booking priority, exclusive invitations and a bi-monthly newsletter. See chapter 1 for details of its play centre and preschool, art, drama, music and enrichment classes. See chapter 4 for its shop 'n' drop facilities and children's parties.

FAMILY TROUBLES

Perhaps one of the greatest taboos. We may be embarrassed to mention even to our closest friends that we are having problems relating to our husband, or that we find difficulty in disciplining our children, or even that our in-laws are making our life a misery.

We often blame ourselves, at least in part, for the way things have turned out, and focus inwards rather than seeking help, which just tends to make matters worse. Nevertheless, in experiencing these problems we are certainly not alone. The vast majority of parents experience similar problems at some stage in their lives.

Here are some organisations you could turn to.

SAMARITANS OF SINGAPORE (SOS)
☎ 1800 221 4444
The main aim of the Samaritans of Singapore is suicide prevention, but the organisation also offers services to those in crisis who may not be suicidal.

ALCOHOLICS ANONYMOUS
☎ 338 2791
Alcoholics Anonymous runs a helpline for alcoholics and their families. Support groups, including a women's group, meet regularly at the Church of St. Peter and Paul.

KAMPONG KAPUR FAMILY SERVICE CENTRE
✉ Sector 20
☎ 299 7662
The Kampong Kapur Family Service Centre offers counselling for

parents and programmes for children. It is run by Methodist Welfare Services.

PAYA LEBAR FAMILY SERVICE CENTRE
Parentline ☎ 289 8811
The Paya Lebar Family Service Centre offers counselling for parents and programmes for children. It is run by Methodist Welfare Services.

TAMPINES FAMILY SERVICE CENTRE
✉ Sector 52
☎ 787 2001
The Tampines Family Service Centre conducts a family life education programme and runs a BASC programme and supervised study centre. It is run by Methodist Welfare Services.

AWARE (ASSOCIATION OF WOMEN FOR ACTION AND RESEARCH)
Helpline ☎ 779 7137
AWARE runs a women's helpline service and provides advice, counselling, information and referral services on appointment. It also produces publications and organises exhibitions and workshops on various topics relevant to women, including women's health.

CARE CORNER
✉ Sector 33
☎ 296 1788
The government-funded Care Corner provides family life education, a child care centre and BASC. Counselling in Mandarin is provided on a case-by-case basis.

FAMILY LIFE SOCIETY
☎ 339 5354
Staff at the Family Life Society offer free counselling in English and Mandarin to those with family or marital problems. The society also organises "Human Sexuality" talks in schools for 14- to 15-year-olds and occasional parenting courses.

FOR CHILDREN AND ADOLESCENTS

PREGNANCY CRISIS CENTRE
☎ 339 9770
The Pregnancy Crisis Centre runs a 24-hour hot line (voice mail outside office hours) aimed mainly at teenage girls faced with unplanned pregnancy. The centre informs them about the options available, coordinating with the Half Way House for Unwed Mothers and the Ministry of Education in order that they may continue their studies.

TINKLE FRIEND
☎ 1800 274 4788
Tinkle Friend is a hot line for primary school children needing to chat or discuss their problems.

NEWCOMERS
To those readers who have recently arrived in Singapore, I offer my understanding and encouragement. When I arrived here I felt very lost and really didn't know where to start. My experiences were the main motivation for writing this book. The following organisations all offer excellent services that will help you settle in more quickly.

AMERICAN ASSOCIATION AND AMERICAN WOMEN'S ASSOCIATION (AWA)
☎ 738 0371/733 6170
Ordinary membership of the American Association is open to Americans. Associate membership is open to all other nationalities, providing that 51% American membership is maintained. There is rarely a long waiting list for associate membership.

The American Association organises annual Fourth of July celebrations, including fireworks and games. The American Women's Association publishes a monthly newsletter, *The Bamboo Telegraph,* with a couple of pages being devoted to recipes and children's activities and events. The association previously published an excellent newsletter for parents, which is likely to be reestablished. Three major parties for members' children of various ages are organised each year, at Easter, Halloween and Christmas. Tours for children are organised from time to time. Additional support services for parents are provided through sister organisation SACAC (see below).

ANZA

☎ 733 1215

ANZA offers ordinary membership to Australians and New Zealanders and associate membership to other nationalities. Sports membership is available for children, to participate in sports programmes (soccer or netball) only. Services provided to members that are particularly relevant to families include:

- Advice on looking for a gynaecologist or paediatrician
- List of play groups (mothers and babies meet in participants' homes)
- List of preschools aimed at or run by expatriates
- Children's activities, especially during school holidays
- Baby-sitting register
- Children's page in monthly newsletter

ANZA also runs a Summer Fun programme during the July/August school holidays, for children from 3 years to teenagers. Activities in-

TRIGGu

clude swimming, tours, rock wall climbing, tennis, cooking, drama and pottery.

BRITISH ASSOCIATION AND BRITISH WOMEN'S ASSOCIATION
☎ 339 8229

Ordinary membership of The British Association is open to Britons. Associate membership is open to all other nationalities. Services provided to members that are particularly relevant to families include:

- Newcomers' coffee mornings for those with small children
- Mums 'n' Tots groups
- Twins Plus—support group for mothers of multiples
- Baby and Child Development Clinic
- Baby-sitting register
- "Kids About Town" page in monthly magazine *The Beam*

SACAC
✉ Sector 22

SACAC is open to all nationalities. Based in the American Club, it runs regular Community Health Programs on topics such as settling in in Singapore, parenting skills and healthy living in Singapore. SACAC also offers a counselling service.

The SACAC library has over 600 books on various topics, includ-

ing parenting skills, families, relocation and women's issues. Use of the library is free to AWA and SACAC members; nonmembers pay a one-off fee of $25.

For information on any of these services, contact Marijean Conrad, Director of Community Health ☎ 733 9249.

THE AMERICAN CLUB
✉ Sector 22
☎ 737 3411

The American Club organises various activities for members' children from three to 16 years at subsidised cost, including:

- Sports lessons
- Games
- Swimming lessons
- Play group
- Art, dance, drama and music classes
- Holiday activities

Facilities include a library, an indoor playroom with play equipment, an outdoor playground , a wading pool in addition to the main pool, and a restaurant that welcomes children.

THE BRITISH CLUB
✉ Sector 28
☎ 467 4311

The British Club organises the following activities for children. All

171

activities are limited to members and their guests.

- Tennis, basketball and netball teams, gymnastics, junior gym, khong chang and junior snooker
- Classical ballet, Music and Movement classes
- Water babies, swimming, and mums and tots classes
- Weekly mother and baby coffee and play sessions
- Activities for under-fives through "BC Club"

A summer programme for children from four to 12 years includes:

- Visits to places of interest
- Cooking and craft sessions
- Horse riding

A child minding service is provided on Mondays, Wednesdays and Fridays from 8.30 a.m. to 11.30 a.m.

Monthly coffee mornings, for newcomers to learn about living in Singapore and make friends, are held in conjunction with two moving companies.

Club facilities for children include a well-equipped indoor playroom, a video and book library, an outdoor play park, a video arcade and a large, shallow baby pool and wet play area in addition to the main pool.

Children's meals are served in the Verandah Café, which has high chairs and booster seats, and all F&B outlets welcome children except the bars. There is a baby changing table in the ladies' toilet and a playpen in the changing rooms.

Antenatal services and a baby clinic are also offered at the club.

HOLLANDSE CLUB
✉ Sector 29
☎ 469 5211

The Hollandse Club, well known for its family oriented atmosphere, has a wide range of children's facilities:

- Attractively decorated supervised play room for 2- to 6-year-olds (The Puppy Club)
- Junior Room for children aged 7 and above, with free computer and Internet access
- Children's library
- Outdoor play area and wading pool

Classes include ballet, gymnastics, baby gym, basketball, floorball, hockey, judo, karate, soccer, tennis, swimming (beginners, mums and tots, and award swimming), sailing and scuba diving.

A summer programme for children aged 4 to 14 is organised.

Antenatal classes and a Mums and Tots group are held weekly. Baby changing facilities and a playpen are available in the ladies' changing room.

Children's meals are served at The Terrace and Juliana's. Both restaurants are equipped with high chairs.

All activities are limited to members and their guests.

THE JAPANESE ASSOCIATION

✉ Sector 28
☎ 468 0066

The Japanese Association's Women's Committee organises a briefing for newcomers to Singapore approximately twice a year.

The association's Sports Committee organises various sports tournaments and an annual sports meet for members and their families.

Activities for children include music classes and concerts and a puppet show held twice a year.

All activities and events are restricted to members only.

PARENTS OF SPECIAL NEEDS KIDS

ASIAN WOMEN'S WELFARE ASSOCIATION (AWWA)

✉ Sector 56, 20 (school)
☎ 454 8919 (TEACH ME)
   291 9706 (School)

The Asian Women's Welfare Association provides assistance to families in distress and runs a special school for multiple disabled children, offering physiotherapy, occupational therapy, speech therapy and educational programmes. It also runs the "TEACH ME" programme, enabling physically handicapped children to attend mainstream preschools and schools. Mobile clinics visit schools and homes to provide the children with therapy and educational services.

HORIZON SCHOOL FOR SPECIAL EDUCATION

✉ Sector 11
☎ 270 1824

The Horizon School for Special Education caters for a wide range of students with special needs. Its multi-disciplinary team of qualified specialists includes special education teachers, a behaviour therapist, speech therapists and a physiotherapist. Opportunities for integration into mainstream schools are available.

MINDS

✉ Sector 14
☎ 479 5655

MINDS (Movement for the Intellectually Disabled of Singapore) runs five schools teaching basic life skills to mentally disabled children from 4 to 18 years. The organisation also runs employment development centres and day activity centres, and provides residential care and support services.

RIDING FOR THE DISABLED

✉ Sector 29

☎ 251 7020

Riding for the Disabled aims to assist disabled people gain balance, movement, muscle tone and self-confidence from learning to ride a horse. Classes are held mornings and afternoons for children (from six years) and adults. This is a charity and welcomes helpers and sponsorship.

SINGAPORE ASSOCIATION FOR THE DEAF

✉ Sector 39

☎ 344 8274

The Singapore Association for the Deaf's Parents Support Group, which meets monthly, is aimed mainly at parents of young children (preschool to P2). They meet on the last Sunday of each month, with a resource speaker each time.

SINGAPORE ASSOCIATION FOR THE VISUALLY HANDICAPPED

✉ Sector 29

☎ 251 4331

The Singapore Association for the Visually Handicapped is closely as-

sociated with the activities of the Singapore School of the Visually Handicapped.

SINGAPORE SCHOOL FOR THE VISUALLY HANDICAPPED

✉ Sector 29

☎ 250 3755

The Singapore School of the Visually Handicapped provides a play group for children from three to five years and offers education from primary age up to 18 years. There is no formal support group for parents, but informal support is offered.

GETTING HELP AT HOME

EMPLOYING A MAID

Most of the women employed here as Foreign Domestic Workers (FDWs), otherwise known as maids or amahs, come from the Philippines, Sri Lanka or Indonesia. You can recruit a maid directly from her country of origin via an employment agency in Singapore. Alternatively, and preferred by most expatriate families, you can recruit a maid who is transferring from an existing employer in Singapore. This has three main advantages: the agency fees are lower, the maid will have more experience and so require less training and, perhaps most important, you can interview her before making a decision rather than relying on biodata from the agency. However, make sure that she has a good reason to be transferring.

The agency can organise the paperwork with the government, arrange insurance for your $5000 bond with the government and organise your maid's medical insurance. Alternatively, you can handle all these matters yourself and pay the agency only for the recruitment process, but in my view it's not worth the hassle.

In order to recruit a maid, you or your spouse must be either a Singapore citizen or a Permanent Resident or have an Employment Pass and be earning at least $36,000 per annum. Once you have recruited a maid, you need to pay the government a monthly levy of $345 by GIRO, in addition to the maid's salary. If you have at least two children under 12 years at home, you can employ two maids.

Before recruiting a full-time, live-in maid, you should consider the following:

Are you sure you want a live-in maid?

Read the paragraph below on employers' responsibilities, and give some thought to how you would feel having a total stranger move into your home. Perhaps if your children

are older and you don't work full-time, you need only part-time help.

What are the main tasks you require a maid to carry out?

These might include cooking, ironing, mopping floors, dusting and washing clothes. Perhaps they also include tasks involving greater responsibility, such as organising regular dinner parties. If so, expect to pay a little more for a suitably experienced person.

Will you require the maid to look after your children?

If so, would this involve taking them out, collecting them from school, caring for them at home or just baby-sitting in the evenings? Language abilities may be particularly important if you want the maid to look after small children for extended periods, where she will need to be able to communicate with them and understand their needs. Some maids even have relevant nursing or child care qualifications.

EMPLOYERS' RESPONSIBILITIES

Your liability

First and foremost, once you sign all the papers and post the bond with the Singapore government, you are ultimately responsible for your maid's welfare. Should she violate the Immigration Act, as the employer you will be liable for the $5000 (insurance for the bond is mandatory) and the cost of her return trip home. If you leave Singapore, you must either sign transfer papers or cancel her work permit.

Salary

Live-in maids are paid between $200 and $1000 a month, with the average being $350 to $400.

Medical expenses

You will need to pay all medical expenses, including the six-monthly medical examination required by the Ministry of Labour, any consultations, hospitalisation (in a public hospital) and medicine she may require. Personal accident/hospitalisation insurance cover is mandatory, and easily available, to cover most eventualities.

Other essentials

You are responsible for providing for your maid's daily needs, including food, toiletries, a suitable place to sleep, bathing and toilet facilities, and a uniform if required. Some employers provide a weekly allowance for food and toiletries ($150 to $180 oer month is recommended). Others prefer to shop for the maid's needs. In this case, remember to keep cupboards stocked so that your maid doesn't go hungry. It can happen!

Setting rules and standards

Many expatriates who have never employed a maid before feel uncomfortable about giving their maid a list of tasks or a rota, but the maid will expect and need some guidance, and a certain amount of discipline is likely to result in a better working relationship—for example, setting the time at which she should return home on a Sunday, clarifying whether or not she can make and receive phone calls and receive visitors, and showing her how you want things to be done. It is advisable to have a contract or written agreement with your maid, which formalises the commitments you have both made.

Having realistic expectations

Don't expect your maid to do something you can't or won't do yourself. This is perhaps particularly important in the area of child care, where parents can sometimes be in danger of expecting the maid to be able to control their children better than they can! If you have more than one child and need the maid to provide child care for extended periods as well as carrying out domestic duties, consider employing two maids, one as a nanny, the other as a domestic maid. Alternatively, look at the child care options available (see chapter 1, "Preschools").

MAIDS' RIGHTS

Following the Flor Contemplacion affair, the case of a Filipino maid who was executed in 1995 for the alleged murder of a fellow maid and her four-year-old charge, the issue of Filipino maids' rights and their protection has become a political issue. The Philippine Embassy has taken various steps in an attempt to protect maids, which unfortunately have also resulted in increased costs being incurred by the employer. Now, in order to recruit a Filipino maid directly from the Philippines, you have to:

1. post a $2000 bond with the Philippine Embassy;
2. undertake to pay for the maid's repatriation (unless she breaks her contract) and agree that her services can be terminated only if she breaks an immigration law.

When you allow your Filipino maid to return to the Philippines for a holiday, either during or at the end of her employment with you, you must make sure her papers are in order and take out a bond for $2000 with the Philippine Embassy (if you have not already done so). You will also have to pay a substantial agency fee (to an accredited agency).

Other countries, such as Sri Lanka, have taken similar measures. Contact the relevant embassy or a reputable maid agency for the most up-to-date information.

HOW TO AVOID PROBLEMS

Several organisations run courses on how to employ a maid and courses for maids on home and child care. These include The Family Place, SACAC (see the "Newcomers" section). See also Professional Nursing Services (chapter 3).

You will probably encounter communication and cultural problems from time to time. In the vast majority of cases these can and should be settled between employer and employee. In the event that matters cannot be resolved between you, contact the agency that supplied the maid, which will in most cases endeavour to resolve the situation. Some agencies offer a free replacement if, after three months, things are not working out. However, I suggest that in most cases it is better to persevere with an existing relationship rather than start again, only to risk having the same problems over again.

IF YOU HAVE TO LEAVE SINGAPORE

Thankfully, maids are no longer penalised for having to transfer between employers more than once. Assuming that you are happy to recommend your maid to others, help her to gain alternative employment by giving her a written reference and, if possible, by advertising in shops and mentioning her availability to friends. Alternatively, you need only pay her return fare home, but give her as much notice as possible (at least a month) so that she has time to investigate the options available. You must sign transfer papers or cancel your maid's work permit before you leave Singapore.

PART-TIME HELP OR BABY-SITTING

The going rate for part-time help or baby-sitting is around $10 an hour (baby-sitting can be less). This can work out as expensive as (or more expensive than) a live-in maid, depending on how much help you need.

I was amused to find that the Yellow Pages Buying Guide contains only one entry under the "Baby Sitters" listing! You could try her, or if she's busy (as I assume she must be) try the following:

- Join one of the national associations listed in the "Newcomers" section. Many have a baby-sitting register.
- Ask your neighbours, or even the condominium security guards (some are great sources of information), if they know of anyone.
- Try contacting an employment agency. Some provide part-time as well as full-time maids, but they don't advertise the fact.

- When we first moved to Singapore we stayed in a serviced apartment for a while. They had a baby-sitting service, and the baby-sitter worked for us again after we left. She was excellent.
- Try contacting your nearest secondary school or international school. You may be able to advertise there, or they may have a list of potential baby-sitters.

APPENDICES

Guidelines to using the following table can be found on pages 14–22.

Sector codes referred to in the table may be located on the map on page 215.

PRESCHOOL SURVEY

Sector Code	Organisation Name	Hours of Operation	Age	Cost	Ratio	Art & Craft	Music & Movement	English	Mandarin	Other Language	Maths	Computer Class
1	Wesley Child Development	Mon.-Fri. Full: 7 a.m.-6.30 p.m. Sat.: 7 a.m.- 2 p.m.	2 yrs.-K2	Full: $450 pm	1:5 to 10	✔	✔	✔	✔		✔	✔
3	Kinderworld Edutainment Concepts	Mon.-Sat. Full: 7.30 a.m.-6.30 p.m. Sat.: 7.30 a.m.-2 p.m. Half: 7.30 a.m.-2 p.m. or 2 p.m.-6.30 p.m.	PG-K2	Full: $750 pm Half: $600-$650 pm	MCD	✔	✔	✔	✔		✔	✔
6	The Moral Child Care Centre	Mon.-Sat. Full: 7.30 a.m.-6.30 p.m. Sat.: 7.30 a.m.-2 p.m.	2½ yrs.-K2	**Full: $400 pm**	Better than MCD	✔	✔	✔	✔		✔	
11	Eternal Life Assembly Child Care	Mon.-Sat. Full: 7 a.m.-7 p.m. Sat.: 7 a.m.-1.30 p.m.	2 yrs.-K2	**Full: $380-$410 pm**	2-3 yrs. 1:12 N 1:15 K1&2 1:20	✔	✔	✔	✔		✔	✔
11	Kinder Corner 1	Mon.-Fri. Full: 7.30 a.m.-6.30 p.m. Half day also available.	PG-K2	Full: $580 pm Half: $480 pm Discount for parents working in Science Park	**1:5 to 12**	✔	✔	✔	✔		✔	
11	Kinder Corner 2	Mon.-Fri. Full: 7.30 a.m.-6.30 p.m. Half day also available.	PG-K2	Full: $580 pm Half: $480 pm Discount for parents working in Science Park	**1:5 to 12**	✔	✔	✔	✔		✔	
12	Brookvale Creche	Full: 7.30a.m.-6.30 p.m. Sat.: 7.30 a.m.-1.30 p.m. Half day also available.	PG-K2	Full: $530-$550 pm Half: $410-$430 pm	PG 1:8 N 1:12 K1&2 1:15	✔	✔	✔	✔		✔	✔

PG: Play group   **N:** Nursery   **K1:** Kindergarten 1   **K2:** Kindergarten 2   **P1:** Primary 1
pa: per annum   **p6m:** per six months   **p20s:** per 20 sessions   **pm:** per month   **pd:** per day

Field Trips	Free Play	Tests	Other Activities	Notes	Food & Drink	Transport	Garden/Outdoor Play Area	Gym Equip	Library	Other Facilities
✓	✓				✓		✓		✓	
✓	✓			75% English, 25% Mandarin	✓		✓		✓	
✓	✓	✓	Drama (E): $40 pm Outdoor programme		✓		✓	✓	✓	
✓	✓	✓	Drama (M): $150 pm Computer classes N-K2		✓		✓	✓	✓	
✓	✓		Cooking, Swimming (K1&2)		✓		✓			Wading pool
✓	✓		Cooking (K1&2)		✓		✓			Wading pool
✓	✓	✓	Cooking. English only, up to 3 years		✓	✓	✓	✓	✓	

Sector Code	Organisation Name	Hours of Operation	Age	Cost	Ratio	Art & Craft	Music & Movement	English	Mandarin	Other Language	Maths	Computer Class
12	KinderWorld EduCare (West Coast)	Mon.-Sat. Full: 7.30 a.m.- 6.30 p.m. Sat.: 7.30 a.m.- 2 p.m. Half: 7.30 a.m.- 2 p.m. or 2 p.m.- 6.30 p.m.	PG-K2	Full: $600 pm Half: $400 or $450 pm BASC: $370 pm	MCD	✔	✔	✔	✔		✔	✔
12	Montessori Creative World	Mon.-Fri. 9 a.m.-5 p.m. Sat. 9 a.m. to 4 p.m. Part: for 2- or 3-hours programmes, 3-5 times per week. 5 times per wk.	2 yrs.-K2	Part: $360-$550 pm	**1:6**	✔	✔	✔	✔		✔	
12	Tenderluv Daycare Child Devt. Centre	Mon.-Fri. Full: 7.30 a.m.- 6.30 p.m. Sat.: 7.30 a.m.-1.30 p.m.	PG-K2	Full: $425-$445 pm Half: $310-$330 pm BASC: $280-$300 pm	MCD	✔	✔	✔	✔		✔	
14	True Way Presbyterian Kindergarten	Mon.-Fri. Part: 8.30 a.m.-11.30 a.m. or 11.45 a.m.-2.45 p.m.	2½ yrs-K2	**Part: $285-$360 pt** Reg: $30 non ref Book and Stationery fee: $150 pa	**Pre-N 1:8 N 1:10 K1&2 1:17**	✔	✔	✔	✔			✔
	Pat's SchoolHouse	Full: 7.30 a.m.-6.30 p.m. Sat.: 7.30 a.m.-1.30 p.m. Half: 7.30 a.m.-12.30 p.m. or 1 p.m. to 6.30 p.m.	2 yrs.-K2	Full: $1270 pm Half: $670 pm Registration: $150	**1:6 to 7**	✔	✔	✔	✔	J	✔	
17	The Family Place	Mon.-Fri. Part: 9 a.m.-12.30 p.m. or 2 p.m.-5.30 p.m.	PG-N	Part: $600-$650 pm	**1:6**	✔	✔	✔	✔			

PG: Play group   **N:** Nursery   **K1:** Kindergarten 1   **K2:** Kindergarten 2   **P1:** Primary 1
pa: per annum   **p6m:** per six months   **p20s:** per 20 sessions   **pm:** per month   **pd:** per day

Field Trips	Free Play	Tests	Other Activities	Notes	Food & Drink	Transport	Garden/Outdoor Play Area	Gym Equip	Library	Other Facilities
✔	✔		Cooking, Science	75% English, 25% Mandarin	✔	✔	✔		✔	
✔	✔		Montessori curriculum, holiday programmes			✔	✔		✔	
✔	✔	✔	Drama (E): $35 pm		✔	✔	✔		✔	Water play
✔	✔		Computer classes: $48 pm		✔	✔	✔			
✔	✔		Cooking, science, P.E., drama (E & M)		✔	✔	✔	✔	✔	
✔	✔		Camps, holiday programmes, cultural activities, parent participation opportunities	Playtime programme	✔			✔	✔	Toy library, reading corner, indoor play area

ps: per session   **p8s:** per eight sessions   **pt:** per term (10 weeks unless otherwise indicated)   185
BASC: before- and after-school care   **A:** Arabic   **H:** Hindi   **J:** Japanese   **Mly:** Malay   **T:** Tamil

Sector Code	Organisation Name	Hours of Operation	Age	Cost	Ratio	Art & Craft	Music & Movement	English	Mandarin	Other Language	Maths	Computer Class
17	The Family Place	Mon.-Fri. Part: 9 a.m.-12.30 p.m. or 2 p.m.-5.30 p.m.	PG-N	Part: $600-$650 pm	**1:6**	✔	✔	✔		J	✔	
17	The Little Skool-House	Mon.-Sat. Full: 7.30 a.m.-7 p.m. Sat.: 7.30 a.m.-2 p.m.	PG-K2	Full: $850 pm	1:6 to 1:18	✔	✔	✔	✔		✔	✔
17	The Little Skool-House	Mon.-Sat. Full: 7.30 a.m.-7 p.m. Sat.: 7.30 a.m.-2 p.m.	PG-K2	Full: $850 pm	1:6 to 1:18	✔	✔	✔		J	✔	✔
18	KinderWorld EduCare (Bras Basah)	Mon.-Sat. Full: 7.30 a.m.-6.30 p.m. Sat.: 7.30 a.m.-2 p.m. Half: 7.30 a.m.-2 p.m. or 2 p.m.-6.30 p.m.	PG-K2	Full: $650 pm Half: $450 or $550 pm BASC: $400 pm	MCD	✔	✔	✔	✔		✔	✔
22	Julia Gabriel Communications	Tues.-Fri.: 9 a.m.-6.30 p.m. Part: (Level 1) 2-hr sessions, twice a week, (Level 2) 2½-hr sessions, daily	PG-3½ yrs.	Part: (Level 1) $790 om (Level 2) $1550 pm	**1:4** to 1:12	✔	✔	✔	✔		✔	
22	Pat's SchoolHouse	Full: 7.30 a.m.-6.30 p.m. Sat.: 7.30 a.m.-1.30 p.m. Half: 7.30 a.m.-12.30 p.m. or 1 p.m. to 6.30 p.m.	2 yrs.-K2	Full: $1270 pm Half: $670 pm Registration: $150	**1:6 to 7**	✔	✔	✔	✔	J	✔	

PG: Play group   **N:** Nursery   **K1:** Kindergarten 1   **K2:** Kindergarten 2   **P1:** Primary 1
pa: per annum   **p6m:** per six months   **p20s:** per 20 sessions   **pm:** per month   **pd:** per day

Field Trips	Free Play	Tests	Other Activities	Notes	Food & Drink	Transport	Garden/Outdoor Play Area	Gym Equip	Library	Other Facilities
✔	✔		Camps, holiday programmes, cultural activities, parent participation opportunities	Hiyoko programme	✔			✔	✔	Toy library, reading corner, indoor play area
✔	✔		Drama (E & M), Moral Education	Bilingual English/Mandarin programme	✔	✔	✔	✔	✔	Use of facilities at The Family Place
✔	✔		Drama (E & M), Moral Education	Bilingual English/Japanese programme	✔	✔	✔	✔	✔	Use of facilities at The Family Place
✔	✔		Cooking, Science	75% English, 25% Mandarin	✔		✔		✔	
	✔		Cooking, P.E.		✔		✔	✔	✔	
✔	✔		Cooking, Science, P.E., Drama (E & M)		✔	✔	✔	✔	✔	

Sector Code	Organisation Name	Hours of Operation	Age	Cost	Ratio	Art & Craft	Music & Movement	English	Mandarin	Other Language	Maths	Computer Class
23	The Kidz Station	Mon.-Fri. Part: 9.30 a.m.-12.30 p.m. or 2 p.m.-5 p.m. 2-5 times per wk. (Also open Saturday p.m. and all day Sunday)	PG-4 yrs.	Part: $250-$500 pm	**1:5 to 8**	✔	✔	✔				
23	The Montessori Workgroup	Part: Mon.-Sat. 10 a.m.-1 p.m. Tues. to Sat. 2 p.m.-5 p.m. 1-2 hr. session, 1-5 times per wk.	2 yrs.-K1	Part: $270-$1200 pt Registration: $40 Deposit: $90 Assessment: $20	**1:5**	✔		✔			✔	
24	The Children's Place	Mon.-Fri. Full: 7.30 a.m.-6 p.m. Half: 7.30 a.m.-1 p.m. or 1 p.m.-6 p.m.	PG-6½ yrs.	Full: $1180 pm Half: $680 pm	**PG 1:6 to 8 N 1:8 to 10** K1&2 1:10 to 15	✔	✔	✔	✔		✔	
25	The Preparatory Place	Mon.-Sat. Full: 7.30 a.m.-6.30 p.m. Sat. 7.30 a.m.-2 p.m. Half: 8.30 a.m.-12.30 p.m. or 1 p.m.-5 p.m.	2 yrs.-K2	Full: $1000 pm Half: $575 pm	**1:8**	✔	✔	✔	✔		✔	
26	Green Pastures Child Centre	Mon.-Fri. Full: 7.30 a.m.-4 p.m. Half: 7.30 a.m.-1.30 p.m.	2½ yrs.-K2	**Full: $400 pm Half: $270 pm**	**N1:9** K1&2 1:22	✔	✔	✔	✔		✔	✔
26	Nanyang Kindergarten	Mon.-Fri. Part: 8 a.m.-11 a.m. or 11 a.m.-2 p.m.	N-K2	Part: $390-$420 pt	1:15	✔	✔	✔	✔		✔	✔

PG: Play group   **N:** Nursery   **K1:** Kindergarten 1   **K2:** Kindergarten 2   **P1:** Primary 1
pa: per annum   **p6m:** per six months   **p20s:** per 20 sessions   **pm:** per month   **pd:** per day

Field Trips	Free Play	Tests	Other Activities	Notes	Food & Drink	Transport	Garden/Outdoor Play Area	Gym Equip	Library	Other Facilities
✔	✔				✔					Indoor playground on level 12, new playground on B1 opens end 1999
			Montessori curriculum							Montessori shop next door
✔	✔		Drama (E or M), Cooking, Science		✔		✔	✔	✔	Parenting resource library
✔	✔				✔	✔	✔	✔	✔	
✔	✔		Cooking		✔	✔	✔	✔		
✔	✔	✔	Holiday camps		✔	✔	✔	✔	✔	

Sector Code	Organisation Name	Hours of Operation	Age	Cost	Ratio	Art & Craft	Music & Movement	English	Mandarin	Other Language	Maths	Computer Class
26	Sunshine Montessori House	Mon.-Fri. Part: 8.30 a.m.-10.45 a.m. or 10.45 a.m.-1 p.m.	2½ yrs.-K2	Contact preschool for details.	**1:8**	✔	✔	✔	✔		✔	
27	Children's Cottage	Mon.-Fri. Full: 7.30 a.m.-6.30 p.m. Half: 8.30 a.m.-12 noon or 1.30 p.m.-5 p.m.	2½ yrs.-K2	Full: $780 pm Half: $480 pm	N 1:11 K1&2 1:13	✔	✔	✔	✔		✔	
27	United Educare (Lotus)	Mon.-Fri. 9 a.m.-5 p.m. Part: 9 a.m.-12 noon, 2, 3 or 5 sessions	PG-K2	Full: $780 pm Part: $380-$650 pm	**Average 1:8**	✔	✔	✔	✔		✔	✔
27	United Educare (Ming Teck)	Mon.-Fri. 9 a.m.-5 p.m. Part: 9 a.m.-12 noon, 2, 3 or 5 sessions	PG-K2	Full: $600 pm Part: $220-$550 pm	**Average 1:8**	✔	✔	✔	✔		✔	✔
29	Pibo's Garden	Mon.-Sat. Full: 7.30 a.m.-6.30 p.m. Sat.: 7.30 a.m.-1 p.m. Part: 3-6 hour sessions, 2-5 times per week	PG-K2	Full: $650 pm Part: $224-$560 pm	**1:6 to 8**	✔	✔	✔	✔		✔	
29	Pat's SchoolHouse	Full: 7.30 a.m.-6.30 p.m. Sat.: 7.30 a.m.-1.30 p.m. Half: 7.30 a.m.-12.30 p.m. or 1 p.m. to 6.30 p.m.	2 yrs.-K2	Full: $1270 pm Half: $670 pm Registration: $150	**1:6 to 7**	✔	✔	✔	✔		✔	
30	Cambridge Child Devt.	Mon.-Fri. Full: 7.30 a.m.-6.30 p.m. Half: 7.30 a.m.-1 p.m. or 1 p.m.-6.30 p.m.	PG-K2	Full: $730-$780 pm Half: $555-$580 pm	**Average 1:10**	✔	✔	✔	✔		✔	✔

PG: Play group   **N:** Nursery   **K1:** Kindergarten 1   **K2:** Kindergarten 2   **P1:** Primary 1
pa: per annum   **p6m:** per six months   **p20s:** per 20 sessions   **pm:** per month   **pd:** per day

Field Trips	Free Play	Tests	Other Activities	Notes	Food & Drink	Transport	Garden/Outdoor Play Area	Gym Equip	Library	Other Facilities
	✔		Montessori curriculum	Afternoon enrichment classes (phonics and maths)	✔	✔			✔	
✔	✔		Gymnastics		✔		✔	✔		
✔	✔		Science		✔	✔	✔	✔	✔	
✔	✔		Science		✔	✔	✔	✔	✔	
✔	✔			In association with Bethlehem Educare Centre. British teachers.	✔	✔	✔	✔	✔	
✔	✔		Cooking, science, P.E., drama (E & M)		✔	✔	✔	✔	✔	
	✔		Drama (E or M), Science		✔	✔	✔	✔	✔	

Sector Code	Organisation Name	Hours of Operation	Age	Cost	Ratio	Art & Craft	Music & Movement	English	Mandarin	Other Language	Maths	Computer Class
30	The Children's Learning Centre	Mon.-Sat. Full: 7.30 a.m.-6.30 p.m. Sat. 7.30 a.m.-1.30 p.m.	PG-K2	Full: $610 pm	**PG-2½ yrs. 1:6 2½ to K2 1:10**	✔	✔	✔	✔	Mly	✔	✔
30	Pat's SchoolHouse	Full: 7.30 a.m.-6.30 p.m. Sat.: 7.30 a.m.-1.30 p.m. Half: 7.30 a.m.-12.30 p.m. or 1 p.m. to 6.30 p.m.	2 yrs.-K2	Full: $1270 pm Half: $670 pm Registration: $150	**1:6 to 7**	✔	✔	✔	✔		✔	
30	Thomson Rd. Baptist Kindergarten	Mon.-Fri. Part: 8 a.m.-11 a.m. or 11 a.m.-2 p.m.	3 yrs.-K2	**Part: $300 pt**	N 1:10 K1 1:20 K2 1:15-16	✔	✔	✔	✔		✔	✔
32	Adventist Child Devt. Centre	Mon.-Fri. Full: 7 a.m.-7 p.m. Sat.: 7 a.m.-2 p.m.	PG-K2	**Full: $400 pm Half: $245 pm**	MCD	✔	✔	✔	✔		✔	✔
32	Care Corner Child Devt.	Mon.-Fri. Full: 7 a.m.-7 p.m.	2½ yrs.-K2	**Full: $360-$380 pm**	MCD	✔	✔	✔	✔		✔	✔
33	Joytech Child Devt. Centre	Mon.-Sat. Full: 7.30 a.m.-6.30 p.m. Sat.: 7.30 a.m.-1.30 p.m.	PG-P1	Full: $430-$480 pm BASC:$250 pm	MCD	✔	✔	✔	✔	Mly		✔
33	Tai Pei Child Care	Mon.-Fri. Full: 7.30 a.m.-6.30 p.m.	N-K2	**Full: $400 pm**	N 1:8 K1&2 1:15	✔	✔	✔	✔		✔	✔
34	Allcare Child Devt. Centre	Mon.-Sat. Full: 7.30 a.m.-6.30 p.m. Sat.: 7.30 a.m.-2 p.m.	PG-K2	Full: $550 pm BASC: $260 pm	MCD	✔	✔	✔	✔		✔	

PG: Play group   **N:** Nursery   **K1:** Kindergarten 1   **K2:** Kindergarten 2   **P1:** Primary 1
pa: per annum   **p6m:** per six months   **p20s:** per 20 sessions   **pm:** per month   **pd:** per day

Field Trips	Free Play	Tests	Other Activities	Notes	Food & Drink	Transport	Garden/Outdoor Play Area	Gym Equip	Library	Other Facilities
✔	✔		Drama (E or M)	Discount for IR staff	✔		✔	✔	✔	
✔	✔		Cooking, Science, P.E., Drama (E & M)		✔	✔	✔	✔	✔	
✔	✔		Computer classes: $120 +		✔	✔	✔		✔	
✔	✔		Drama (E), Health, Moral stories, Optional reading programme	Provides BASC	✔		✔	✔	✔	Computers
✔	✔		Drama (E): $20 pm		✔				✔	Use of public playground
✔	✔				✔		✔		✔	
✔	✔	✔	Science, Cooking, Moral Education	Vegetarian food	✔	✔			✔	Computers (5) for use of K1&2 children
✔	✔		Computer class planned		✔	✔	✔	✔	✔	

ps: per session   **p8s:** per eight sessions   **pt:** per term (10 weeks unless otherwise indicated)
BASC: before- and after-school care   **A:** Arabic   **H:** Hindi   **J:** Japanese   **Mly:** Malay   **T:** Tamil

Sector Code	Organisation Name	Hours of Operation	Age	Cost	Ratio	Art & Craft	Music & Movement	English	Mandarin	Other Language	Maths	Computer Class
35	Strawberry's Child Devt. Centre	Mon.-Sat. Full: 7.30 a.m.-6.30 p.m. Sat.: 7.30 a.m.-1.30 p.m. Half: 7.30 a.m.-1.30 p.m. or 12 noon-6.30 p.m.	PG-K2	Full: $461 pm Half: $261 or $311	**Average 1:8**	✔	✔	✔	✔		✔	✔
37	MacPherson Moral Child Care	Mon.-Sat. Full: 7 a.m.-6.30 p.m. Sat.: 7 a.m.-2 p.m.	2 yrs.-K2	**Full: $385 pm**	1:8, 1:12, 1:15	✔	✔	✔	✔		✔	✔
41	1-2-3 Kids Childcare & Devt.	Full: 7.30 a.m.-6.30 p.m. Sat.: 7.30 a.m.-2 p.m. Half: 7.30 a.m.-1 p.m. or 1 p.m.-6.30 p.m. Sat.: 7.30 a.m.-1 p.m.	PG-K2	Full: $800 pm Half: $500 pm BASC: $300 pm	**PG-N 1:4 to 8** K1-P1 1:12	✔	✔	✔	✔		✔	✔
41	Kinderjoy Educare	Mon.-Sat. Full: 7 a.m.-7 p.m. Sat. 7 a.m.-2 p.m.	2 yrs.-K2	Full: $450 pm	1:12, 1:15	✔	✔	✔	✔		✔	
41	Kinderland Child Care	Mon.-Sat. Full: 7.30 a.m.-6.30 p.m. Sat.: 7.30 a.m.-2 p.m.	PG-K2	Full: $700 pm BASC: $320 pm	MCD	✔	✔	✔	✔		✔	✔
41	KinderWorld EduCare (Kembangan)	Mon.-Sat. Full: 7.30 a.m.-6.30 p.m. Sat.: 7.30 a.m.-2 p.m. Half: 7.30 a.m.-2 p.m. or 2 p.m.-6.30 p.m.	PG-K2	Full: $580-$680 pm BASC: $370 pm	MCD	✔	✔	✔	✔		✔	✔
42	Little Fairyland Child Care & Devt.	Mon.-Sat. Full: 7.30 a.m.-6.45 p.m. Sat.: 7.30 a.m.-1.30 p.m.	PG-P1	Full: $510-$535 pm BASC: $260 pm	N 1:10 to 12 K1 1:15 **K2 1:10**	✔	✔	✔	✔		✔	

PG: Play group **N:** Nursery **K1:** Kindergarten 1 **K2:** Kindergarten 2 **P1:** Primary 1
pa: per annum **p6m:** per six months **p20s:** per 20 sessions **pm:** per month **pd:** per day

Field Trips	Free Play	Tests	Other Activities	Notes	Food & Drink	Transport	Garden/Outdoor Play Area	Gym Equip	Library	Other Facilities
✔			Swimming, Computer classes: $50 pm		✔		✔	✔		
✔	✔	✔	Computer classes: $120 +		✔		✔		✔	
✔	✔		Montessori, Swimming, Cooking, Science, Drama (E & M), Computer aided learning	Offers BASC	✔	✔	✔	✔	✔	
✔			Drama (E) for extra charge		✔	✔			✔	Near public playground
✔	✔		Abacus, Exercise Program, Children's Music Course Drama (E): $60 pm		✔	✔	✔	✔	✔	
✔	✔		Cooking, Science	75% English, 25% Mandarin	✔	✔	✔		✔	
✔	✔		Drama (E)		✔		✔	✔	✔	

Sector Code	Organisation Name	Hours of Operation	Age	Cost	Ratio	Art & Craft	Music & Movement	English	Mandarin	Other Language	Maths	Computer Class
42	St Hilda's Kindergarten	Mon.-Fri. Part: 8.30 a.m.-11.30 a.m. or 12 noon-3 p.m.	3 yrs.-K2	**Part: $240-$255 pt**	N 1:15 K1 1:20 K2 1:25	✔	✔	✔	✔		✔	✔
43	Etonhouse Pre-School (Newton)	Mon.-Fri. Full: 7.30 a.m.-6.30 p.m. Half-day morning and afternoon sessions also available.	2 yrs.-K2	Full: $1300 pm Half: (a.m.) $750 pm (p.m.) $650 pm	**2 yrs.-N 1:6** **N 1:10** K1 1:12 K2 1:15	✔	✔	✔	✔	J	✔	
43	Playhouse Child Devt.	Mon.-Sat. Full: 7.30 a.m.-6.30 p.m. Sat. 7.30 a.m.-1.30 p.m. Half: 7.30 a.m.-1 p.m.	PG-K2	Full: $495-$550 pm Half: $380-$480 pm BASC: $380-$550 pm	PG-3 yrs. **1:5** **N 1:8** **K1 1:10** **K2 1:12**	✔	✔	✔	✔		✔	✔
43	Wonder Kids Child Care & Devt.	Full: 7 a.m.-7 p.m. Sat.: 7 a.m.-1.30 p.m. Half: 7 a.m.-1 p.m. or 1 p.m.-7 p.m.	PG-K2	Full: $410 pm Half: $310 pm BASC: $310 pm Registration: $50	PG-3 yrs. 1:8 N 1:15 K1&2 1:20	✔	✔	✔	✔	Mly A	✔	✔
44	Mandarin Gardens Kindergarten	Mon.-Fri. Half: 8.30 a.m.-3 p.m.	N-K2	Half: $405-$435 pt	1:15 to 25	✔	✔	✔	✔		✔	✔
44	Montessori Creative World (East)	Mon.-Sat., 9 a.m.-5 p.m. Part: 1-2 hr. sessions, 3-5 times per wk.	2 yrs.-K2	Part: $360-$550 pm	**1:6**	✔	✔	✔	✔		✔	
44	Tung Ling Kindergarten	Mon.-Fri. Part: 8.30 a.m.-11.30 a.m. or 11.30 a.m.-2.30 p.m.	N-K2	**Part: $270 pt** Registration: $30	Average 1:13	✔	✔	✔	✔		✔	✔

PG: Play group   **N:** Nursery   **K1:** Kindergarten 1   **K2:** Kindergarten 2   **P1:** Primary 1
pa: per annum   **p6m:** per six months   **p20s:** per 20 sessions   **pm:** per month   **pd:** per day

Field Trips	Free Play	Tests	Other Activities	Notes	Food & Drink	Transport	Garden/Outdoor Play Area	Gym Equip	Library	Other Facilities
✔	✔		Activity stations: Cooking, P.E., educational videos Computer classes: $100 + (K1 & 2 only)		✔	✔	✔	✔	✔	
✔	✔		Holiday activities		✔	✔	✔	✔	✔	4 acre site
✔	✔		Montessori, Drama (E), Letterland phonics, Swimming, Chinese calligraphy		✔		✔			
✔	✔		Science, Cooking, Drama (E): $45 pm		✔		✔	✔	✔	
✔	✔		Holiday programmes		✔	✔	✔			
✔	✔		Montessori curriculum, holiday programmes			✔	✔		✔	
✔	✔				✔	✔	✔		✔	

Sector Code	Organisation Name	Hours of Operation	Age	Cost	Ratio	Art & Craft	Music & Movement	English	Mandarin	Other Language	Maths	Computer Class
45	Abel Child Devt. & Learning	Mon.-Sat. Full: 7.30 a.m.-6.30 p.m. Sat.: 7.30 a.m.-1.30 p.m. Half: 7.30 a.m.-1 p.m.	PG-K2	Full: $530 pm Half: $385 pm Registration: $50	MCD	✔	✔	✔	✔		✔	✔
45	Bethesda (Katong) Kindergarten	Mon.-Fri. **Part: 8.15 a.m.-11.15 a.m. or 11.30 a.m.-2.30 p.m.**	N-K2	**Part: $120 pm**	**N: 1:10** K1 1:12 K2 1:13	✔	✔	✔	✔		✔	✔
45	Pitter Patter Child Care & Devt.	Mon.-Sat. Full: 7.30 a.m.-6.30 p.m. Sat.: 7.30 a.m.-2 p.m.	PG-K2	Full: $530-$570 pm	**2-3 yrs. 1:8** N 1:15 K1&2 1:25	✔	✔	✔	✔		✔	✔
46	Good Shepherd Childcare	Mon.-Sat. Full: 7.30 a.m.-6.30 p.m. Sat.: 7.30 a.m.-1.30 p.m.	2 yrs.-K2	**Full: $375 pm**	MCD	✔	✔	✔	✔		✔	✔
46	Honeykids Child Care & Devt.	Mon.-Sat. Full: 7 a.m.-7 p.m. Sat.: 7 a.m.-1.30 p.m. Half day care also available	PG-K2	Full: $495-$525 pm BASC: $200-$225 pm	MCD	✔	✔	✔	✔		✔	✔
46	Little Genius Childcare & Devt.	Mon.-Sat. Full: 7 a.m.-6.30 p.m. Sat.: 7 a.m.-1.30 p.m. Mon.-Fri. Half: 7 a.m.-1 p.m.	PG-K2	**Full: $405 pm Half: $270-$290 pm** BASC: $240 pm	MCD	✔	✔	✔	✔		✔	✔
46	Mothergoose Child Devt.	Mon.-Sat. Full: 7.30 a.m.-6.30 p.m. Sat.: 7.30 a.m.-1.30 p.m.	PG-K2	Full: $530-$570 pm	MCD	✔	✔	✔	✔		✔	✔

PG: Play group   **N:** Nursery   **K1:** Kindergarten 1   **K2:** Kindergarten 2   **P1:** Primary 1
pa: per annum   **p6m:** per six months   **p20s:** per 20 sessions   **pm:** per month   **pd:** per day

Field Trips	Free Play	Tests	Other Activities	Notes	Food & Drink	Transport	Garden/Outdoor Play Area	Gym Equip	Library	Other Facilities
✔	✔				✔	✔	✔		✔	
✔	✔				✔	✔	✔	✔		
✔	✔		Montessori activities, phonics		✔	✔	✔	✔	✔	
✔	✔		Drama (E): $22 pm		✔		✔	✔	✔	
✔			Drama (E)		✔	✔	✔	✔		
✔	✔	✔			✔				✔	Near public playground
✔	✔		Drama (E or M)		✔	✔	✔	✔		

ps: per session   p8s: per eight sessions   pt: per term (10 weeks unless otherwise indicated)
BASC: before- and after-school care   A: Arabic   H: Hindi   J: Japanese   Mly: Malay   T: Tamil

Sector Code	Organisation Name	Hours of Operation	Age	Cost	Ratio	Art & Craft	Music & Movement	English	Mandarin	Other language	Maths	Computer Class
46	Sasco Child Care	Mon.-Sat. Full: 7.30 a.m.-6.30 p.m. Sat.: 7.30 a.m.-2 p.m.	2 yrs.-K2	**Full: $385 pm**	MCD	✔	✔	✔	✔		✔	
47	Eastmen Child Care & Devt.	Mon.-Sat. Full: 7 a.m.-6.30 p.m. Sat.: 7 a.m.-1.30 p.m. Half: 7 a.m.-12.30 or 1 p.m.-6.30 p.m.	PG-K2 BASC: 7-12 yrs.	Full: $610 pm Half: $350 pm BASC: $300 pm Emergency care: $30 pd	MCD	✔	✔	✔	✔		✔	✔
47	Taman Bacaan Child Care & Devt.	Mon.-Sat. Full: 7 a.m.-7 p.m. Sat.: 7 a.m.-2 p.m.	N-K2	**Full: $330 pm** BASC: $150 pm ($230 during school holidays)	N 1:15 K1&2: 1:20	✔	✔	✔		Mly	✔	
47	Young Talents Child Care & Devt.	Mon.-Sat. Full: 7 a.m.-7 p.m. Sat.: 7 a.m.-2 p.m. Half: 7 a.m.-12.30 p.m. or 12.30 p.m.-7 p.m.	PG-P1	**Full: $390-$420 pm Half: $260-$280 pm** BASC: $225 pm	MCD	✔	✔	✔	✔		✔	
50	KinderWorld EduCare (Toh Crescent)	Mon.-Sat. Full: 7.30 a.m.-6.30 p.m. Sat.: 7.30 a.m.-2 p.m. Half: 7.30 a.m.-2 p.m. or 2 p.m.-6.30 p.m.	PG-K2	Full: $550 pm Half: $350 or $450 pm BASC $370 pm"	MCD	✔	✔	✔	✔		✔	✔
51	Jude Child Care & Child Devt.	Mon.-Sat. Full: 7 a.m.-7 p.m. Sat.: 7 a.m.-2 p.m.	PG-K2	**Full: $380-$420 pm** BASC: $180 pm	MCD	✔	✔	✔	✔	Mly A	✔	✔

PG: Play group   **N:** Nursery   **K1:** Kindergarten 1   **K2:** Kindergarten 2   **P1:** Primary 1
pa: per annum   **p6m:** per six months   **p20s:** per 20 sessions   **pm:** per month   **pd:** per day

Field Trips	Free Play	Tests	Other Activities	Notes	Food & Drink	Transport	Garden/Outdoor Play Area	Gym Equip	Library	Other Facilities
✔	✔		Drama (E): $30 pm		✔		✔		✔	
✔	✔	✔	Abacus class (K2), Computer sided learning, Gym workshop		✔		✔	✔	✔	
✔	✔	✔			✔			✔	✔	
✔	✔	✔	Drama (M), Drama (E): $30 pm		✔	✔			✔	
✔	✔		Cooking, Science	75% English, 25% Mandarin	✔	✔	✔		✔	
✔		✔		Malay upon request	✔	✔	✔	✔	✔	

Sector Code	Organisation Name	Hours of Operation	Age	Cost	Ratio	Art & Craft	Music & Movement	English	Mandarin	Other Language	Maths	Computer Class
52	Taman Bacan Sang Nila Utama Child Care	Mon.-Sat. Full: 7 a.m.-7 p.m. Sat.: 7 a.m.-2 p.m.	N-K2	**Full: $330 pm**	N 1:12 K1&2 1:20	✔	✔	✔		Mly	✔	
53	Junior Playworld Child Care & Devt.	Mon.-Sat. Full: 7.30 a.m.-7 p.m. Sat.: 7.30 a.m.-2 p.m.	PG-K2	Full: $420 pm	**1:6** to 12	✔	✔	✔	✔		✔	✔
53	Pakson Childcare Centre	Mon.-Sat. Full: 7 a.m.-7 p.m. Sat.: 7 a.m.-2 p.m. Half day also available.	PG-K2	Full: $500 pm **Half: $250 pm**	MCD	✔	✔	✔	✔		✔	✔
53	Paya Lebar Methodist Church Covenant Kindergarten	Mon.-Fri. Part: 8 a.m.-11 a.m. or 11.15 a.m.-2.15 p.m.	N-K2	**Part: $315 pt**	N 1:20 K1 & 2 1:25	✔	✔	✔	✔		✔	✔
53	Rhymesland Educare	Mon.-Sat. Full: 7 a.m.-7 p.m. Sat.: 7 a.m.-2 p.m.	PG-K2	**Full: $390-$420 pm**	MCD	✔	✔	✔	✔		✔	
53	T P B C Kindergarten	Mon.-Fri. Part: 8.15 a.m.-11.15 a.m. or 11.30 a.m.-2.30 p.m.	N-K2	**Part: $110 pm**	1:13	✔	✔	✔	✔		✔	✔
54	Pat's SchoolHouse	Full: 7.30 a.m.-6.30 p.m. Sat.: 7.30 a.m.-1.30 p.m. Half: 7.30 a.m.-12.30 p.m.or 1 p.m. to 6.30 p.m.	2 yrs.-K2	Full: $1270 pm Half: $670 pm Registration: $150	**1:6 to 7**	✔	✔	✔	✔		✔	

PG: Play group   **N:** Nursery   **K1:** Kindergarten 1   **K2:** Kindergarten 2   **P1:** Primary 1
pa: per annum   **p6m:** per six months   **p20s:** per 20 sessions   **pm:** per month   **pd:** per day

Field Trips	Free Play	Tests	Other Activities	Notes	Food & Drink	Transport	Garden/Outdoor Play Area	Gym Equip	Library	Other Facilities
✔	✔		Regular assessments		✔		✔		✔	
✔	✔		Drama (E): $30 pm		✔	✔	✔	✔	✔	
✔	✔		Computer class for K1+		✔		✔	✔		
✔	✔		Computer classes: $120 pm		✔	✔	✔	✔	✔	Mini road safety park
✔	✔	✔			✔		✔		✔	
✔	✔	✔	Science, Computer classes: $80 p8s		✔	✔	✔	✔	✔	
✔	✔		Cooking, Science, P.E., Drama (E & M)		✔	✔	✔	✔	✔	

ps: per session   **p8s:** per eight sessions   **pt:** per term (10 weeks unless otherwise indicated)
BASC: before- and after-school care   **A:** Arabic   **H:** Hindi   **J:** Japanese   **Mly:** Malay   **T:** Tamil

Sector Code	Organisation Name	Hours of Operation	Age	Cost	Ratio	Art & Craft	Music & Movement	English	Mandarin	Other Language	Maths	Computer Class
55	Chen Su Lan Methodist Children's Home	Mon.-Fri. Full: 7 a.m.-7 p.m. Sat. 7 a.m.-2p.m. Half day also available.	N-K2	**Full: $400 pm** **Half: $250 pm** BASC: $200 pm	1:15	✔	✔	✔	✔		✔	
55	Creative Child Devt.	Mon.-Sat. Full: 7 a.m.-6.30 p.m. Sat.: 7 a.m.-2 p.m. Half: 7 a.m.-1 p.m. or 1 p.m.-6.30 p.m.	PG-K2	Full: $520 pm Half: $380 pm BASC (P1-P6): $380 pm	PG-N 1:8 K1&2 1:15	✔	✔	✔	✔		✔	✔
55	Joewe Playhouse & Child Devt.	Mon.-Sat. Full: 7 a.m.-7 p.m. Sat. 7 a.m.-2 p.m.	PG-K2	**Full: $390-$420 pm**	MCD	✔	✔	✔	✔		✔	✔
55	Wesley Child Development	Mon.-Fri. Full: 7 a.m.-6.30 p.m. Sat. 7 a.m.-2 p.m.	2 yrs.-K2	**Full: $400 pm**	**1:5 to 10**	✔	✔	✔	✔		✔	✔
55	Zion Kindergarten	Mon.-Fri. Part: 8.30 a.m.-11.30 a.m. or 11.45 a.m.-2.45 p.m.	3 yrs.-K2	**Part: $240 pt** Registration: $30	2:25-30	✔	✔	✔	✔		✔	✔
56	Intellect Child Care & Devt.	Mon.-Sat. Full: 7 a.m.-7 p.m. Sat.: 7 a.m.-2 p.m. Half day also available.	2 yrs.-K2	**Full: $390-$420 pm** **Half: $250-$275 pm**	1:15	✔	✔	✔	✔		✔	
56	KinderWorld EduCare (Techpoint)	Mon.-Sat. Full: 7.30 a.m.-6.30 p.m. Sat.: 7.30 a.m.-2 p.m.	PG-K2	Full: $580-$680 pm BASC: $300-$350 pm	MCD	✔	✔	✔	✔		✔	✔

PG: Play group   **N:** Nursery   **K1:** Kindergarten 1   **K2:** Kindergarten 2   **P1:** Primary 1
pa: per annum   **p6m:** per six months   **p20s:** per 20 sessions   **pm:** per month   **pd:** per day

Field Trips	Free Play	Tests	Other Activities	Notes	Food & Drink	Transport	Garden/Outdoor Play Area	Gym Equip	Library	Other Facilities
✔	✔				✔		✔	✔	✔	Music room
✔	✔				✔		✔	✔	✔	
✔	✔	✔			✔		✔	✔	✔	
✔	✔	✔	Science and nature study, Cooking		✔		✔		✔	
✔	✔		Holiday programmes, Sunday school, Saturday activities		✔	✔	✔	✔	✔	
✔	✔		Drama (E)		✔		✔			
✔	✔		Cooking, Science	75% English, 25% Mandarin	✔		✔		✔	

Sector Code	Organisation Name	Hours of Operation	Age	Cost	Ratio	Art & Craft	Music & Movement	English	Mandarin	Other Language	Maths	Computer Class
56	Praises Child Devt. Centre	Mon.-Sat. Full: 7 a.m.-7 p.m. Sat.: 7 a.m.-2 p.m.	2 yrs.-K2	**Full: $375-$395 pm**	1:15	✔	✔	✔	✔			
57	KinderWorld EduCare (Macritchie)	Mon.-Sat. Full: 7.30 a.m.-6.30 p.m. Sat.: 7.30 a.m.-2 p.m. Half: 7.30 a.m.-2 p.m. or 2 p.m.-6.30 p.m.	PG-K2	Full: $530 pm Half: $330 or $430 pm BASC: $350 pm	MCD	✔	✔	✔	✔		✔	✔
57	Teeny Tiny Child Care & Devt.	Mon.-Sat. Full: 7 a.m.-6.30 p.m. Sat.: 7 a.m.-2 p.m.	PG-K2	**Full: $400 pm**	MCD	✔	✔	✔	✔		✔	✔
58	Joyce Goh's Playgroup	Mon.-Fri. Half: 8 a.m. to 1 p.m. or 8.15 a.m.-11.30 a.m.	2 yrs.-K2	Contact preschool for details.	1:6-12	✔	✔	✔	✔			
61	Jurong Calvary Kindergarten	Mon.-Fri. 8.15 a.m.-2.30 p.m. Part: 3 hrs., morning or afternoon	3½ yrs.-K2	**Full: $390-$420**	Average 2:28 (1:14)	✔	✔	✔	✔		✔	✔
65	LV-U Child Care & Devt. Centre	Mon.-Sat. Full: 7 a.m.-7 p.m. Sat.: 7 a.m.-1.30 p.m.	PG-K2	**Full: $390-$410 pm**	MCD	✔	✔	✔	✔		✔	✔
65	Smartie Child Care Centre	Mon.-Sat. Full: 7 a.m.-7 p.m. Sat.: 7 a.m.-2 p.m.	PG-K2	**Full: $380 pm**	PG-2½ yrs. MCD N-K2 1:15	✔	✔	✔	✔		✔	✔

PG: Play group **N:** Nursery **K1:** Kindergarten 1 **K2:** Kindergarten 2 **P1:** Primary 1
pa: per annum **p6m:** per six months **p20s:** per 20 sessions **pm:** per month **pd:** per day

Field Trips	Free Play	Tests	Other Activities	Notes	Food & Drink	Transport	Garden/Outdoor Play Area	Gym Equip	Library	Other Facilities
✔	✔		Drama (E): $5 registration and $30 pm		✔				✔	Public playground
✔	✔		Cooking, Science	75% English, 25% Mandarin	✔	✔	✔		✔	
✔	✔		Computer classes: $40 pm		✔		✔		✔	
	✔					✔	✔			
✔	✔		Reading programme, Holiday camps		✔	✔	✔	✔	✔	
✔	✔		Computer classes for K1&2		✔		✔	✔	✔	
✔			Optional computer classes: $40 pm		✔		✔	✔	✔	

Sector Code	Organisation Name	Hours of Operation	Age	Cost	Ratio	Art & Craft	Music & Movement	English	Mandarin	Other Language	Maths	Computer Class
65	Sonshine Child Care Centre	Mon.-Sat. Full: 7 a.m.-7 p.m. Sat. 7 a.m.-1.30 p.m. Half day also available.	2 yrs.-K2 BASC: 7-12 yrs.	**Full: $390 pm** **Half: $265 pm** BASC: $200 pm	**PG 1:6** **N 1:10** K1 1:22 K2 1:18	✔	✔	✔	✔		✔	✔
65	St. Clare Kindergarten	Mon.-Fri. Part: 8.20 a.m.-11.20 a.m. or 11.20 a.m.-2.20 p.m.	3 yrs.-K2	**Part: $300 pt**	N 1:12 K1&2 1:14	✔	✔	✔	✔		✔	✔
67	Jan & Elly - The Learning Place	Mon.-Fri. Part: 12 noon-2.45 p.m. or 3 p.m.-5.45 p.m.	2-7 yrs.	Part: $260-$290 pm Registration: $25	1:5 to 10	✔	✔	✔	✔		✔	
67	Kids Haven Child Care & Devt. Centre	Mon.-Sat. Full: 7 a.m.-7 p.m. Sat. 7 a.m.-2 p.m. Half: 7 a.m.-2 p.m. or 2 p.m.-7 p.m.	PG-K2	**Full: $390-$420 pm** **Half: $260-$280 pm** Registration: $50 Uniform: $20	MCD	✔	✔	✔	✔		✔	✔
68	Gloryland Child Devt.	Mon.-Sat. Full: 7 a.m.-6.30 p.m. Sat.: 7 a.m.-1.30 p.m.	PG-K2	Full: $550 pm	MCD	✔	✔	✔	✔		✔	✔
68	Ichiban Montessori Child Care Centre	Full: 7.30 a.m.-6.30 p.m. Sat.: 7.30 a.m.-2 p.m. Half: 7.30 a.m.-1 p.m. or 1 p.m.-6 p.m. Sat.: 7.30 a.m.-2 p.m.	PG-K2	Full: $630 pm Half: $450 pm	1:8	✔	✔	✔	✔		✔	✔

PG: Play group   **N:** Nursery   **K1:** Kindergarten 1   **K2:** Kindergarten 2   **P1:** Primary 1
pa: per annum   **p6m:** per six months   **p20s:** per 20 sessions   **pm:** per month   **pd:** per day

Field Trips	Free Play	Tests	Other Activities	Notes	Food & Drink	Transport	Garden/Outdoor Play Area	Gym Equip	Library	Other Facilities
✔	✔		Science, Moral Studies. Computer classes: $30 pm	Recently renovated and extended	✔		✔	✔		
✔	✔		P.E., Computer classes: $90 pt		✔	✔	✔	✔		
✔			Science, Language arts, School holiday workshops			✔		✔		
✔	✔		Science		✔		✔		✔	
✔	✔	✔	Reading and phonics programmes		✔	✔	✔	✔	✔	Maths, science corners, water and sand play areas
✔	✔	✔	Montessori curriculum		✔		✔		✔	

Sector Code	Organisation Name	Hours of Operation	Age	Cost	Ratio	Art & Craft	Music & Movement	English	Mandarin	Other Language	Maths	Computer Class
73	New Life Kindergarten	Mon.-Fri. Part: 8.30 a.m.-11.30 a.m. or 11.45 a.m.-2.45 p.m.	N-K2	**Part: $330 pt**	Average 1:15	✔	✔	✔	✔	T	✔	✔
75	Greentree Montessori Kindergarten	Mon.-Fri. Part: 8 a.m.-11 a.m. and 11 a.m.-2 p.m.	N-K2	Part: $300 pm	**1:10**	✔	✔	✔	✔		✔	✔
75	His Little Kingdom Child Care & Devt. Centre	Mon.-Sat. Full: 7 a.m.-6.30 p.m. Sat.: 7 a.m.-1.30 p.m.	PG-K2	Full: $460 pm	**Average 1:8**	✔	✔	✔	✔		✔	✔
76	Alyson & Goofy Child Care	Mon.-Sat. Full: 7 a.m.-7 p.m. Sat.: 7 a.m.-3 p.m.	PG-K2	Full: $415-$445 pm	MCD	✔	✔	✔	✔		✔	✔
76	Bethlehem Educare Centre	Mon.-Sat. Full: 7 a.m.-7 p.m. Sat.: 7 a.m.-2 p.m.	PG-K2	**Full: $355 pm** BASC: $250 pm	**Average 1:6-8**	✔	✔	✔	✔		✔	
76	Everjoy Child Care	Mon.-Sat. Full: 7.30 a.m.-6.30 p.m. Sat.: 7.30 a.m.-2 p.m.	2 yrs.-K2	**Full: $400 pm**	MCD	✔	✔	✔	✔		✔	
76	KinderWorld EduCare (Yishun)	Full: 7.30 a.m.-6.30 p.m. Sat.: 7.30 a.m.-2 p.m. Half: 7.30 a.m.-2 p.m. or 2 p.m.-6.30 p.m. Sat.: 7.30 a.m.-2 p.m.	PG-K2	Full: $680 pm Half: $480 or $580 pm BASC: $300-$350 pm	MCD	✔	✔	✔	✔		✔	✔

PG: Play group **N:** Nursery **K1:** Kindergarten 1 **K2:** Kindergarten 2 **P1:** Primary 1
pa: per annum **p6m:** per six months **p20s:** per 20 sessions **pm:** per month **pd:** per day

Field Tripst	Free Play	Tests	Other Activities	Notes	Food & Drink	Transport	Garden/Outdoor Play Area	Gym Equip	Library	Other Facilities
✔	✔		Computer class: $120 pt + book		✔	✔	✔			
✔	✔		Montessori curriculum		✔	✔	✔	✔	✔	
✔	✔		Computer class for N-K2		✔	✔	✔	✔	✔	
✔	✔	✔	Computer classes for N2-K2: $40 pm		✔		✔	✔		
✔	✔				✔					Use of public playground
✔	✔				✔	✔	✔	✔		
✔	✔		Cooking, Science	75% English, 25% Mandarin	✔	✔	✔	✔	✔	

Sector Code	Organisation Name	Hours of Operation	Age	Cost	Ratio	Art & Craft	Music & Movement	English	Mandarin	Other Language	Maths	Computer Class
76	Everjoy Child Care	Mon.-Sat. Full: 7.30 a.m.-6.30 p.m. Sat.: 7.30 a.m.-2 p.m.	2 yrs.-K2	**Full: $400 pm**	MCD	✔	✔	✔	✔		✔	
76	KinderWorld EduCare (Yishun)	Full: 7.30 a.m.-6.30 p.m. Sat.: 7.30 a.m.-2 p.m. Half: 7.30 a.m.-2 p.m. or 2 p.m.-6.30 p.m. Sat.: 7.30 a.m.-2 p.m.	PG-K2	Full: $680 pm Half: $480 or $580 pm BASC: $300-$350 pm	MCD	✔	✔	✔	✔		✔	✔
76	The Little Skool-House	Mon.-Sat. Full: 7.30 a.m.-7 p.m. Sat.: 7 a.m.-2 p.m. Part: 3 hrs. per day	PG-K2 Part: 2½-4 yrs.	Full: $680 pm Part: call preschool for details.	**PG 1:6** N 1:8-13 K1&2 1:18	✔	✔	✔	✔		✔	✔
80	Kiddy Junction Child Devt. & Learning	Full: 7.30 a.m.-6.30 p.m. Sat.: 7.30 a.m.-2 p.m. Half: 7.30 a.m.-1 p.m. or 1 p.m.-6.30 p.m.	PG-K2	Full: $950 pm Half: $600 pm	**PG to N 1:6** K1-K2 1:12	✔	✔	✔	✔		✔	✔
82	Bridges Montessori	Mon.-Fri. Part: 8.15 a.m.-11.15 a.m. or 11.15 a.m.-2.15 p.m.	2 yrs.-K2	Part: $900 pt	**1:8**	✔	✔	✔	✔		✔	
Call NTUC	NTUC Childcare Co-operative	Mon.-Sat. Full: 7 a.m.-7 p.m. Sat.: 7 a.m.-2 p.m.	PG-K2	**Full: $400** or $470 pm BASC: $220 pm Registration: $50 Deposit: $200	**PG 1:8 N 1:8** K1 1:15 K2 1:20	✔	✔	✔	✔		✔	✔
Call PCF	PCF Education Centres	Education Centres offer either 2-hour or 4-hour sessions.	K1-K2	**Part: from $30 or $80 pm**	Average 1:30	✔	✔	✔	✔	Mly T	✔	✔

212   **PG:** Play group   **N:** Nursery   **K1:** Kindergarten 1   **K2:** Kindergarten 2   **P1:** Primary 1
pa: per annum   **p6m:** per six months   **p20s:** per 20 sessions   **pm:** per month   **pd:** per day

Field Trips	Free Play	Tests	Other Activities	Notes	Food & Drink	Transport	Garden/Outdoor Play Area	Gym Equip	Library	Other Facilities
✔	✔				✔	✔	✔	✔		
✔	✔		Cooking, Science	75% English, 25% Mandarin	✔	✔	✔	✔	✔	
✔	✔		Swimming, Moral Education	Parenting seminars, monthly newsletter	✔	✔	✔	✔	✔	Swimming pool, indoor playground
✔	✔			Director runs parenting workshops.	✔	✔	✔	✔	✔	
✔	✔		Montessori curriculum			✔	✔	✔	✔	
✔	✔		Drama, Moral Education, Computer-Assisted Learning (most centres)	Newsletter, workshops, parent-teacher conferences	✔		✔	✔	✔	
✔	✔		Computer classes (some centres), trips out (most centres)	70% English, 30% Mandarin, some offer Malay or Tamil. 310 centres					✔	

MAP OF SINGAPORE
GUIDE TO SECTOR CODES

P. UBIN

SENTOSA

01 02 03 04 05 06 07 08 09 10 11 12 12 14 15 16 17 18 19 20 21 22 23 24 25 26 27 28 29 30 31 32 33 34 35 36 38 39 40 41 41 42 43 44 45 46 47 48 49 50 51 52 53 54 55 56 57 58 59 60 61 62 63 63 64 65 66 67 68 69 70 71 72 73 74 75 76 77 78 79 80 81

LIST OF ADDRESSES

5678
53B Robinson Road
3rd Floor
Singapore 068886
☎ 738 2668
Fax: 738 7896

1-2-3 Kids Childcare & Development
1 Jalan Yasin
Singapore 417958
☎ 745 1230
Fax: 745 1220

Abel Child Development & Learning
6 Jalan Ulu Siglap
Singapore 457127
☎ 446 0038

ACT 3 Drama Academy
126 Cairnhill Road
Singapore 229707
☎ 735 9986
Fax: 736 1196
E-mail: act3@pacific.net.sg

ACT 3 Drama Academy
10 Tampines Street 23
Tampines East Community Club, Level 3
Singapore 520000
☎ 788 2282
E-mail: act3@pacific.net.sg

ACT 3 Drama Academy
41 Sunset Way
Clementi Arcade #02-05
Singapore 597071
☎ 469 0608
E-mail: act3@pacific.net.sg

Adoptive Families of Singapore
☎ 462 1237

Adventist Child Development Centre
120 Balestier Road
Singapore 329680
☎ 299 6542
Fax: 299 4571

Alcoholics Anonymous
☎ 338 2791

Allcare Child Development Centre
22 Lichi Avenue
Singapore 348796
☎ 283 3830
Fax: 283 2292

Alyson & Goofy Child Care
Block 865 Yishun Street 81
#01-21
Singapore 760865
☎ 758 5493

American Association & American Women's
Association
21 Scotts Road
The American Club
Singapore 228219
☎ 733 6170
Fax: 733 6190

AMP Centre
25 Jalan Tembusu
Singapore 438234
☎ 346 0911
Fax: 346 0922

Anglo-Chinese School
60 Barker Road
Singapore 309919

Ang Mo Kio Community Library
4300 Ang Mo Kio Avenue 6
Singapore 569834
☎ 553 5503
Fax: 375 5128
Website: www.lib.gov.sg

Ang Mo Kio Swimming Complex
1771 Ang Mo Kio Avenue 1
Singapore 569978
☎ 456 6821

ANZA (Australian and New Zealand Asso-
ciation)
19 Tanglin Road
Tanglin Shopping Centre #06-27
Singapore 247909
☎ 733 1215
Fax: 735 9695
E-mail: anza@pacific.net.sg

Aprisin Singapore
257 Selegie Road
Selegie Complex #01-261
Singapore 188350
☎ 336 8311

Aquaducks
Block 10-B Braddell Hill
#09-07
Singapore 579721
☎ 356 8715
Fax: 356 8716

Archery Club of Singapore
5 Binchang Walk
Singapore 579857
☎ 258 1140

Asian Civilisations Museum
39 Armenian Street
Singapore 179941
☎ 332 3015
Fax: 883 0732
E-mail: juniper_chua@nhb.gov.sg
Website: www.museum.org.sg/nhb

Asian Women's Welfare Association
(AWWA) Special School
9 Norris Road
Singapore 208252
☎ 291 9706
Fax: 392 5271
E-mail: awwass@singnet.com.sg

Asian Women's Welfare Association
(AWWA) TEACH ME Services
Block 619, #01-1073
Ang Mo Kio Avenue 4
Singapore 560619
☎ 454 8919
Fax: 454 9346
E-mail: nc0075d@cyberway.com.sg

ATT Language Centre
19 Tanglin Road
Tanglin Shopping Centre #08-01
Singapore 247909
☎ 235 5222
Fax: 738 1257

List of Addresses

Australian International School
201 Ulu Pandan Road
Singapore 596468
☎ 462 7611
Fax: 463 9555
E-mail: aisenrol@mbox4.singnet.com.sg
Website: www.ais.com.sg

AWARE
Block 5 Dover Crescent
#01-22
Singapore 130005
☎ 779 7137
Fax: 777 0318
E-mail: aware@pacific.net.sg
Website: www.aware.org.sg

Balloon Baron Specialities
☎ 785 4929

Bedok Community Library
21 Bedok North Street 1
Singapore 469659
☎ 244 4901
Fax: 244 4917
Website: www.lib.gov.sg

Bedok Sports Hall
3 Bedok North Street 2
Singapore 469643
☎ 443 1787

Bedok Swimming Complex
901 New Upper Changi Road
Singapore 467335
☎ 443 5511

Bethesda (Katong) Kindergarten
2 La Salle Street
Singapore 456929
☎ 442 2622

Bethlehem Educare Centre
Block 311 Yishun Ring Road
#01-1286
Singapore 760311
☎ 257 3875

Bike Haus
553 Bukit Timah Road
Singapore 269693
☎ 468 3908

Bishan Swimming Complex
1 Bishan Street 14
Singapore 579778
☎ 353 6117

Bookaburra
583 Orchard Road
#02-05 Forum Galleria
Singapore 238884
☎ 235 9232
Fax: 286 1292
E-mail: bookaburra@pacific.net.sg
Website: www.bookaburra.com.sg

Boon Lay Swimming Complex
88 Boon Lay Place
Singapore 649883
☎ 261 0964

Bouncy Castles
253 Holland Road
Singapore 278602
☎ 469 6409/9511 2849 (pgr)

Breastfeeding Club
☎ 736 1636

Breastfeeding Mothers Support Group
96 Waterloo Street
Singapore 187967
☎ 339 3558 (hotline)
    337 0508 (registration)
E-mail: bmsg@iname.com
Website: www.members.tripod.com/~bmsg

Bridges Montessori Kindergarten
200 Punggol Seventeenth Avenue
Singapore 829646
☎ 384 0292
Fax: 384 0291

British Association & British Women's
Association
1 Selegie Road
#08-26 Paradiz Centre
Singapore 188306
☎ 339 8229
Fax: 339 1167

Brookvale Creche
111 Faber Drive
Singapore 129423
☎ 774 6784

Bukit Batok Community Library
1 Bukit Batok Central Link
#03-01 West Mall
Singapore 658713
☎ 794 6292
Fax: 794 6291
Website: www.lib.gov.sg

Bukit Batok Swimming Complex
2 Bukit Batok Street 22
Singapore 659581
☎ 561 0939

Bukit Merah Community Library
3779 Jalan Bukit Merah
Singapore 159462
☎ 375 5111
Fax: 375 5111
Website: www.lib.gov.sg

Bukit Merah Swimming Complex
3500A Bukit Merah Central
Singapore 159837
☎ 273 4549

Bukit Panjang Community Library
1 Jelebu Road
Bukit Panjang Plaza #04-16/17
Singapore 677743
☎ 767 1020
Fax: 767 1030
Website: www.lib.gov.sg

Bukit Timah Nature Reserve
177 Hindhede Drive
Singapore 589333
☎ 1800 468 5736
Fax: 462 0723
E-mail: Nparks_Mailbox@nparks.gov.sg
Website: www.nparks.gov.sg

Buona Vista Swimming Pool
76 Holland Drive
Singapore 278938
☎ 778 0244

Cambridge Child Development
1 Novena Terrace
Singapore 307903
☎ 355 0555

List of Addresses

Canadian International School
5 Toh Tuck Road
Singapore 596679
☎ 467 1732
Fax: 467 1729
E-mail: admissions@cis.edu.sg
Website: www.cis.edu.sg

Capers Restaurant
The Regent Hotel
1 Cuscaden Road
Singapore 249715
☎ 739 3019

Care Corner
112 Lavender Street
Chuan Building #04-01
Singapore 338728
☎ 296 1788
Fax: 291 1127

Care Corner Child Development
Block 14 St. George's Road
#01-70
Singapore 320014
☎ 298 2543

Cecilia Hon Ballet Theatre
9 Greenmead Avenue
Singapore 289402
☎ 466 4365

Central Community Library
91 Stamford Road
Singapore 178896
☎ 332 3645
Fax: 332 3642
Website: www.lib.gov.sg

Chatsworth International School
37 Emerald Hill Road
Singapore 229313
☎ 737 5955
Fax: 737 5655

Chen Su Lan Methodist Children's Home
202 Serangoon Garden Way
Singapore 556057
☎ 289 1070

Cheng San Community Library
90 Hougang Avenue 10
NTUC Hougang Mall #03-11
Singapore 538766
☎ 488 4100
Fax: 488 4109
Website: www.lib.gov.sg

Child Care Information
☎ 1800 258 5812

Childbirth Education and Parentcraft
19 Tanglin Road
#04-04 Tanglin Shopping Centre
Singapore 247909
☎ 736 1636
Fax: 736 3500
E-mail: anna@mail.childbirth-ed.com.sg
Website: www.childbirth-ed.com.sg

Children's Art Society
Block 87 Zion Road
#19-174
Singapore 160087
☎ 733 3414

Children's Cottage
2 Mt. Sinai Road
Singapore 276837
☎ 469 6681

Children's World
68 Race Course Road
Singapore 218571
☎ 294 6868
Fax: 294 4009

Chinese and Japanese Gardens
Yuan Ching Road
Jurong Park
Singapore 610108
☎ 264 3455
Fax: 265 8133

Choa Chu Kang Community Library
21 Choa Chu Kang Avenue 4
#03-01 Lot 1 Shoppers Mall
Singapore 689812
☎ 765 8616
Fax: 765 8617
Website: www.lib.gov.sg

C. K. Tang
320 Orchard Road
Singapore 238865
☎ 737 5500
Fax: 735 1130

Clementi Sports Hall
518 Clementi Avenue 3
Singapore 129907
☎ 776 2560

Clementi Swimming Complex
520 Clementi Avenue 3
Singapore 129908
☎ 779 0577
Website: www.ssc.gov.sg

Community Children's Library (Aljunied)
Block 125 Hougang Ave 1
#01-1470
Singapore 530125
☎ 280 3245
Fax: 230 1269
Website: www.lib.gov.sg

Community Children's Library (Ang Mo Kio)
Block 211 Ang Mo Kio Ave 3
#01-1446
Singapore 560211
☎ 452 7450
Fax: 452 7552
Website: www.lib.gov.sg

Community Children's Library (Bishan East)
Block 115 Bishan Street 12
#01-70
Singapore 570115
☎ 356 3937
Website: www.lib.gov.sg

Community Children's Library (Bishan-Toa Payoh North)
Block 238 Bishan Street 22
#01-232
Singapore 570238
☎ 553 1293
Fax: 553 1730
Website: www.lib.gov.sg

Community Children's Library (Braddell Heights)
Block 235 Serangoon Ave 3
#01-08
Singapore 550 235
☎ 284 2415
Fax: 284 2415
Website: www.lib.gov.sg

Community Children's Library (Bukit Batok)
Block 229 Bukit Batok East Avenue 3
#01-118
Singapore 650229
☎ 563 1303
Website: www.lib.gov.sg

Community Children's Library (Bukit Panjang)
Block 270 Bangkit Road
#01-22
Singapore 670270
☎ 764 4539
Website: www.lib.gov.sg

Community Children's Library (Bukit Timah)
Block 13 Toh Yi Drive
#01-07
Singapore 590013
☎ 467 3346
Fax: 466 0365
Website: www.lib.gov.sg

Community Children's Library (Changi Simei)
Blk 120 Simei Street 1
#01-476
Singapore 520120
☎ 426 9395
Fax: 426 9395
Website: www.lib.gov.sg

Community Children's Library (Changkat)
Blk 316 Tampines St 33
#01-186
Singapore 520316
☎ 2608180
Fax: 2607009
Website: www.lib.gov.sg

Community Children's Library (Clementi)
Block 322 Clementi Avenue 5
#01-235
Singapore 120322
☎ 776 1887
Website: www.lib.gov.sg

Community Children's Library (Eunos)
Block 606 Bedok Reservoir Road
#01-716
Singapore 470606
☎ 445 7303
Website: www.lib.gov.sg

Community Children's Library (Hong Kah East)
Blk 312 Jurong East St 32
#01-319
Singapore 600312
☎ 565 9217
Fax: 565 7193
Website: www.lib.gov.sg

Community Children's Library (Hong Kah North)
Block 222 Bukit Batok Street 33
#01-06
Singapore 650322
☎ 563 2471
Website: www.lib.gov.sg

Community Children's Library (Hong Kah West)
Block 836 Jurong West Street 81
#01-65
Singapore 640836
☎ 791 7683
Website: www.lib.gov.sg

Community Children's Library (Jalan Besar)
Blk 103 Towner Road
#01-296
Singapore 322103
☎ 296 2654
Fax: 296 1954
Website: www.lib.gov.sg

Community Children's Library (Jurong)
Blk 334 Kang Ching Road
#01-260
Singapore 610334
☎ 261 4726
Fax: 261 4726
Website: www.lib.gov.sg

Community Children's Library (Kaki Bukit)
Blk 554 Bedok North St 2
#01-211
Singapore 460554
☎ 244 0242
Fax: 244 0242
Website: www.lib.gov.sg

Community Children's Library (Marsiling)
Blk 301 Woodlands St 31
#01-231
Singapore 730301
☎ 365 3772
Fax: 365 3772
Website: www.lib.gov.sg

Community Children's Library (Mountbatten)
Block 12 Kampong Arang
#01-01
Singapore 431012
☎ 345 9798
Website: www.lib.gov.sg

Community Children's Library (Nee Soon Central)
Blk 644 Yishun Street 61
#01-312
Singapore 760644
☎ 757 0286
Fax: 752 4469
Website: www.lib.gov.sg

Community Children's Library (Nee Soon East)
Block 356 Yishun Ring Road
#01-1828
Singapore 760356
☎ 753 1870
Website: www.lib.gov.sg

Community Children's Library (Nee Soon South)
Block 812 Yishun Ring Road
#01-4155
Singapore 760812
☎ 755 9705
Website: www.lib.gov.sg

Community Children's Library (Pasir Ris Central)
Block 105 Pasir Ris Street 12
#01-87
Singapore 510105
☎ 581 1916
Website: www.lib.gov.sg

Community Children's Library (Pasir Ris Elias)
Blk 613 Elias Road
#01-130
Singapore 510613
☎ 581 6713
Fax: 581 6713
Website: www.lib.gov.sg

Community Children's Library (Pasir Ris South)
Blk 479 Tampines St 44
#01-241
Singapore 520479
☎ 260 7287
Fax: 260 7287
Website: www.lib.gov.sg

List of Addresses

Community Children's Library (Paya Lebar)
Blk 234 Hougang Ave 1
#01-252
Singapore 530234
☎ 281 0257
Fax: 281 5620
Website: www.lib.gov.sg

Community Children's Library (Punggol
Central)
542 Hougang Avenue 8
#01-1289
Singapore 540542
☎ 385 3938
Website: www.lib.gov.sg

Community Children's Library (Punggol
South)
Blk 662 Hougang Ave 4
#01-411
Singapore 540542
☎ 387 8251
Fax: 387 8252
Website: www.lib.gov.sg

Community Children's Library
(Sembawang)
Blk 716 Woodlands Drive 70
#01-124
Singapore 730716
☎ 365 1466
Fax: 365 1466
Website: www.lib.gov.sg

Community Children's Library (Serangoon)
Blk 125 Serangoon North Ave 1
#01-127
Singapore 550125
☎ 284 8142
Website: www.lib.gov.sg

Community Children's Library (Tampines
Central)
Blk 860 Tampines Ave 5
#01-635
Singapore 520860
☎ 260 0985
Fax: 260 0985
Website: www.lib.gov.sg

Community Children's Library (Tampines
East)
Block 254 Tampines Street 21
#01-464
Singapore 521254
☎ 787 9893
Website: www.lib.gov.sg

Community Children's Library (Tampines
West)
Block 938 Tampines Avenue 5
#01-155
Singapore 520938
☎ 782 6370
Website: www.lib.gov.sg

Community Children's Library (Thomson)
Block 308 Shunfu Road
#01-165
Singapore 570308
☎ 258 0170
Website: www.lib.gov.sg

Community Children's Library (Toa Payoh
East)
Blk 231 Toa Payoh Lorong 8
#01-192
Singapore 310231
☎ 356 3120
Fax: 356 3120
Website: www.lib.gov.sg

Community Children's Library (Whampoa)
Block 85 Whampoa Drive
#01-260
Singapore 320085
☎ 254 3823
Website: www.lib.gov.sg

Community Children's Library (Yew Tee)
Block 787 Choa Chu Kang North 6
#01-206
Singapore 682787
☎ 762 3269
Website: www.lib.gov.sg

Community Children's Library (Yio Chu Kang)
Blk 610 Ang Mo Kio Ave 4
#01-1237
Singapore 560610
☎ 452 9983
Fax: 452 9983
Website: www.lib.gov.sg

Community Children's Library (Yuhua)
Blk 229 Jurong East St 21
#01-701
Singapore 600229
☎ 566 4310
Fax: 566 4310
Website: www.lib.gov.sg

Coronation Music School
587 Bukit Timah Road
Coronation Shopping Plaza #03-10
Singapore 269707
☎ 467 3883

Corrine Private School
257 Selegie Road
Selegie Complex #04-277
Singapore 188350
☎ 337 5564
Fax: 337 1625

Council for the Development of the Singapore Muslim Community
51 Kee Sun Avenue
Wisma Mendaki
Singapore 457057
☎ 240 2130/240 2133

Creative Child Development
275A Lorong Chuan
Singapore 556770
☎ 280 8919

Crestar Learning Centre
Block 87 Marine Parade Central
#03-202
Singapore 440087
☎ 340 4114
Fax: 345 2112
E-mail: crestar@sungnet.com.sg

Cristofori Music School
Block 3014 Bedok Industrial Park E
#02-2148
Singapore 489980
☎ 243 9555

Cristofori School of Fine Arts
North Bridge Road
Funan Centre #03-01
Singapore 179097
☎ 339 5621
Fax: 348 0062

Daimaru
177 River Valley Road
Liang Court
Singapore 179030
☎ 339 1111

Dance Arts
277 Orchard Road
Specialists' Shopping Centre #05-31/34
Singapore 238858
☎ 235 4218

Delta Sports Hall
900 Tiong Bahru Road
Singapore 158790
☎ 474 7472
Website: www.ssc.gov.sg

Delta Swimming Complex
900 Tiong Bahru Road
Singapore 158790
☎ 474 7573
Website: www.ssc.gov.sg

Deutsche Schule Singapur
72 Bukit Tinggi Road
Singapore 289760
☎ 469 1131
Fax: 469 0308

Discovery Station
386 Upper Bukit Timah Road
The Rail Mall
Singapore 678043
☎ 765 4988
E-mail: edfas@mbox5.singnet.com.sg

Dover Court Preparatory School
Dover Road
Singapore 139644
☎ 775 7664
Fax: 777 4165

East Shore Hospital
321 Joo Chiat Place
Singapore 427990
☎ 344 7588
Fax: 345 4966
Website: www.esh.parkway.com.sg

Eastmen Child Care & Development
Block 743 Bedok Reservoir Road
#02-3083
Singapore 470743
☎ 442 5887

Eco Kids
9 Sandwich Road
Singapore 139158
☎ 778 2239

Eternal Life Assembly Child Care
132 Pasir Panjang Road
Singapore 118549
☎ 471 1727

EtonHouse Pre-School
51 Broadrick Road
Singapore 439501
☎ 346 6922
Fax: 346 6522
E-mail: ~etonhouse@pacific.net.sg
Website: www.etonhouse.com.sg

EtonHouse Pre-School and International
School
39 Newton Road
Singapore 307966
☎ 352 3322
Fax: 356 7822
E-mail: ~etonhouse@pacific.net.sg
Website: www.etonhouse.com.sg

Everjoy Child Care
7 Jalan Hikayat
Singapore 769852
☎ 755 2068

Excel-World Language School
50 East Coast Road
Singapore 428769
☎ 354 1774/247 7275

Family Life Society
257 Selegie Road
Selegie Complex #02-273
Singapore 188350
☎ 339 5354

Fantastic Sam's
176 Orchard Road
Centrepoint #03-24
Singapore 238843
☎ 235 6106

Fantastic Sam's
583 Orchard Road
Forum Galleria #02-35
Singapore 238884
☎ 737 9925

Fantasy Island
11 Sentosa East Mall
#02-01
Singapore 099054
☎ 275 1088

Farrer Park Swimming Complex
2 Rutland Road
Singapore 218253
☎ 299 1002
Website: www.ssc.gov.sg

Formation Centre
34 Holland Grove Road
Henry Park Suite 02
Singapore 278808
☎ 468 1211
Fax: 468 4112
E-mail: formain@pacific.net.sg
Website: home1.pacific.net.sg/~formatn

Formation Centre
32 Watten Rise
Singapore 287332
☎ 469 0607
Fax: 463 2961
E-mail: formain@pacific.net.sg
Website: home1.pacific.net.sg/~formatn

Formation Centre
36H Dunearn Road
Chancery Court #02-46
Singapore 309433
☎ 251 1300
Fax: 251 9190
E-mail: formain@pacific.net.sg
Website: home1.pacific.net.sg/~formatn

Forms Ballet and Dance Centre
12 West Coast Walk
West Coast Recreation Centre #02-17
Singapore 127157
☎ 778 0689

Forum Galleria Hip Kids Club
583 Orchard Road
Singapore 238884
☎ 732 2479

Fuji Ice Palace
2 Jurong East Street 13
Jurong Entertainment Centre #03-01
Singapore 609731
☎ 565 1905

Geylang East Community Library
50 Geylang East Avenue 1
Singapore 389704
☎ 842 8071
Fax: 842 8081
Website: www.lib.gov.sg

Geylang East Swimming Complex
601 Aljunied Crescent
Singapore 389862
☎ 745 7175
Website: www.ssc.gov.sg

Gician
Block 3015 Ubi Road 1
#04-224
Singapore 408704
☎ 744 1945
Fax: 744 2700

Gleneagles Hospital
6A Napier Road
Singapore 258500
☎ 473 7222
Fax: 475 1832
Website: www.ghl.parkway.com.sg

Gloryland Child Development
8 Hong San Walk
Singapore 688999
☎ 760 0895

Good Shepherd Childcare
Block 542 Bedok North Street 3
#01-1296
Singapore 460542
☎ 242 5695

Green Pastures Child Centre
28-30 Dukes Road
Singapore 268910
☎ 467 2380

Greentree Montessori Kindergarten
45 Jalan Mata Ayer
Singapore 759130
☎ 756 4382

Gymboree
163 Tanglin Road
Tanglin Mall #03-17
Singapore 247933
☎ 735 5290/737 2856
Fax: 737 7059
E-mail: gymboreesg@pacific.net.sg

Hard Rock Café
50 Cuscaden Road
#02-01
Singapore 249724
☎ 235 5232

His Little Kingdom Child Care & Development Centre
29/31 Jalan Lengkok Sembawang
Singapore 759218
☎ 756 8298

Hollandse Club
22 Camden Park
Singapore 299814
☎ 469 5211
Fax: 468 6272
E-mail: hcsg@hollandseclub.org.sg
Website: www.hollandseclub.org.sg

Hollandse School
65 Bukit Tinggi Road
Singapore 289757
☎ 466 0662
Fax: 467 7582

Honeykids Child Care & Development
440A Upper East Coast Road
Singapore 466497
☎ 444 4170

Horizon School for Special Education
8/9 Winchester Road
Singapore 117782
☎ 270 1824
Fax: 271 7242

Hougang Sports Hall
93 Hougang Avenue 4
Singapore 538832
☎ 286 0449
Website: www.ssc.org.sg

Hougang Swimming Complex
95 Hougang Avenue 4
Singapore 538830
☎ 386 5010
Website: www.ssc.org.sg

Ice World Kallang
No. 5 Stadium Walk #03-06/07
Singapore 397693
☎ 348 7928
Fax: 348 7949

Ichiban Montessori Child Care Centre
57 Hong San Walk
Singapore 689046
☎ 765 8426

IKEA
317 Alexandra Road
IKEA Building
Singapore 159965
☎ 474 0122
Fax: 474 3200

Inlingua School of Languages
1 Grange Road
Orchard Building #04-01
Singapore 239693
☎ 737 6666
Fax: 737 6007
E-mail: inlingua@singnet.com.sg
Website: web.singnet.com.sg/inlingua

Inlingua School of Languages
41 Sunset Way
Clementi Arcade #02-01/04
Singapore 597071
☎ 463 0966
Fax: 467 5483
E-mail: inlingua@singnet.com.sg
Website: web.singnet.com.sg/inlingua

Intellect Child Care & Development
Block 320 Ang Mo Kio Avenue 1
#01-1521
Singapore 560320
☎ 451 4789

International Community School
3 Mt. Faber Road
Singapore 099196
☎ 270 3378
Fax: 270 3370
E-mail: intlcoms@mbox4.singnet.com.sg

International School of Singapore (ISS)
21 Preston Road
Singapore 109355
☎ 475 4188
Fax: 273 7065
E-mail: ISS@pacific.net.sg

International School of Singapore (ISS)
25 Paterson Road
Singapore 238510
☎ 235 5844
Fax: 273 7065
E-mail: ISS@pacific.net.sg

In the States
176 Orchard Road
Centrepoint #03-02
Singapore 238843
☎ 235 0221

In the States
261a Holland Avenue
Singapore 278986
☎ 462 6011

Isetan Scotts
350 Orchard Road
Shaw House
Singapore 238868
☎ 733 1111

List of Addresses

Isetan Katong
80 Marine Parade Road
Parkway Parade
Singapore 449269
☎ 345 5555

Isetan Tampines
4 Tampines Central 5
Tampines Mall
Singapore 525910
☎ 788 7777

Jan & Elly - The Learning Place
432 Upper Bukit Timah Road
The Rail Mall
Singapore 678058
☎ 762 7783
Fax: 762 7781
E-mail: ellysim@singnet.com.sg

Joewe Playhouse & Child Development
Block 553 Serangoon North Avenue 3
#01-75
Singapore 550553
☎ 484 1078

John Little
277 Orchard Road
Specialists' Shopping Centre, Levels 1 to 4
Singapore 238858
☎ 737 2222
Fax: 734 1767
Website: www.johnlittle.com.sg

John Little
1 Pasir Ris Central Street 3
White Sands #02-01/06
Singapore 518457
☎ 585 0922
Website: www.johnlittle.com.sg

John Little
Yishun Avenue 2
Northpoint Shopping Centre #02-15
Singapore 769098
☎ 752 9288
Website: www.johnlittle.com.sg

John Little
1 Woodlands Square
#02-41/42 Causeway Point
Singapore 738099
☎ 894 0900

Joyce Goh's Playgroup
1A Bukit Ayer Molek
Singapore 589696
☎ 466 4471

Joytech Child Development Centre
11 Beng Wan Road
Singapore 339843
☎ 298 9682

Jude Child Care & Child Development
Block 104 Pasir Ris Street 12
#01-141
Singapore 510104
☎ 582 0285

Julia Gabriel Communications
583 Orchard Road
Forum Galleria #04-00
Singapore 238884
☎ 733 4322
Fax: 733 2334

Juliet McCully School of Language and
Communications
277 Orchard Road
Specialists' Shopping Centre #05-48
Singapore 238858
☎ 732 5510
Fax: 733 7718

Junior Playworld Child Care & Development
2 & 4 Jalan Lye Kwee
Singapore 537822
☎ 281 7865

Jurong BirdPark
2 Jurong Hill
Singapore 628925
☎ 265 0022
Fax: 261 1869
E-mail: birdpark@singnet.com.sg
Website: www.birdpark.com

Jurong Calvary Kindergarten
1 Tao Ching Road
Singapore 618720
☎ 265 6193

Jurong East Community Library
Jurong Town Hall Road
Singapore 609430
☎ 665 0303
Fax: 665 0312
Website: www.lib.gov.sg

Jurong Town Swimming Complex
4, 4th Chin Bee Road
Singapore 619698
☎ 265 0586
Website: www.ssc.gov.sg

Jurong West Community Library
1 Jurong West Central 2
Jurong Point #04-01/04
Singapore 648886
☎ 793 6900
Fax: 793 6906
Website: www.lib.gov.sg

Kallang Basin Swimming Complex
21 Geylang Bahru Lane
Singapore 339627
☎ 295 4261
Website: www.ssc.gov.sg

Kallang Roller Disco
Stadium Walk
Kallang Leisure Park #03-05
Singapore 397693
☎ 348 6793

Kampong Kapur Family Service Centre
Block 2 Kitchener Road
#03-89
Singapore 200002
☎ 299 7662

Kangaroo Creek Gang Roadshow
8 Kim Keat Lane
Singapore 328865
☎ 354 6635
Fax: 354 6820
E-mail: monco8@mbox2.singnet.com.sg

Katong Swimming Complex
111 Wilkinson Road
Singapore 436752
☎ 344 9609
Website: www.ssc.gov.sg

Kiddy Junction Child Development &
Learning
Seletar Hills Estate
33 Kasai Road
Singapore 808280
☎ 484 6781

Kids Haven Child Care & Development Centre
Block 450 Bukit Panjang Ring Road
#01-595
Singapore 670450
☎ 765 1264

Kinder Corner 1
85 Science Park Drive
#01-01
Singapore 118259
☎ 775 3112

Kinder Corner 2
21 Science Park Road
#02-05 The Aquarius
Singapore 117628
☎ 776 0103

Kinderjoy Educare
Block 656 Jalan Tenaga
#01-104
Singapore 410656
☎ 745 7723

Kinderland Child Care
15, 17 Jalan Lana
2nd Floor entrance at Chai Chee Drive
Singapore 419041
☎ 442 2033

Kindermusik
293 Holland Road
Jelita Cold Storage #01-08
Singapore 278628
☎ 467 1789
Fax: 467 5560
E-mail: kindermusik@pacific.net.sg
Website: www.kindermusik.com.sg

KinderWorld EduCare
12 West Coast Walk
West Coast Recreation Centre #01-05
Singapore 127157
☎ 774 4146
Website: www.kinderworld.com.sg

KinderWorld EduCare
18 Middle Road
Singapore 188929
☎ 339 5270
Website: www.kinderworld.com.sg

KinderWorld EduCare
14 Lengkong Lima
Singapore 417552
☎ 448 7877
Website: www.kinderworld.com.sg

KinderWorld EduCare
58/58A Toh Crescent
Singapore 507965
☎ 543 0767
Website: www.kinderworld.com.sg

KinderWorld EduCare
10 Ang Mo Kio Street 65
Techpoint #01-04
Singapore 569059
☎ 484 1849
Website: www.kinderworld.com.sg

KinderWorld EduCare
33 Westlake Avenue
Singapore 574244
☎ 250 5048
Website: www.kinderworld.com.sg

KinderWorld EduCare
100 Yishun Central
Yishun Medical Centre #03-01/05
Singapore 768826
☎ 759 6540
Website: www.kinderworld.com.sg

KinderWorld Edutainment Concepts
3 Temasek Boulevard
Suntec City Mall #02-001/2
Singapore 038983
☎ 337 7595/334 2433
Website: www.kinderworld.com.sg

Kinokuniya, Books
391 Orchard Road
#03-09 Ngee Ann City
Singapore 238872
☎ 737 5021
Fax: 738 0487
Website: www.kinokuniya.com

Kinokuniya
177 River Valley Road
Liang Court #03-08
Singapore 179030
☎ 337 1300
Website: www.kinokuniya.com

Kinokuniya
250 North Bridge Road
Sogo Raffles City #03-01
Singapore 179101
☎ 330 8173
Website: www.kinokuniya.com

Kinokuniya
200 Victoria Street
Parco Bugis Junction #03-09
Singapore 188021
☎ 339 1790
Website: www.kinokuniya.com

KK Women's and Children's Hospital
100 Bukit Timah Road
Singapore 229899
☎ 293 4044
Fax: 293 7933
E-mail: info@kkh.com.sg
Website: www.kkh.com.sg

La Salle - SIA College of the Arts
90 Goodman Road
Junior School of Creative Arts
Singapore 439053
☎ 344 4300
Fax: 346 5708
E-mail: lasalle@singnet.com.sg
Website: www.lasalle.edu.sg

Little Fairyland Child Care & Development
509 East Coast Road
Singapore 429063
☎ 447 1088

Little Genius Childcare & Development
Block 64 New Upper Changi Road
#01-1158
Singapore 460064
☎ 445 4930

LV-U Child Care & Development Centre
Block 501 Bukit Batok Street 52
#01-71
Singapore 650501
☎ 569 2880

MacPherson Moral Child Care
Block 93 Paya Lebar Way
#01-3039
Singapore 370093
☎ 741 8359

Mandarin Gardens Kindergarten
9 Siglap Road
Mandarin Gardens
Singapore 448910
☎ 443 5428

Mandeville Music School
442 Orchard Road
Orchard Hotel Shopping Arcade #02-12
Singapore 238879
☎ 733 3517
Fax: 733 2351
E-mail: artistes@pacific.net.sg

Marine Parade Community Library
6 Marine Parade Central
Singapore 449411
☎ 346 2125
Fax: 346 2130
Website: www.lib.gov.sg

Maternity Support Services
25 First Avenue
Singapore 268759
☎ 463 4285/9817 1010

Metro Marina
6 Raffles Boulevard
Marina Square #02-300
Singapore 039594
☎ 337 2868
E-mail: metro@metro.com.sg

Metro Far East
40 Scotts Road
Far East Plaza #01-01
Singapore 228213
☎ 733 3322
E-mail: metro@metro.com.sg

Metro Paragon
290 Orchard Road
Paragon by Sogo #02-08
Singapore 238859
☎ 835 3322
E-mail: metro@metro.com.sg

Metro Tampines
2 Tampines Central 5
Century Square #01-03
Singapore 529509
☎ 783 8433
E-mail: metro@metro.com.sg

MINDS
844 Margaret Drive
Singapore 149308
☎ 479 5655

Monkeys Café
400 Orchard Road
#01-20 Orchard Towers
Singapore 238875
☎ 735 3707

Montessori Creative World
154 West Coast Road
Ginza Plaza #B1-40
Singapore 127371
☎ 773 2031

Montessori Creative World
1 Marine Parade Central
Parkway Builders Central #03-06
Singapore 449408
☎ 348 8173

Morris Allen Study Centre
1 Newton Road
Goldhill Plaza #02-47/49
Singapore 307943
☎ 253 5737
Fax: 253 2698

Morris Allen Study Centre
112 East Coast Road
Katong Mall #02-13/18
Singapore 428802
☎ 440 8586
Fax: 345 9854

Morris Allen Study Centre
5 Tampines Central 6
#01-02 Telepark
Singapore 529482
☎ 786 9595
Fax: 785 2488

Mothercare
6 Raffles Boulevard
Marina Square #02-100
Singapore 039594
☎ 337 0388/337 0389

Mothercare
3 Temasek Boulevard
Suntec City Mall #02-003/5/7
Singapore 039893
☎ 337 5138

Mothercare
176 Orchard Road
Centrepoint #01-34/39
Singapore 238843
☎ 732 7566/732 7567

Mothercare
80 Marine Parade Road
Parkway Parade #02-34B
Singapore 449269
☎ 447 2355/447 2356

Mothergoose Child Development
2 Jalan Hajijah
Singapore 468697
☎ 445 6628

Mount Alvernia Hospital
820 Thomson Road
Singapore 574623
☎ 359 7923/359 7810
Fax: 356 1151
Website: www.mtalvernia-hospital.org

Mount Elizabeth Hospital
3 Mt. Elizabeth
Singapore 228510
☎ 737 2666
Fax: 737 1189
Website: www.meh.parkway.com.sg

Mövenpick Marché Restaurant
260 Orchard Road
#01-03 The Heeren
Singapore 238855
Fax: 235 6138

MPH Bookstores
63 Robinson Road
Afro-Asia Building #01-01/02
Singapore 068894
☎ 222 6423
Fax: 222 5035

MPH Bookstores
71-77 Stamford Road
Singapore 178894
☎ 336 3633
Fax: 334 0592

MPH Bookstores
8 Bishan Place
#03-07 Junction 8
Singapore 579839
☎ 354 4430

MPH Bookstores
435 Orchard Road
#04-30 Wisma Atria
Singapore 238877
☎ 835 0039

MPH Bookstores
80 Marine Parade Road
Parkway Parade #B1-155/157
Singapore 449269
☎ 348 1483
Fax: 440 0669

List of Addresses

MRT Information Centre
☎ 1800 336 8900

Nanyang Kindergarten
118 King's Road
Singapore 268155
☎ 466 3375

National University Hospital
5 Lower Kent Ridge Road
Singapore 119074
☎ 779 5555
Fax: 779 5678

New Life Kindergarten
10 Marsiling Lane
Singapore 739147
☎ 368 9567

New Mothers' Support Group
22 Camden Park
The Dutch Club
Singapore 299814
☎ 462 6203/468 3727/256 4791

Novel Learning Centre
271 Bukit Timah Road
Balmoral Plaza #B1-01
Singapore 259708
☎ 732 7115
Fax: 732 3135

NTUC Childcare Co-operative
Block 192 Toa Payoh Lorong 4
#02-872
Singapore 310192
☎ 256 8361
Fax: 250 0883

NTUC Childcare Co-operative Publications
Unit
Block 66 Kallang Bahru
#05-473
Singapore 330066
☎ 293 9161

Nurture Craft
3 Temasek Boulevard
Suntec City Mall #02-004
Singapore 039893
☎ 336 8717
E-mail: info@nurture.com.sg
Website: www.nurture.com.sg

Nurture Craft
583 Orchard Road
Forum Galleria #B1-12
Singapore 238884
☎ 734 3610
E-mail: info@nurture.com.sg
Website: www.nurture.com.sg

Nurture Craft
101 Thomson Road
United Square #B1-51
Singapore 307591
☎ 252 1321
E-mail: info@nurture.com.sg
Website: www.nurture.com.sg

Nurture Craft
4 Tampines Central 5
Tampines Mall #03-09
Singapore 529510
☎ 786 3020
E-mail: info@nurture.com.sg
Website: www.nurture.com.sg

Nurture Craft
90 Hougang Avenue 10
NTUC Hougang Mall #03-19
Singapore 538876
☎ 387 2602
E-mail: info@nurture.com.sg
Website: www.nurture.com.sg

Nurture Craft
301 Upper Thomson Road
Thomson Plaza #01-25
Singapore 574408
☎ 456 9727
E-mail: info@nurture.com.sg
Website: www.nurture.com.sg

Nurture Craft
1 Jalan Anak Bukit
Bukit Timah Plaza #B2-12
Singapore 588996
☎ 466 7179
E-mail: info@nurture.com.sg
Website: www.nurture.com.sg

Nurture Craft
1 Jurong West Central 2
Jurong Point #B1-01
Singapore 648886
☎ 793 5156
E-mail: info@nurture.com.sg
Website: www.nurture.com.sg

One Plus One Schoolhouse
104 Pemimpin Place
Singapore 576101
☎ 353 3200

Overseas Family School
25F Paterson Road
Singapore 238515
☎ 738 0211
Fax: 733 8825
Website: www.ofs.edu.sg

Pakson Childcare Centre
7 Lorong Batawi
Singapore 536668
☎ 382 0560

Palais Dance Studio
557 Bukit Timah Road
#02-16
Singapore 269694
☎ 467 7788
E-mail: tkteo@pacific.net.sg

Pandan Garden Swimming Complex
200 Pandan Gardens
#01-00
Singapore 609336
☎ 560 2372
Website: www.ssc.gov.sg

Party Land
370 Alexandra Road
B1-36/37 Anchorpoint
Singapore159953
☎ 479 3911

Partylink
26 Cheng Soon Crescent
Singapore 599898
☎ 479 6127

Pat's SchoolHouse
9 Halifax Road
Singapore 229261
☎ 299 0372

Pat's SchoolHouse
121B Whitley Road
Singapore 297814
☎ 250 7623

Pat's SchoolHouse
7 Buckley Road
Singapore 309763
☎ 256 7404

List of Addresses

Pat's SchoolHouse
2C Lim Ah Pin Road
Singapore 547813
☎ 282 4270

Pat's Schoolhouse
18B Fort Road
Singapore 439084
☎ 346 7675/346 7845
Fax: 346 7875

Pat's Schoolhouse
11 Canning Walk
Singapore 178881
☎ 339 6989
Fax: 339 7226

Paya Lebar Family Service Centre
☎ 289 8811

Paya Lebar Methodist Church Covenant Kindergarten
521 Upper Paya Lebar Road
Singapore 535000
☎ 285 3730

Paya Lebar Swimming Complex
19 Aroozoo Avenue
Singapore 539830
☎ 283 2319
Website: www.ssc.gov.sg

PCF Education Centres
Block 57B New Upper Changi Road
#01-1402
Singapore 463057
☎ 244 4600
Fax: 444 4459

Piano Master
Block 1016 Geylang East Avenue 3
#01-143/02-147
Singapore 389731
☎ 747 7695/ 747 9163

Pibo's Garden
1 Dunearn Close
Singapore 299574
☎ 466 2639

Pitter Patter Child Care & Development
41 Frankel Avenue
Singapore 458172
☎ 241 4143

Playhouse Child Development
1 Bournemouth Road
Singapore 439659
☎ 348 0897

Popular Book Company
Block 231 Bain Street
Bras Basah Complex #04-23/33
Singapore 180231
☎ 338 2339
Fax: 338 6364

Popular Book Company
437 Orchard Road
Orchard MRT Station #B1-08
Singapore 238878
☎ 838 0820
Fax: 235 0279

Popular Book Company
Block 190 Toa Payoh Central Lorong 6
#03-512
Singapore 310190
☎ 354 2645
Fax: 353 5776

Popular Book Company
Block 86 Marine Parade Central
#02-101/102
Singapore 440086
☎ 344 9884
Fax: 345 0831

Popular Book Company
Block 205 Hougang Street 21
#04-02
Singapore 530205
☎ 287 1664
Fax: 287 6284

Popular Book Company
10 Jurong East Street 12
Jurong East MRT Station #01-01
Singapore 609690
☎ 665 1290
Fax: 565 3136

Popular Book Company
1 Jurong West Central 2
Jurong Point #03-07
Singapore 648886
☎ 793 5280
Fax: 793 5284

Praises Child Development Centre
Block 645 Ang Mo Kio Avenue 6
#01-4991
Singapore 560645
☎ 454 8327

Pregnancy Crisis Centre
☎ 339 9770

Presbyterian Welfare Services (PWS)
1 Sophia Road
#04-34 Peace Centre
Singapore 228149
☎ 334 4445

Prime Gymnastics Club
Block 36 Holland Drive
#02-395
Singapore 270036
☎ 773 2901
Fax: 872 2158
E-mail: primegym@pacific.net.sg
Website: www.ipbnet.com/primegym

Professional Nursing Services
Block 2 Woking Road
#01-01
Singapore 138942
☎ 479 1044/463 6678/9604 1530 (pgr)/
9833 7470 (h/p)

Queenstown Community Library
53 Margaret Drive
Singapore 149297
☎ 471 9046
Fax: 471 9973
Website: www.lib.gov.sg

Queenstown Swimming Complex
473 Stirling Road
Singapore 148948
☎ 473 2555
Website: www.ssc.gov.sg

Radiance Training Centre
Block 501 Jurong West Street 51
#04-255
Singapore 640501
☎ 567 6730
Fax: 569 1942

Rhymesland Educare
Block 406 Hougang Avenue 10
#01-1124
Singapore 530406
☎ 385 2518

Riding for the Disabled
5 Jalan Mashhor
Singapore 299114
☎ 251 7020
Fax: 354 2396

River Valley Swimming Complex
1 River Valley Road
Singapore 179018
☎ 337 6275

List of Addresses

Robinsons
176 Orchard Road
Centrepoint
Singapore 238843
☎ 733 0888
Fax: 734 1767
Website: www.robinsons.com.sg

SACAC (Singapore American Community
Action Council)
21 Scotts Road
The American Club
Singapore 228219
☎ 733 9249 (community health)
363 6454 (sports)
Fax: 733 9321
Website: www.sacac.com

Sagacity Arts & Crafts Centre
Block 231 Bain Street
Bras Basah Shopping Centre #02-93/97
Singapore 180231
☎ 337 0909

Samaritans of Singapore (SOS)
☎ 1800 221 4444

Sasco Child Care
Block 93 Bedok North Avenue 4
#01-1477
Singapore 460093
☎ 449 0020

School of Physical Education
21 Evans Road
Singapore 259366
☎ 468 8393/460 5380 (pool)
Website: www.ssc.gov.sg

School of Young Talents
1a Short Street
Department of Junior Art
Singapore 188210
☎ 337 6636

School of Young Talents
111 Middle Road
Singapore 188969
☎ 337 6636
Fax: 337 3920

School of Young Talents
11 Upper Wilkie Road
Singapore 228120

Seiyu Wing On
230 Victoria Street
Bugis Junction
Singapore 188024
☎ 223 2222
Free hot line: 1800 337 6096

Sentosa Development Corporation
1 Garden Avenue
#03-00
Singapore 099621
☎ 275 0388
Website: www.sentosa.com.sg

Serangoon Swimming Complex
35-A Yio Chu Kang Road
Singapore 545552
☎ 288 4606
Website: www.ssc.gov.sg

Singapore Art Museum
71 Bras Basah Road
Singapore 189555
☎ 375 2510
Fax: 334 3054
Website: www.museum.org.sg/sam

Singapore Association for the Deaf
227 Mountbatten Road
Singapore 397998
☎ 344 8274
E-mail: dawn@rainbow.sad.org.sg

Singapore Association for the Visually
Handicapped
47 Toa Payoh Rise
Singapore 298104
☎ 251 4331

Singapore Badminton Hall
100 Guillemard Road
Singapore 399718
☎ 345 7554

Singapore Ballet Academy
Cox Terrace
Level 2 Fort Canning Centre
Singapore 179618
☎ 337 9125

Singapore Children's Society
302 Tiong Bahru Road
Tiong Bahru Plaza #06-10/11
Singapore 168732
☎ 272 3229
Fax: 272 7371
E-mail: info@childrensociety.org.sg
Website: www.childrensociety.org.sg

Singapore Discovery Centre
510 Upper Jurong Road
Singapore 638365
☎ 792 6188
Fax: 792 1233
Website: www.sdc.com.sg

Singapore General Hospital
Outram Road
Singapore 169608
☎ 222 3322/326 5605 (O&G)
Fax: 222 1720
Webaite: www.sgh.gov.sg

Singapore History Museum
93 Stamford Road
Singapore 178897
☎ 375 2510
Fax: 334 3054
Website: www.museum.org.sg/shm

Singapore Judo Club
5B Portsdown Road
Singapore 139296
☎ 475 6406

Singapore Malay Youth Library Association
Block 136 Bedok Reservoir Road
#01-1425
Singapore 470136
☎ 744 8457

Singapore Maritime Showcase
World Trade Centre
Harbour Promenade #01-131
Singapore 099253
☎ 321 1053

Singapore Repertory Theatre
182 Cecil Street
TA Performing Arts Centre
Singapore 069547
☎ 221 5585
Fax: 221 1936

Singapore Rugby Union
469 Bukit Timah Road
School of Physical Education
Singapore 259756
☎ 467 4038
Fax: 467 0283
E-mail: sru@pacific.net.sg
Website: www.sru.org.sg

List of Addresses

Singapore School for the Visually
Handicapped
51 Toa Payoh Rise
Singapore 298106
☎ 250 3755

Singapore Science Centre and Omni-Theatre
15 Science Centre Road
Singapore 609081
☎ 560 3316 (Science Centre)
 568 9188 (Omni-Theatre)
Fax: 565 9533
Website: www.sci-ctr.edu.sg

Singapore Zoological Gardens
80 Mandai Lake Road
Singapore 729826
☎ 269 3411
Fax: 367 2974
E-mail: singzoo@pacific.net.sg
Website: www.singzoo.com

Smartie Child Care Centre
Block 368 Bukit Batok Street 31
#01-485
Singapore 650368
☎ 565 5898

Sonshine Child Care Centre
Block 211 Bukit Batok Street 21
#01-252
Singapore 650211
☎ 565 0844
Fax: 561 3917

Spageddies Italian Kitchen
163 Tanglin Road
Tanglin Mall #02-22/23
Singapore 247933
☎ 733 5519

St. Clare Kindergarten
5 Bukit Batok East Avenue 2
Singapore 659915
☎ 567 4770

St. Hilda's Kindergarten
83 Ceylon Road
Singapore 429740
☎ 344 3119

Stamford Café
2 Stamford Road
Westin Stamford Hotel
Singapore 178882
☎ 338 8585
Website: www.westinsingapore.com

STPB Tourist Information Centre
328 North Bridge Road
Raffles Hotel Arcade #02-34
Singapore 188719
☎ 1800 334 1335

Strawberry's Child Development Centre
1 Youngberg Terrace
Avon Park #01-02
Singapore 357741
☎ 288 5421

Sungei Buloh Nature Park
301 Neo Tiew Crescent
Singapore 718925
☎ 793 7377
Fax: 793 7271
E-mail: sbnp@pacific.net.sg
Website: www.sbnp.org

Sunsafe Swimwear
16B Margoliouth Road
Chatelet #09-03
Singapore 258542
☎ 733 1667

Sunshine Montessori House
20/22/24 Watten Rise
Singapore 287307
☎ 466 6608/468 8066
Fax: 466 6618

Swimfast Aquatic School
☎ 472 1011
Website: www.cyberway.com.sg/~swimfast

Swiss School Association
38 Swiss Club Road
Singapore 288140
☎ 468 2117
Fax: 466 5342
E-mail: ssaspore@singnet.com.sg

T P B C Kindergarten
20 Lorong Ah Soo
Singapore 536698
☎ 283 0196

Tai Pei Child Care
Block 77 Lorong Limau
#01-51
Singapore 320077
☎ 352 6510

Takashimaya Singapore
391A Orchard Road
Ngee Ann City
Singapore 238873
☎ 738 1111

Taman Bacaan Child Care & Development
Block 136 Bedok Reservoir Road
Tun Sri Lanang Centre #01-1425
Singapore 470136
☎ 744 8457

Taman Bacan Sang Nila Utama Child Care
Block 939 Tampines Avenue 5
#01-167
Singapore 520939
☎ 787 7977

Tampines Family Service Centre
470 Tampines Street 44
#01-194
Singapore 520470
☎ 787 2001

Tampines Regional Library
31 Tampines Avenue 7
Singapore 529620
☎ 788 8266
Fax: 375 5128
Website: www.lib.gov.sg

Tampines Swimming Complex
505 Tampines Avenue 5
Singapore 529652
☎ 786 1151
Website: www.ssc.gov.sg

Tang Dynasty City
2 Yuan Ching Road
Singapore 618641
☎ 261 1116
E-mail: tdcsales@mbox2.singnet.com.sg

Teeny Tiny Child Care & Development
Block 140 Bishan Street 12
#01-484
Singapore 570140
☎ 353 1712

Tenderluv Daycare Child Development
Centre
25 West Coast Road
Singapore 127310
☎ 779 6370

The American Club
21 Scotts Road
Singapore 228219
☎ 737 3411
Fax: 732 8308

The Battle Box
51 Canning Rise
Fort Canning Park
Singapore 179872
☎ 338 1212
Fax: 334 3020
E-mail: battle42@mbox4.singnet.com.sg
Website: www.battlebox.com.sg

The Boys' Brigade in Singapore
105 Ganges Avenue
BB Campus
Singapore 169695
☎ 737 0377

The British Club
73 Bukit Tinggi Road
Singapore 289761
☎ 467 4311
Fax: 468 6161
E-mail: memberbritclub@pacific.net.sg
Website: www.britishclub.org.sg

The Children's Learning Centre
55 Newton Road
5th Floor Revenue House
Singapore 307987
☎ 258 7130

The Children's Place
19 Kay Siang Road
Singapore 248935
☎ 472 3788

The Disney Store
391A Orchard Road
Ngee Ann City #B1-00
Singapore 238873
☎ 737 0790

The Family Place
177 River Valley Road
Liang Court #05-01
Singapore 179030
☎ 334 3937
E-mail: skoolhouse@pacific.net.sg
Website: www.ntuc-childcare.com.sg

The Japanese Association
120 Adam Road
Singapore 289899
☎ 468 0066
E-mail: info@jas.org.sg
Website: www.jas.org.sg

The Kidz Station
583 Orchard Road
Forum Galleria #B1-07
Singapore 238884
☎ 735 6340

The Learning Connection
Block 279 Bishan Street 24
#01-44
Singapore 570279
☎ 459 2464

The Little Skool-House
177 River Valley Road
Liang Court #05-01
Singapore 179030
☎ 339 3488
E-mail: skoolhouse@pacific.net.sg
Website: www.ntuc-childcare.com.sg

The Little Skool-House
1 Orchid Club Road
Orchid Country Club
Singapore 769162
☎ 759 0393
E-mail: skoolhouse@pacific.net.sg
Website: www.ntuc-childcare.com.sg

The Montessori Shop
9 Penang Road
Park Mall #B1-14/15
Singapore 238459
☎ 337 9438

The Montessori Workgroup
9 Penang Road
Park Mall #B1-14/15
Singapore 238459
☎ 337 9438

The Moral Child Care Centre
19c Boon Tat Street
Singapore 069619
☎ 227 9694

The Mother and Child Centre
583 Orchard Road
Forum Galleria #02-34
Singapore 238884
☎ 836 0063

The Nature Society
601 Sims Drive
PAN-I Complex #04-05
Singapore 387382
☎ 741 2036
Fax: 741 0871
E-mail: natsoc@mbox2.singnet.com.sg

The Preparatory Place
11 Ewe Boon Road
Singapore 259321
☎ 737 6427

Singapore American School
40 Woodlands Street 41
Woodlands Campus
Singapore 738547
☎ 363 6303
Fax: 363 3408
Website: www.sas.edu.sg

Thomson Road Baptist Kindergarten
45 Thomson Road
Singapore 307584
☎ 255 0111

Times the Bookshop
3 Temasek Boulevard
Suntec City Mall #02-054/056/058/060
Singapore 038983
☎ 336 9391
Fax: 336 9394
Website: www.ecomz.com/timesbookshop/

Times the Bookshop
1 Raffles Place
OUB Centre #03-01
Singapore 048616
☎ 533 8407
Fax: 538 5075
Website: www.ecomz.com/timesbookshop/

Times the Bookshop
252 North Bridge Road
Raffles City Shopping Centre #02-24
Singapore 179103
☎ 339 3787
Fax: 334 4653
Website: www.ecomz.com/timesbookshop/

Times the Bookshop
68 Orchard Road
Plaza Singapura #03-13/14
Singapore 238839
☎ 837 0552
Fax: 837 0556
Website: www.ecomz.com/timesbookshop/

List of Addresses

Times the Bookshop
176 Orchard Road
Centrepoint #04-08/16
Singapore 238843
☎ 734 9022
Website: www.ecomz.com/timesbookshop/

Times the Bookshop
6 Scotts Road
#03-09/13 Scotts Shopping Centre
Singapore 228202
☎ 834 2989
Fax: 834 2987
Website: www.ecomz.com/timesbookshop/

Times the Bookshop
101 Thomson Road
United Square #B1-23/29
Singapore 307591
☎ 250 4044
☎ 734 9022
Website: www.ecomz.com/timesbookshop/

Times the Bookshop
2 Tampines Central 5
Century Square #04-01
Singapore 529509
☎ 787 4561
Fax: 787 4762
Website: www.ecomz.com/timesbookshop/

Times the Bookshop
4 Tampines Central 5
Tampines Mall #03-26/27
Singapore 529510
☎ 783 3106
Fax: 783 3917
Website: www.ecomz.com/timesbookshop/

Times the Bookshop
930 Yishun Avenue
Northpoint Shopping Centre #03-05/06/06A
Singapore 769098
☎ 754 5976
Fax: 754 4249
Website: www.ecomz.com/timesbookshop/

Times the Bookshop
Singapore Changi Airport Terminal 1
Departure Transit East Terminal
Singapore 819142
☎ 543 0712
Fax: 543 2236
Website: www.ecomz.com/timesbookshop/

Times the Bookshop
Singapore Changi Airport Terminal 2
Arrival Hall Level 1 #016-010
Singapore 819643
☎ 545 4847
Website: www.ecomz.com/timesbookshop/

Times the Bookshop
Singapore Changi Airport Terminal 2
Departure Hall Level
Singapore 819643
☎ 545 0867
Fax: 545 0758
Website: www.ecomz.com/timesbookshop/

Tinkle Friend
☎ 1800 274 4788

Toa Payoh Community Library
Toa Payoh Central
Singapore 319191
☎ 332 3255
Fax: 354 5067
Website: www.lib.gov.sg

Toa Payoh Swimming Complex
301 Lorong 6 Toa Payoh
Singapore 319392
☎ 259 4808
Website: www.ssc.gov.sg

Toys R Us
583 Orchard Road
Forum Galleria #03-00
Singapore 238884
☎ 235 4322

Toys R Us
6 Raffles Boulevard
#01-202/203 Marina Square
Singapore 039594
☎ 333 9468

Toys R Us
4 Tampines Central 5
Tampines Mall #03-17
Singapore 529510
☎ 787 0662

Toys R Us
930 Yishun Avenue 2
Northpoint Shopping Centre #04-01
Singapore 769098
☎ 754 7707

True Way Presbyterian Kindergarten
156B Stirling Road
Singapore 148947
☎ 471 0781/474 3527

Tumble Tots
277 Orchard Road
Specialists' Shopping Centre #03-41/41
Singapore 238858
☎ 733 9066
E-mail: ttots@pacific.net.sg

Tumble Tots
80 Marine Parade Road
Parkway Parade #05-06/07
Singapore 449269
☎ 344 5191
E-mail: ttots@pacific.net.sg

Tumble Tots
Block 208 Hougang Street 21
Hougang Centre #03-223
Singapore 530208
☎ 288 1085
E-mail: ttots@pacific.net.sg

Tumble Tots
301 Upper Thomson Road
Thomson Plaza #03-11
Singapore 574408
☎ 459 1462
E-mail: ttots@pacific.net.sg

Tumble Tots
15A West Coast Road
#01-131/132 Ginza Plaza
Singapore 127371
☎ 773 0775
E-mail: ttots@pacific.net.sg

Tumble Tots
1/A Tampines St 92
SAFRA Tampines Centre
Singapore 528883
☎ 784 0241
E-mail: ttots@pacific.net.sg

Tumble Tots
2 Jurong East Street 21
#02-07 IMM Building
Singapore 609601
☎ 562 4578
E-mail: ttots@pacific.net.sg

List of Addresses

Tumble Tots
Block 258 Pasir Ris Street 21
#02-311A Loyang Point
Singapore 518970
☎ 582 8366
E-mail: ttots@pacific.net.sg

Tumble Tots
10 Jalan Serene
#02-01A/02
Singapore 258748
☎ 469 3933
E-mail: ttots@pacific.net.sg

Tumble Tots
30 Woodlands Avenue 1
#02-12 The Woodgrove
Singapore 739065
☎ 364 0488
E-mail: ttots@pacific.net.sg

Tung Ling Kindergarten
145 Marine Parade Road
Singapore 449274
☎ 345 1469

Twinkle Thinkers (HQ)
102F Pasir Panjang Road
#05-02 Citilink Warehouse Complex
Singapore 118530
☎ 275 5722
Fax: 275 2577

Twinkle Thinkers
301 Upper Thomson Road
#01-03 Thomson Plaza
Singapore 574408
☎ 455 5565

Twinkle Thinkers
80 Marine Parade Road
B1-35 Parkway Parade
Singapore 449269
☎ 345 6278

Twinkle Thinkers
583 Orchard Road
B1-23 Forum Galleria
Singapore 238884
☎ 733 3143

Twinkle Thinkers
100 Bukit Timah Road
#01-23 KK Women's & Children's Hospital
Singapore 229899
☎ 392 3032

Uni-3 Montessori (East)
50 East Coast Road
#01-110/#03-14 New Roxy Square
Singapore 428769
☎ 348 3329/348 1955
Fax: 348 1959

Uni-3 Montessori (West)
6 Jubilee Road
Singapore 128531
☎ 773 6029
Fax: 773 6347

United Educare
35 Lotus Avenue
Singapore 277618
☎ 467 9877

United Educare
45 Ming Teck Park
Singapore 277412

Victor Doggett Music Studios
1 Jalan Kechil
#01-05
Singapore 438468
☎ 344 8324

Warner Bros. Studio Store
3 Temasek Boulevard
Suntec City Galleria #01-007/011
Singapore 039893
☎ 337 0228

Warner Bros. Studio Store
435 Orchard Road
Wisma Atria Shopping Centre #02-21/03-18
Singapore 238877
☎ 733 7710

Wesley Child Development
Block 29 Telok Blangah Rise
#01-231
Singapore 019029
☎ 271 1216

Wesley Child Development
Block 504 Serangoon North Avenue 4
#01-470
Singapore 550504
☎ 481 8455

Wetheby Pre-School
7 Seraya Lane
Singapore 437275
☎ 440 5100
Fax: 440 4085

Wonder Kids Child Care & Development
861 Mountbatten Road
Singapore 437842
☎ 447 4350

Woodlands Sports Hall
2 Woodlands St 12
Singapore 738620
☎ 365 2707
Website: www.ssc.gov.sg

Woodlands Swimming Complex
3 Woodlands Street 13
Singapore 738600
☎ 269 4192
Website: www.ssc.gov.sg

Yan Kit Swimming Complex
5 Yan Kit Road
Singapore 088261
☎ 221 3532
Website: www.ssc.gov.sg

Yio Chu Kang Sports Hall
214 Ang Mo Kio Ave 9
Singapore 569780
☎ 483 4294
Website: www.ssc.gov.sg

Yio Chu Kang Swimming Complex
202 Ang Mo Kio Avenue 9
Singapore 569771
☎ 481 9054
Website: www.ssc.gov.sg

Yishun Community Library
Blk 290 Yishun St 22
#03-401
Singapore 760290
☎ 756 9298
Fax: 756 9290
Website: www.lib.gov.sg

Yishun Sports Hall
101 Yishun Ave 1
Singapore 769130
☎ 756 7416
Website: www.ssc.gov.sg

Yishun Swimming Complex
351 Yishun Avenue 3
Singapore 769057
☎ 752 5513
Website: www.ssc.gov.sg

List of Addresses

Young Talents Child Care & Development
Block 718 Bedok Reservoir Road
#01-4572
Singapore 470718
☎ 442 6332

YWCA
150 Orchard Road
Orchard Plaza #08-08
Singapore 238841
☎ 235 8822

Zion Kindergarten
5 Tavistock Avenue
Singapore 555108
☎ 288 0733

Useful Publications

Chapter 1

Every Child a Star

A true-life account of bringing up children in Singapore, with a focus on the school system

Written by Carol Lim

Published by Brit Aspen Publishing

Chapter 2

The STPB (Singapore Tourist Promotion Board) publishes the following booklets:

Festivals and Events (annual guide),

Family Fun Island,

Educational Tourism Guide (aimed mainly at visiting students and school parties, but has some good suggestions for visits suitable for schoolchildren).

Discover Singapore and *Let's Celebrate!*

Two excellent interactive children's books which will help you find interesting places to explore with your kids.

Published by Small Books.

Chapter 3

Dangerous Plants

A useful reference guide to poisonous plants in Singapore

Written by Gopalkrishnakone, P. and Wee Yeow Chin

Published by Ridge Books

Chapter 4

The Singapore Party Book

Ideas on how to plan creative children's parties. Includes suggestions for children's celebrations to coincide with national festivals and how to find materials, entertainers and venues.

Written by Alison Gable and Marti Sevier

Published by Armour Publishing

Chapter 5

Programmes on Family Life and Parent Education

☎ 1800 258 4741

The Public Education and Sports Branch, Ministry of Community Development, compiles this regular quarterly bulletin, giving details of educational programmes for parents planned by various organisations. It will also help find a speaker on a parenting topic for a company's or organisation's meeting.

Living in Singapore

An invaluable source of information for newcomers, this book covers everything from settling in to moving out and includes useful guides to house hunting, local food, recreation, employing a maid and more. It's also the only book on Singapore aimed at expatriate residents rather than tourists.

Published by the American Association

The Finder

A monthly guide funded by advertising, which includes information aimed mainly at expatriates, including contacts for maid agencies, kindergartens, holidays and shopping.

The Expat

☎ 463 6268

A monthly magazine which includes a regular events column and occasional features on education and parenting topics.

INDEX

Index

Index

THE AUTHOR

Nicola Supka (née Green)

Nicola is a freelance writer living and working in Singapore. She has a son, Rory, aged five, and a daughter, Holly, aged two.

Once upon a time, there was a little girl called Nicola Helen Green. She lived not in Singapore but far away in Leicester, a medium-sized town in England. Nicola was a very happy but rather cautious and shy child.

One day at school, when Nicola was about eight years old, a woman came into the classroom and asked if anyone was interested in learning to play the violin. Nicola put up her hand, and was amazed to find later that she was one of a few children who had been selected to have violin lessons after school.

At the end of the class, Nicola left the violin she had been given in the entrance hall as instructed. Only later, when she got home, did she begin to feel rather confused. How was she going to practise what she had learned before the next class?

The next week, Nicola arrived for the violin class. She was really excited but a bit worried when everybody else arrived carrying a violin. She asked the teacher and found out that she should have taken the violin home with her and that it had been taken away as one of the "extras". Nicola was too embarrassed and too upset to say any more. She never got the violin back, and she never played the violin again. Now over 30 years old, she has never really forgotten the disappointment she felt that day.

P.S. Making your dreams come true is so important, for little girls and boys, and for adults of all ages. This book is one of mine.